C000124470

Riding The Rover Coaster

The Inside Story Of Tranmere's Turbulent Decade

By Matt Jones

Edited by Nick Hilton

Photos and cover design by Richard Ault

To Sadie

Introduction

A few minutes before 6pm on Saturday May 25, 2019, Connor Jennings headed a winning goal in the last minute of extra time to secure Tranmere Rovers success in a tense League Two play-off final at Wembley.

Celebrations of unbounded joy broke out among the thousands of members of the Super White Army who had travelled to the ground they could once again refer to as Prenton Park South.

The 1-0 victory over Newport County meant Tranmere would return, in 2019/20, to the League One status they had relinquished five years before.

Those five years in-between were the most dramatic and traumatic in Tranmere's history. Although the club's decline over the preceding decade had, initially, been gradual in terms of results on the field, the descent suddenly became a hurtling fall with back to back relegations in 2013/14 and 2014/15.

The second of those demotions cost Rovers the Football League status they had proudly boasted since 1921. Supporters were entitled to feel they had hit rock bottom. They would be entering an unknown and unwelcome territory and had no idea if there was any way back.

Yet the drop into non-league football allowed Tranmere to build strength and momentum, on and off the field, that led to three successive play-off final appearances and back-to-back promotions in 2017/18 and 2018/19.

This ride on the Rover Coaster has been tearful, anxious and exhilarating for supporters and players, staff, management and the custodians of the club at boardroom level.

The purpose of this book is to tell the story of Tranmere Rovers' giddy journey from a range of perspectives: how it looked for people who spend their lives supporting the club; how it looked from inside the dressing room, the coaching room or the manager's office and from inside the boardroom.

I've tried to look beyond what happened and to focus on the how and why by interviewing individuals who were at the centre of events or in a position to observe the whirlwind change of fortunes blowing around them.

I have to thank a long list of people who gave their time, recollections and opinions freely in preparing for this book: Chairman Mark Palios and former chairman Peter Johnson, manager Micky Mellon and former manager Les Parry, long serving coach Shaun Garnett, current players Liam Ridehalgh, Scott Davies and Connor Jennings, former players Steve Jennings, Danny Holmes, Ian Goodison and Iain Hume.

Attempts were made to contact former managers Ronnie Moore and Micky Adams for the book but neither responded.

For the fans' viewpoint I turned to Mark Bartley, chairman of the Tranmere Rovers Official Supporters Club, and Dave Kennedy, who helped to run the Cowsheds forum.

I also sought out an independent expert in football finances, Kieran Maguire, who lectures at the University of Liverpool. He was able to provide a view on how Tranmere survived the turbulent decade and emerged stronger while other clubs of similar stature encountered deeper difficulties.

I've chosen as a starting point for this story the final match of the 2008/09 season when Tranmere narrowly missed out on making the League One play-offs. You could argue the years of decline began some years earlier and that Rovers had been treading water for much of the 21st century. But I think it is fair to say that the 2009/10 season set the pattern for many of the campaigns that followed.

My first book, 'Back Where We Belong', published in the summer of 2018, covered the National League years and the promotion season of 2017/18 in depth so that phase is reported in less detail here. More emphasis is placed on the 2018/19 campaign.

The time-frame of this book does lead us to an uplifting conclusion., with Jennings' header one that will live long in the memory of every supporter who was at Wembley that day. But of course, it is not the end of the story. We cannot be sure of where the Rover Coaster is heading next.

Part One
The Downfall

Chapter One
A Surprise Sacking

Sunshine followed the Super White Army eastwards across England as they made the trip along the M62 to Glanford Park, home of Scunthorpe United, on May 2nd 2009. They packed out a claustrophobic away end to watch Tranmere in the final game of the regular League One season.

Except this was not just any old season finale. A place in the play-offs was at stake. Rovers had given themselves a chance of sneaking into the top six at the last minute courtesy of a run of one defeat in seven games. Victory here was all they needed to extend their season for only the second time since being relegated from the Championship. Scunthorpe, on the other hand, required only a draw to pip Ronnie Moore's side to sixth position.

Tranmere were depleted, with talismanic centre-back Ian Goodison suspended after being sent off against Hereford in mid-April, whilst Bas Savage and Chris Shuker were both out injured. That meant Craig Curran, a young, up and coming forward was handed a rare start in attack alongside Ian Thomas-Moore.

Curran, though, made his mark. Without a goal since the end of August, he ended the long drought in the 39th minute, heading home a cross from his strike partner to put the visitors 1-0 up. The traveling fans were already in party mode and this sent them into delirium. Hold onto that lead and their side were into the play-offs.
They had chances to double the advantage, Steven Jennings in particular coming close, before Gareth Edds saw red late in the second half, dismissed for a second bookable offence after a foul on Martyn Woolford on the right flank. There were, however, only three minutes left. Rovers could hold on, surely?

No. Scunthorpe equalised from the resulting free-kick, with Grant McCann curling the ball onto the head of captain Cliff Byrne, who in turn beat goalkeeper Danny Coyne to send his side back into sixth place and into the play-offs.

As is always the case with such occasions in sport, the emotions on display could not have been more polarised. Whilst the home supporters danced with glee, there were tears at the opposite end of the pitch. Jennings was one of those who collapsed to the ground, emotionally and physically sapped of the ability to walk.

It had been a phenomenal season for Tranmere. Moore had built a solid team with a dependable spine. Ben Chorley, on-loan Ryan Shotton and Andy Taylor, as well as Goodison, were like a brick wall in defence, whilst Antony Kay, converted to a central midfielder, had been a revelation, finishing the campaign as the club's top scorer with 12 goals.

The problem for Rovers was this was a one-time chance. As exciting a season as it had been, and as close as they had come to the top six, the opportunity to go up had passed.

Within weeks, the team started to break up. Chorley, pining for a return to London, joined Leyton Orient, Kay moved to Huddersfield and Jennings departed for Motherwell. All three of them were out of contract, all three of them departed on free-transfers.

And whilst none of those moves came as a surprise, the news that hit the headlines on June 5th, little over a month after that Scunthorpe game, shocked fans and signalled a change in how Tranmere would operate over the following years. Manager Ronnie Moore, after three years at the helm, had been sacked.

"I found out just before I went off on holiday," reveals Jennings, who was still hoping to pen a new deal at Prenton Park at the time. "I was sat on an airplane ready to take off and I was just scrolling through my phone. It came up on BBC Sport that Tranmere had sacked him.

"I had to turn my phone off when I was flying and I was in No Man's Land for a couple of hours. It was really strange to find out that way.

"To be honest, Ronnie being sacked probably did have an impact on my decision to leave. Knowing that he'd gone and we'd be starting fresh over again, it would have been strange. I think I got the call to go to Motherwell and I just weighed them up. Tranmere didn't have a manager at the time and it was an easier decision."

Les Parry had been Tranmere's physio for nearly 20 years, arriving at Prenton Park initially under Johnny King. He knew Moore as well as anybody at the club, and he too was stunned by the news.

"I was listening to the radio in the garden," he recalls. "It was a sunny day. And I said to my wife 'did I just hear that right, that Ronnie's gone?' Then I started getting text messages and it was obviously true.

"I worked with a lot of managers, so I saw quite a lot getting the sack. Generally, you could see it coming. That one, I didn't see it coming at all. I thought we'd be back the next season. Pre-season with Ronnie would be the same and we'd go again, so I was really surprised.

"I contacted him straight away. We've always got on really well. He was there when I first started at the club as John King's assistant, so you're talking over 20 years that we'd known each other.

"The first thing you always do when a manager goes is contact them because you don't like to see people lose their jobs. He was just as shocked. I remember saying to him that it's actually not a bad time to get the bullet, when you've done something good, because your stock is up.

"He saw that side of it a little bit, although Ronnie's a very proud man. He wouldn't have wanted it on his CV, that he'd been sacked. He's always been that way; very proud and very competitive."

The decision to change manager had come completely out of the blue. Tranmere had just had their most successful campaign since finishing in third place under Brian Little in 2005. Jennings admits the players were just as stunned as everybody else.

"It was really baffling how anybody could sack somebody after a good season," Jennings continued. "Tranmere was a good place to be plying your trade. We had a lot of big characters in the team, we always have whenever I've been here since I left school.

"I think that's part of the make-up. To make it as a footballer at any level you've got to have character, and Tranmere didn't lack any of that. We had had a few mediocre seasons when we were 9th, 10th or 11th and tailed off late on into the season, but in that year, we had some great lads in the team who I still keep in contact with now. It was a very good place to be around."

Moore's departure did not go down well with a large section of the Tranmere fanbase. He was a club legend, having enjoyed two stints at Prenton Park as a player, as well as serving as part of Johnny King's backroom staff for the best part of a decade.

"I grew up watching him play," says Dave Kennedy, who at the time was running fan site The Cowsheds. "I always thought he was a good guy. He was Tranmere through and through and I really rated him.

"I was disappointed because it was getting mooted at the time that Peter Johnson was keen to forge closer links with Liverpool and what happened next just smacked of that."

Chapter Two
The John Barnes Experiment

With Ronnie Moore out the door, rumours started to circulate, almost straight away, as to who was going to replace him as Tranmere manager. There was one name that carried more noise than any other, and it was not a particularly popular one: John Barnes.

Within days, the appointment had been confirmed. The former Liverpool and England winger, then aged 45, brought in as his assistant another ex-Red in Jason McAteer, who had spent the later years of his playing career at Prenton Park.

Barnes had been working as manager of the Jamaica international team before accepting the Rovers role, but it had been some time since he was involved in club football. A decade earlier, a stint in the hot-seat at Celtic had turned into something of a calamity.

"He was our first choice for the position," Tranmere chairman Peter Johnson said in a statement. "John and Jason bring a wealth of experience, knowledge and contacts within the game. They are a Wirral-based partnership who are very enthusiastic about what they offer Tranmere and I look forward to watching their team play next season."

The pair, however, inherited a squad that contained just eleven contracted players. They needed to build the numbers, and quickly, but their knowledge of the lower leagues was limited. Indeed, after giving his first press conference as Tranmere boss, once the microphones had been turned off, Barnes asked the attending media whether they could recommend any new signings.

His intention had been to use his links with Liverpool as a way of attracting talent to Prenton Park. Loan players were expected to arrive from Anfield, but they never materialised. The project looked destined to fail from the start.

"I was disappointed when he got the job," says Dave Kennedy. "Barnes' previous experiences as a manager were grim, to say the least. I think it was a bad appointment at the wrong time for our club.

"I think Peter Johnson was trying to move the club in a different direction and it was one none of us were really used to. We'd had former Liverpool players as managers before, like Ron Yeats back in the 1970s, but this was a really odd one.

"I couldn't quite put my finger on what Peter was actually doing. I certainly didn't think it was for the good of the club, or what was going to happen on the pitch. I knew we had no money and I knew John Barnes would struggle under a tight budget and so it proved."

Within the dressing room, or at least among those who remained after a mass exodus that summer, there were mixed feelings. Some were excited over Barnes' arrival. Les Parry, physiotherapist at the time, was intrigued to see how he did.

"I quite like John Barnes," he says. "I knew Jason really well. In fact I knew they were coming in before it was announced, because Jason called around to my house with his girlfriend, who's now his wife, and said they'd been approached by Tranmere.

"I thought, to be honest, it was quite a good appointment. I was unsure about the fans. I wasn't too sure how they'd take to it. Those concerns ended up being realised. But I thought it was a decent appointment."

Club legend Ian Goodison meanwhile was still trying to get over the shock of a change of manager. "I was in Jamaica at the time and I got the news that John Barnes was going to be the new manager," he says. "It was very shocking. Ronnie Moore had done very well in the previous season, so I was surprised."

Barnes and McAteer had a huge job on their hands to get a decimated squad ready for the new campaign. Steve Jennings, Antony Kay, Ben Chorley and Danny Coyne were just a handful of the senior players who had left the club.

Somebody who had already signed that summer headed off to pastures new without even playing a first team fixture. Mark Allott joined Tranmere from Oldham on a two-year contract just a handful of days before Ronnie Moore was given the sack.

It was evident that he did not fit into Barnes' plans, because by the end of July he had left, joining Chesterfield. No doubt it was a fun eight weeks on the Wirral for the midfielder, anyway.

The new management team had limited knowledge of the lower divisions but former Liverpool youngster John Welsh, arriving on a free transfer from Hull, was a known entity, as was fellow midfielder Paul McLaren, who returned to Tranmere for a second spell after leaving Bradford.

Another familiar face rocked up at Prenton Park. Alan Mahon was part of John Aldridge's Tranmere squad when they reached the League Cup final in 2000. He left at the end of that season, joining Sporting Lisbon before returning to England with Blackburn.

His fitness record was not great. The midfielder had started only 26 games during a three year stint with Burnley, where his contract had expired. His pedigree, could not be questioned, it was just a case of getting him on the pitch.

"Recruitment didn't go greatly in the summer," Parry continues. "To bring Alan Mahon in, he got rid of the left-back Andy Taylor to Sheffield United. He was one of our big earners and he was a half decent player.

"But I don't think he was that concerned about defence to be quite honest with you. He wanted people who could keep the ball. I think John's thinking is that if you've got the ball, you don't need to defend.

"I thought we'd start the season decently to be honest. In pre-season, the results were a little bit up and down, but we were messing around with the team. To lose to Yeovil on the opening day wasn't great."

Other signings were made after the season had started, including the recruitment of former England striker Michael Ricketts, whose best days were long behind him, and a Grenada international called Kithson Bain.

Goalkeeper Luke Daniels, meanwhile, arrived on loan from West Brom, whilst full-back Shay Logan joined on a temporary deal from Manchester City. All good business, but done very late in the day.

***

Tranmere's start to the season was an absolute calamity. They rocked up at Huish Park to take on Yeovil in the opening game of the campaign with a squad of just 17 players. Five were academy products who had barely played a first team match between and made up the substitutes' bench.

"The preparation, or lack of, during the summer, cost us dearly," says Kennedy. "It led to John Barnes' swift demise. We lost 2-0 at Yeovil with only two recognised defenders and it could have been worse.

"At a time when he should have been building a squad and doing training and everything else involved in managing a football club, it was very much the John Barnes show. I certainly saw him in London one day doing a sponsorship for Mars. It was all about John Barnes and not about preparation."

A couple of wins followed the horror show at Huish Park, much to the relief of everybody, firstly against Grimsby in the League Cup as Rovers ran out impressive 4-0 winners. A first league victory of the season followed a handful off days later, 4-2 against Gillingham.

"That one was quite a good game," continues Kennedy, who starts scrolling through the starting line-ups for the match. "But it's probably the only one. There were flashes of really good stuff, particularly the passing game, but it just wasn't consistent enough.

"I don't believe the players were good enough to adapt to his required tactics, although I use the word tactics loosely, because I didn't see many of them. It just didn't work."

The final sentiment is something Goodison agrees with. The defender had been part of some seriously good teams during his career, but this one simply could not do what the manager wanted.

"John Barnes mostly wanted to play football," he says. "He wanted to start from the back. At that time, I don't think we had the players to play that way. He just wanted to pass and play proper passing football, but I don't think we had the players. We tried, but it didn't go very well."

The Gillingham victory was pretty much as good as it got for Barnes. Tranmere lost their next seven matches, failing to score in the first five. They were absolutely woeful, and were lucky that some of the losing margins were as slender as they were.

"We lost 3-0 at Leeds," says Parry. "It could have been 30. I remember one of the goals, and it typifies John's approach really. We had to play out from the back and keep possession. For one of them, we made 20 odd consecutive passes, and then lost the ball on the edge of our own area. They scored.

"Even though we were getting walloped, he kept on wanting to play, play, play. That was just his philosophy. I don't believe you can get players at that level of football to play that style of football and be successful, and I think I probably said it to John.

"I really like John Barnes as a manager. He had a lot going for him. But he did get a little bit frustrated when players couldn't do what he could do. I think he expected players to be able to retain possession like Liverpool could, and it was a little bit optimistic."

Every game was a nightmare. As well as that defeat at Elland Road, Tranmere got stuffed 4-0 at home by Charlton, 3-0 away by Carlisle and put in a dismal display in a 2-1 loss down at Exeter.

There was some respite for the boss when Rovers ended the losing streak by drawing 1-1 at home to Colchester, whilst an early strike from Ian Thomas-Moore then earned a 1-0 victory down at Wycombe. But the dye had already been cast.

Next up was a trip to The Den to take on Millwall. Tranmere were obliterated. It finished 5-0, with four of those goals coming in a wretched opening 27 minutes.

"That was another one where they squeezed us to death and stopped us playing out," recalls Parry. "Barnes was ahead of his time really, because playing out from the back is what you see in modern football.

"But they were squeezing us and teams kept doing it all the time. They knew we weren't going to turn them. That was another game where you were happy it was only five."

"That game was the worst one of the lot," adds Kennedy, getting visibly angry as he recalls a shambolic 90 minutes of football. "It was an absolute disgrace. It should have been about 15.

"You won't see a worse game, if you're a Tranmere fan, than that. It epitomised his tenure as manager. It was absolutely disgraceful. We were woeful. Utterly woeful.

"The away end was vitriolic that day, and it continued to be that way. In fact it was all the way throughout. He didn't really have much of a chance before a ball had been kicked. It turned very nasty, very quickly. It started in the first game at Yeovil."

Kennedy has just tripped on an interesting point. Was Barnes ever given a fair crack of the whip as Tranmere manager, or were the odds stacked against him from the start? In the end, the football was awful and the results were worse, but plenty of supporters had made their minds up before the season even got underway.

"I don't think the fans were ever accepting of John Barnes," he admits. "That's possibly because of his links to Liverpool, but I also think a lot of that will have been because of his lack of experience at our level.

"As fans, all that you want is something that would be for the good of the club. I didn't think, and I know many others didn't think that this type and style of appointment was a shrewd move.

"He had very little managerial experience. As a player, he'd probably been one of the best I've ever seen. As a manager, he was an absolute calamity. He just looked like he didn't know what he was doing."

What also did not help Barnes was that he had replaced a club legend in Ronnie Moore. The majority of fans had not wanted a change in the first place, let alone for an appointment like this to be made.

"It would have been tough for any manager coming in," Kennedy concedes. "We'd had a really good season and Ronnie Moore was very popular indeed. It wasn't that he was going to be a tough act to follow, it's because of his popularity, his links and history with the club.

"It was a shock when he was fired, especially after us coming to within a couple of minutes of the play-offs. Whoever was appointed was always going to have their work cut out, but if it had been anybody with a modicum of experience at the time, I think it would have been a lot better.

"John Barnes started the season trying to make third division players play like Brazil. There were flashes from the quality players. I could see what he was trying to do. But in the third division football, It's not something that will get you promoted. It's a recipe for disaster. It was just leaving us wide open all the time. You knew what he was trying to do but he just didn't have enough quality in that side to do it and that was a big part in his downfall.

"I had a couple of Facebook Memories pop up recently from ten years ago. One of them just said 'Sod off Barnes and take McAteer with you'. It wasn't frustrating. It was bitterly annoying.

"There were fans who were paying a lot of good money for season tickets and travelling to away games and they ended up with nothing. Their team weren't even scoring goals. They were just seeing clinical defeats where we weren't even in the game.

"He looked clueless on the sidelines. When things were going wrong, he didn't know what to do to make it right. It was all very disappointing."

Parry reckons those supporters would have backed the manager eventually, though. All he needed to do was produce results.

"It was always going to be difficult," he adds. "I know the fans didn't take to him, but had he won some games, they'd have come around. If you look at history, from a fan point of view, the worst appointments in the world have turned out to be good ones if they win games. Unfortunately, we didn't, and that didn't help."

After the embarrassment at Millwall, Tranmere's next game was a Johnstone's Paint Trophy clash with Bury and the knives were out. Rovers took the lead through Craig Curran after just four minutes, but even that was not enough to stop some fans chanting for the manager to be sacked.

In the second half, the Shakers hit back, with former Tranmere youngster Mike Jones netting a late winner. The fact that the hosts won 2-1 is not remarkable. But each of their goals was cheered loudly by the away fans.

"In 20 odd years at Tranmere, it's the only time I'd ever experienced something like that," says Parry. "Since I've left, it might have happened, I don't know. But whilst I was there, I can't remember our fans ever cheering adversity.

"I can honestly say I didn't know the writing was on the wall for him at any point. I'd have given him more time. I think had the fans not been so aggressive with him and so anti-John Barnes, he might have got a little bit more time. But the fans didn't hide their feelings.

"Even when we were winning, the fans were still singing 'you're getting sacked in the morning'. We'd do things right and the fans didn't react. I just thought that it was fan banter, because I'd heard them sing that a hundred times, but as it turns out, it wasn't.

"I suppose in hindsight you look back and I should have read into it a little bit more, because it was odd. You really feel sorry for a manager when you're sitting there and they're giving him stick, normal stick, when you're not doing well and you get the odd chant. You feel sorry. But when that's happening, it takes it up to another level."

Kennedy was in the away end that night, situated down one side of Gigg Lane and on the opposite touchline to the dugouts.

"As a fan, I could never cheer an opposition goal," he says. "Inwardly, of course, I was seething. I was livid. But it's not something I would do personally. I can't condone it but I can understand it.

"It wasn't just 'get out' or chants of 'you don't know what you're doing'. This was anger, real anger. It was horrible as a fan to witness it to be honest, but I can understand it because we were that bad.

Cheering an opposition goal though? I can't agree with that."

***

Tranmere had a little bit of a break after the Bury game. Their trip to Gigg Lane had taken place on a Tuesday night. Next up was a home match against Stockport County, live on Sky Sports six days later.

Rovers sat deep in the relegation zone and their visitors were themselves only two points above the dotted line. Even at such an early stage in the season, mid-October, it looked like a crucial game for all the wrong reasons.

"The Cowsheds was a big part in the Tranmere community at the time," says Kennedy. "The Trust were active then, but as a forum, it grew very quickly and we dealt with quite a few things, such as player sponsorships and getting money into the club.

"We bought that massive flag that travelled around the country, which everyone chipped in for. It was great. I ran the website with a friend of mine, Chris Nolan.

"Within about 12 months of starting, there were about 3,500 members, of which about 2,500 were active every day. We were a big part of the Tranmere community and I got to meet a lot of people through that very medium.
"We ran a poll on The Cowsheds forum asking if people wanted John Barnes to stay or go. It got a massive response and 97% wanted him sacked immediately. We contacted the club and asked for a meeting for Chris and I, as representatives, to present the fans feelings. I don't think we heard anything straight away."

The club soon got in touch, though. The Stockport game was being televised to the nation. It looked like the perfect opportunity for any supporters to make their feelings known. They knew it, and so did Peter Johnson, who was worried.

"It was all over the forums," Kennedy continues. "The fans were going to make a very vocal protest about John Barnes and wanting him out. Then, out of nothing, we got a call from Sue Beedles, who's a good friend of mine and was working at the club at the time. She's somebody I always felt very sorry for, because she was doing the work of about 20 people, but did everything for the club.

"We were invited to the boardroom the following day to speak to Peter Johnson and Mick Horton, the chief executive. We dropped everything and collected some questions from the forum that we could put to him.

"Obviously we had the poll results and some posts from the members who we classed as the most reliable ones, not those who were just gobbing off. But even when you put those aside, you were still left with pretty much everybody calling for Barnes to be sacked. We were able to put some of the questions to him."

Nolan and Kennedy found it a surreal experience as two fans invited to chat to the chairman about their feelings on the current management team. You often find clubs holding question and answer sessions with supporters if things are going well, but not if the team is falling off a cliff. For football, let alone Tranmere, this was unique.

"Sitting in the boardroom with Mr Johnson and Mr Horton was quite an experience," he laughs. "Peter was such a gentleman in the meeting, he really was. It was him who poured the coffees and he was very amiable.

"He's a good guy. I'd spoken to him a few times in the past. He used to wander around outside with the fans before big games. I remember sitting on the wall outside the Prenton Park pub with a can of beer and he came up to us and was chatting away during one of our play-off pushes in the 1990s. He was always good for a chat and he came across like that during the interview.

"However, I was quite nervous to be sat in front of him, because as nice as he was with the fans, it was a very rare thing that he would come out and speak. It was unusual.

"We were chatting about various different things, such as past players, and when it came down to the key part of it, I presented the poll to him and quoted a lot of the posts from fans and people I'd spoken to.

"It wasn't just a select group that we were talking about. The Cowsheds didn't speak for everybody, but it was certainly enough for me to sit in front of the chairman to tell him it was going wrong.

"Peter was keen to find out what plans were in place for the protest at the Stockport game. You could see he was visibly concerned about that. He didn't want a protest in the stands for a televised live game, but it was certainly coming and he knew it.

"He listened to everything that we said and we'd spoken to him about the previous season with Ronnie getting sacked and his wanting to forge closer links with Liverpool at the time, hence the appointment of John Barnes and Jason McAteer. He spoke really well, but you could see the concern etched on his face.

"I just came out and asked 'are you going to dismiss him' and he wouldn't be drawn on that. When the meeting ended, I asked Mick Horton the same question and he just shrugged his shoulders and said 'I don't know'.

"Mick didn't have any, or very little, input into the meeting itself. It was all about Peter Johnson. He just kept saying that he wanted to gauge how the fans were feeling, which later came back and bit me a little bit.

"The meeting finished and I went back to the computer to type out what had happened; that we'd presented everybody's point of view as much as we possibly could. It was warmly received. We didn't want any credit for it."

On 9th October, John Barnes and Jason McAteer were sacked by Tranmere Rovers, roughly 24 hours after Johnson's meeting with Kennedy and Nolan. They left the club with a record of two wins and eight defeats from eleven league matches in charge, conceding 26 goals in the process, the most in the division.

Peter Johnson released a brief statement confirming the news, saying: "Unfortunately results have not gone our way this season and we are at the wrong end of the table. We must now focus on finding the best possible candidate to help us climb the division."

The news came on a Friday morning, three days out from the clash with Stockport. Despite what had happened at Bury, Les Parry admits to being somewhat surprised when he was told.

"It was a normal day," he recalls. "Everyone was in and I was in my room. John and Jason called us in and he said 'we've been sacked'. Obviously you sound surprised, because we were.

"I think it was just me and Shaun Garnett in there and he said he had to get out straight away. Then we had the debacle over the bike, because he used to ride in everyday!"

Barnes was trying to put his bike in the back of McAteer's 4x4. Unfortunately, or fortunately, depending on how you look at it, they just could not work out how to squeeze it into the boot. And the Sky Sports cameras caught it all.

"I sensed that the sack was imminent," said McAteer in one interview with Sky Sports a few years later. "John was in the office early, as he always was, and the chairman called him into his office. I had a funny feeling it was going to be bad news.

"I went to put my training kit on and by the time I got back into the manager's office, John looked me up and down in my kit and said 'it's all over. We've been sacked.'

"I said to him 'let's go for a coffee' but he wanted to ride out on his bike. I knew he couldn't do that because if the press saw him riding out, there was their headline: 'on your bike'.

"So I said 'we'll put the bike in the car, we'll go for a coffee and I'll drop you off at home'. We got downstairs to the car, lifted the boot up and we were trying to get it in the car.

"John was on his phone and I couldn't get it in. It was like the Krypton Factor. Then my phone goes and it was my mate: 'Macca, turn the wheel the other way and the bike will go in!'

"I looked around the car park and I said 'where are you?' He said 'I'm at home. You're live on Sky. Turn the wheel the other way and it will go in!' So I said 'cheers mate', put my phone in my pocket, turned the wheel and of course it went in. We were only live on Sky being sacked!"

"Watching that was painful," says Kennedy, his head slumped in his hands at the memory. "It summed up the whole debacle of their appointment, watching them trying to work that bike into the car."

Tranmere's fans were generally pleased with the news that Barnes had gone. The heartache of his tenure had lasted only a few months, although the damage it caused was potentially serious in terms of the club's League One status.

"I definitely praise Peter Johnson for making the decision to sack Barnes as quickly as he did," says Kennedy. "But I think it was more because of the fear of the club getting shown up on TV. He pulled me and Chris in for this meeting and basically made it look like it was on the back of the fans' behest, but I think he was going to sack him anyway. In fact I'm in no doubt that he was going to sack John Barnes.

"But he had a couple of fans in to present all these pieces of information, feelings and fan polls, with their dislike, disregard and in some respects hatred for John Barnes. He made it look like it was on the back of what we'd said to him, when I don't think it was."

Chapter Three
From Physio To Manager

Little more than a few minutes after John Barnes' sacking, Les Parry was asked to go for a chat with Peter Johnson. The owner needed somebody in charge for that televised match against Stockport, giving him some breathing space to find a permanent boss.

Parry was the man Johnson had decided upon as his caretaker, assisted by Centre of Excellence boss Shaun Garnett. The physiotherapist was a surprise choice, especially as he had never played football professionally.

But it was an opportunity he could not allow to pass. A boyhood Tranmere fan, Parry had been employed by Rovers since 1991, when he was appointed to Johnny King's medical team, originally on a part-time basis.

He was a popular figure at Prenton Park, thanks in part to his witty column in the match day programme and his insistence on wearing shorts when in the dug-out, even on the coldest of nights.

"I went up to Peter Johnson's office," recalls Parry. "He said 'you've probably heard, we've had to release John and Jason. Listen, could you just look after the team until I find a manager?'

"Obviously being a Tranmere fan, I was delighted. I thought just one game managing the team I support? Yeah, I'll have a little bit of that! Shaun Garnett was probably a little bit disappointed that he wasn't asked. Really, there was only me or him that it could have been, but I think Peter's thinking was that I knew all the first team lads, whilst Shaun had been with the youths.

"So he asked me and I obviously dragged Shaun in as well. It was

Stockport on Sky Sports on the Monday night, so we had a few days to prepare. It was just a case of get on with it, get the TV game out of the way and we can get back to our jobs when a manager comes in."

The thought of being in charge of a Tranmere side thrilled Parry. This was a lifetime ambition being fulfilled at a point when he was thinking about moving away from football after so many years in the job.

Not everybody was thrilled, though. "I was appalled," says Dave Kennedy. "I like him, I do, but I was appalled. I know what happened with the survival that he took us through, an unlikely one, but I couldn't support the physiotherapist who said that he was experienced enough to be a manager because he'd heard nearly 1,000 teamtalks.

"I couldn't agree with that as far as credentials go for appointing a manager. So for Peter Johnson, as much as it was brave to sack Barnes and McAteer, he shouldn't have sacked Ronnie in the first place, which was a mistake, he shouldn't have appointed Barnes and he made another mistake by appointing Les Parry."

Parry did have some credentials though. "I was an A Licence coach between 1989 and 1991," he reveals. "When I started as a physio, because you have to do a refresher course, I didn't do mine. So in reality, no I didn't have any badges, because if somebody said 'are you a currently qualified coach', the answer would have been no.

"I actually started them again, in my second year, when it came out that you needed them. They agreed to fast track me back on to my A Licence, because I'd had it before. But things changed as it wasn't long before I left."

***

As far as Parry was concerned, he was only going to be in the job for one game, maybe two at most. Once the Stockport match had been and gone, he would be heading back to his physio room and working under a new manager.

So he set his sights on doing the job as best as he possibly could. He took a look at the players at his disposal and alongside Garnett, formulated a way of playing that he felt best suited the squad.

"Me and Shaun had a little chat," Parry continues. "We were like 'this will be great, we've got a game!' We were thinking that if we could get an away game out of it, that would be even better!

"We sat down and decided what way we should play. I'm not sure what our goal difference was then, but it was minus a lot. So we decided that we needed to stop the goals.

"All we did was put a picture of all the players we had on the wall and picked which ones we'd take to war with us and made a team out of those. That's how the formation was decided upon. We looked at what was available and it pointed to a 4-3-3.

"It's only a conscious decision, a formation. Sometimes, you have to have a formation that fits the players available, especially when we needed certain players who were going to dig in for us."

Parry made six changes from the side who had lost 2-1 at Bury. Rovers were spirited, and they were tough to beat, but they lost 1-0. The goal was a penalty, with Carl Baker converting from the spot midway through the second half after Luke Daniels had brought down Luke Vincent in the box.

"I think we did quite well," Parry muses. "The lad Baker who scored, he went on to have a good career with Coventry. But we did okay. We didn't look like we were going to get turned over.

"We weren't happy about losing, because we wanted to win. That was one of the three aims for myself and Shaun; get a game, get an away game, get a win."

A week later, that win came. Tranmere were at home to Brighton, who sat just outside the League One relegation zone. Rovers were several points from safety, but goals from Gareth Edds and John Welsh either side of half-time earned a 2-1 win. Parry was in dreamland.

"That was it then," he smiles. "It was fantastic. I was happy. Bring somebody in now! It was unbelievable getting a win as a manager. Because we hadn't won for so long, the dressing room was buzzing.

"It was a great feeling. For me, it was up there with the League Cup semi-final win over Bolton in 2000 or beating Stockport later in the season."

***

The Brighton match should have been Les Parry's final one as caretaker manager of Tranmere. Keith Hill had been lined up to replace him, and he looked like a sound appointment.

He was in charge of Rochdale, a club who perennially occupied the bottom tier of the Football League. Indeed, they had not been promoted since being invited into the pyramid in 1921, the same year as Tranmere.

But in 2008, Hill guided the club to the League Two play-off final, only to suffer defeat to Stockport at Wembley, before falling at the semi-final stage a year later.

"After the win over Brighton, I was made up," Parry continues. "The chairman calls me in to say well done, and he also told me a new manager was coming in the next day. I didn't care. I'd won a game! That's all I wanted!

"The manager he had lined up was Keith Hill. I turned up for training on the Monday morning ready to jump back in my room, which I'd never left really, and there was no new manager.

"The chairman calls me again and says 'it's fallen through'. I think it had something to do with his assistant not agreeing terms. It was something to do with money anyway, so they weren't coming.

"I was asked to keep going until somebody else was found. I then go and tell Shaun Garnett 'we're going to get an away game here!' So that's how it was extended. I've never spoken to Keith Hill about it. I see him all the time. But I've never asked him. I should do really!"

"Everybody was waiting for another manager, some other name or something," adds Ian Goodison. "Then Les got the job until the end of the season. It surprised everybody.

"He was very old school as a manager. He had been around for years before me and he knew a lot of managers. He wanted to be rough and get the result, that type of manager. He was okay."

Tranmere had a bit of a wobble after that. They were beaten 1-0 up at Hartlepool in Parry's first away game, before suffering a humiliating 4-1 defeat to Swindon in the club's 125 year anniversary match.

But by the middle of November, the caretaker manager started to have an impact. He got a win in the first round of the FA Cup, beating Leyton Orient 1-0 in a replay, before further victories followed against Southend and Brentford in the league.

Eventually, having had to take things game to game, Parry was given the reins until the end of the season, with Peter Johnson unsuccessful in finding a more experienced boss who was willing to take charge.
"It was getting into Christmas when that happened," says Parry. "The only reason I know is because I hadn't appointed a physio. I thought 'sod that, I'm not appointing a physio, only for me to get put back in!'

"We used Chris Malkin a few times. He was setting his practice up at the time. He came in and we spoke and I tried to get him in as physio permanently. He was dragging it on, so in the end I dropped it. But he came in a few times.

"When he did cover games for us, he was great. He loves Tranmere. He's good around the lads, which is why I wanted him as physio, because apart from him being a good physio, he's just good to have around the place."

When Malkin was not around, Parry would carry out physiotherapy duties himself. That led to some particularly amusing moments on a match day, when he would charge on to treat an injured player. If he was unhappy at the performance of the officials, he would give the referee both barrels on the way back to the technical area.

"There was a question on A Question Of Sport," Parry laughs. "Who's the only league manager who's allowed to enter the field of play? And it was obviously me, because I was doing the physio job too.

"You get to know the referees. I still see a lot of them now. We used to laugh about it. I'd be giving instructions when I was on too!

"Before the game, I used to do the rubs and the strappings. I had help from Ken Langley and George Cain, who was a former referee himself. We'd then go in and do the set plays and give the team talk before going out and running on the pitch if needed. At half-time, we'd go in and give another team talk.

"Just to give an idea of what it was like, we had Bas Savage at that time. There was one game when I was screaming at the lads. We had a run where we were winning games and then conceding. So I was shouting 'has anybody got anything to say?' Bas sticks his hand up and says 'have you got some ice for me knee?'

"So from October until January, I was doing all that, and I was writing up my pHd as well, all at the same time. So when people tell me they haven't got time to do something, I tell them they have."

Chapter Four
Stockport Survival

With Les Parry now knowing he would be Tranmere manager until the end of the season, he was tasked with keeping the club in League One. A run of just one defeat in eight matches between November and New Year certainly increased their chances, but a poor January meant they remained firmly in the relegation zone.

"We didn't string results together," admits Parry. "We'd have a win, a draw and then maybe a defeat. That lifted us out of the bottom four at one point. But once we did that, people kind of breathed a sigh of relief, and suddenly we were back in it and in trouble. At that point, I thought it wouldn't be easy to drag around."

Come the end of February, Tranmere were still at risk of going down and the squad was lacking a little bit in the final third. In a bid to help the manager, the Supporters Trust launched 'Les Aid', a fundraising initiative whereby the fans essentially paid for a new player.

The target was £12,000 and before the transfer window shut in March, it had been reached. Parry used the money to bring Andy Robinson back to Prenton Park, on loan from Leeds until the end of the season.

Robinson had actually started his professional career with Tranmere, joining them aged 22 from local Non League side Cammell Laird. Manager Ray Mathias would only hand him one appearance for the club, though, and in 2003 he was released, joining League Two side Swansea City.

In South Wales, the forward quickly became a lower league star. He forged a brutal partnership with Lee Trundle in attack and helped the club into the Championship, winning the Football League Trophy along the way.

After five years with the club, he moved onto Leeds, but found his opportunities limited at Elland Road once they too were promoted to the second tier. He was looking for some game time and a return home to Tranmere was ideal. It was just a case of Rovers being able to afford him.

"Les Aid saw us do some fundraising and we raised quite a bit of money with that," says Mark Bartley, who was vice chairman of the Tranmere Rovers Supporters Trust at the time.

"We sold the shares that had been donated to the Trust by former director Fred Williams. We sold them to distribute to as many fans as possible. We had some buckets at the games too, which I'm never that big a fan of, but it got us a few hundred pounds. We had a fundraising night as well. It was a big success."

"It was brilliant," reflects Parry. "We didn't have any money. People talk about low budgets, but we really did have a low budget. John Barnes had spent all the money, so there wasn't a penny.

"I was having to scrimp and save everything to get somebody in. Peter Johnson ran quite a tight ship. People criticise him for that sometimes. I'm of the opposite opinion.

"Tranmere Rovers are still going today. There isn't a phoenix club. That's because they were run well and a big part of that is the playing budget. To get the money off the fans was absolutely brilliant."

Robinson joined on 26th March, with Parry saying of his arrival: "He's a class player. We would have liked to get him around Christmas time but finances dictated we were not able to do it.

"The money from the supporters has enabled us to bring in a quality player we would not have been able to afford otherwise. It's been a brilliant initiative and I would like to thank them for it."

There were ten games left in the campaign. Rovers had drawn their previous match against Hartlepool 0-0, leaving them with 38 points and very much in trouble. Robinson had to make an immediate impact.

Unfortunately, the second debut was not a dream one for the returning forward. He was sent off as Tranmere were beaten 3-0 by Brighton, dismissed for a poor tackle on Inigo Calderon, perhaps down to a hint of frustration at his side being two goals down with only 12 minutes left.

"Andy Robinson was a great signing," says Parry. "He just lifted the place. But away to Brighton, he put in a stupid tackle and got the heave-ho.

"That nailed us a little bit, because we lost him for three games and we didn't have that long to go. We were doing alright in the game, too. We got beat 3-0, but we were doing alright."

Robinson would be out of action for a month, not returning until he came on as a second half substitute in a 2-1 defeat down at Brentford. He missed five matches in total, three of which Tranmere lost, but crucially they also recorded victories at home to Norwich and down at Exeter.

"We won 3-1 and that was a big game for us," says Parry of the latter. "They were on the back of a few wins on the bounce and were on the edge of the play-offs. Their manager was expecting them to win, because after the game he just shot off. He didn't say anything. To be fair, he emailed me the following day apologising."

Robinson would have his day, though. Tranmere's penultimate game of the season was at home to high-flying Millwall, themselves fighting for an automatic promotion spot.

Rovers were still in the relegation zone. They absolutely had to win to have a hope of going into the final game of the season with a chance of staying up.

Thankfully, their loan signing finally delivered. Ian Thomas-Moore had given the hosts the lead on the stroke of half-time, but Millwall were beginning to get a foothold and showed signs of a fight back after the break.

And that is when Robinson struck. The Rock Ferry born forward became a hometown hero at last when he received a delicate lay-off from Thomas-Moore before turning and unleashing a vicious, dipping shot that soared past goalkeeper David Forde and flew into the top corner.

"The Millwall game was one where nobody expected us to win," continues Parry. "We played really well. I thought the lads would be nervous, but they weren't.

"There was a big change that day because of the way the results went. It sort of swayed it towards us for the last game of the season. We could still go down, don't get me wrong, but it brought other teams into it as well.

"So it wasn't a case of us needing to win and other results having to go our way. If we won, and still went down, it would have taken a few results to go wrong for us. So I think that was what was important about the Millwall game."

"What a fantastic goal that was," adds Bartley. "That sort of kept us up, in my opinion, because it galvanised us. It was worth doing Les Aid just for that."

***

The final game of the season was against already relegated Stockport. The equation for Tranmere was simple: they needed to win, and hope that one of Exeter or Gillingham lost in order to stay up.

It was a do or die clash. Rovers' League One status was on the line, just like it was in 2005/06 when they only narrowly avoided going down on the penultimate day of the season by winning 2-1 at MK Dons.

In anticipation of such a big game, Tranmere's fans snapped up 3,000 tickets for Edgeley Park. They would occupy one stand behind the goal, as well as down one side of the pitch.

"I was trying to just do everything exactly the same," says Parry, "Just forgetting we needed to win. It was another game of football. But the anticipation around the place was huge.

"You heard how many tickets we'd sold and then it's all over the radio and the TV all the time. It was only that that made you realise what a big game it was. We were playing it down completely.

"We didn't even go overnight. The chairman asked if we wanted to, but we said no, because we'd normally do Stockport on the day, so we did it on the day. But even going to the stadium it was different. I can't describe it, but there was a different feel about the game."

Parry had a near fully fit squad to choose from. He packed his starting line up with experience, playing Marlon Broomes alongside Ian Goodison in the heart of the defence. Gareth Edds was joined by the youthful exuberance of Joss Labadie and Ashton Taylor in midfield, whilst Robinson started in a front three that also included Ian Thomas-Moore and Bas Savage.

It was a tense opening half an hour, as you might expect given the occasion. Stockport arguably started the stronger of the two teams, and they actually had the ball in the back of the net early on, but thankfully for the visitors Jabo Ibhere was flagged offside.

Tranmere took the lead just before half-time though, Goodison smashing a loose ball into the back of the net after County struggled to defend Zoumana Bakayogo's long throw.

The travelling fans went wild, as did the goalscorer, who celebrated by playing the air guitar. One up and already a good omen was on Rovers' side: they had never lost a game in which the Jamaican had scored.

"It was a good feeling," says the goal hero. "The supporters were so awesome to me at Tranmere. They were always backing me. For me to score the first goal in such an important game was so vital.

"It made me feel so good, especially as I knew how it made the supporters feel. They are very passionate fans. It was a good goal for them. They ran on the pitch and jumped on me. Everything about that day was for the supporters and the club."

"Before the game, it probably got to the lads a little bit," admits Parry. "It was a little bit quieter than normal. But when we got out and started playing, our fans were just fantastic. When we scored, it relaxed everybody."

Tranmere were still reliant on results from elsewhere, though. This was an age when social media was beginning to become an influence on people's lifestyles, and fans were desperately checking Twitter in the hope that Gillingham or Exeter would lose their games.

The news from St James' Park was not great; Paul Tisdale's side were drawing 1-1. But on the stroke of half-time, a huge cheer erupted from the Rovers fans as Gillingham went 1-0 down.

"I didn't have a radio or anybody telling me what the other scores were," Parry laughs. "We agreed that before the game. We didn't want that affecting us.

"But our fans, over on the far side and over to my left, they were letting you know what was happening. There would be a passage of play, just a little bit of passing, and the next thing you know, an almighty cheer would go up and they'd be dancing. Well it wasn't for a five yard pass!"

The news got better and better after the break. Ian Thomas-Moore scored Tranmere's second after 53 minutes. Meanwhile Alan Bennett and Kevin Betsy put Wycombe into a 3-0 lead over Gillingham.

There was no chance Rovers were letting this one slip, surely? Stockport were playing like a team who knew they were down and out, while the visitors showed they had something to fight for.

They made it 3-0 with less than a quarter of an hour left to play when Joss Labadie poked the ball past Lloyd Rigby. Game over. The Tranmere fans could start to celebrate, the players could breathe a sigh of relief.

When the final whistle went, it confirmed that Parry had guided his side to safety, as they finished one point above the relegation zone. They had achieved what many people believed to be impossible when he took over; The Great Escape.

"That was one of my most enjoyable days in football," concludes Parry. "Should you celebrate staying in a division? After the year that we'd had, yes, probably. It was an achievement.

"When I first took over, I looked at what the press were saying. The gist of it was that we didn't stand a chance of staying up. The fact that we did is a massive feather, not in my hat, but the hats of the staff and players."

"When Les Parry took over, we were struggling," adds Goodison. "We were definitely playing for him to make sure that we could stay up. We knew how hard it would be to get back up if we went down.

"We never thought we would fall so much in twelve months. When Ronnie was there, I think I won player of the season three times in a row. We just missed out on the play-offs by a couple of points. From that position, to fall down the league, it was very disappointing. The fans were expecting more."

Tranmere's fans were a little too exuberant in their celebrations. Hundreds of them invaded the pitch, and the club were left having to fork out to buy Stockport a new set of goal posts after some supporters decided to swing on the cross bar, snapping it in the process.

"Staying up was a miracle," admits Dave Kennedy. "We came out of there, and as much as it looked like everybody was really celebrating, I was walking out with a sense of massive relief.

"It was more that we shouldn't have been in that position in the first place. It was a season I was glad to see the back of. Another one!

"But whilst Les did perform a miracle to keep Tranmere up, I don't think it was down to his tactical genius, I think there was enough quality to stay up. In fact, there was enough quality there probably to do far better than just surviving on the last day.

"I'd love to give Les credit for doing that, and rightly so, but I think it was mainly down to the squad that he took on. He should have done better."

For everybody, it brought to a close a long, hard season, the kind of campaign nobody envisaged 12 months earlier. From being a team that fought valiantly for promotion in 2008/09, Tranmere became a team that survived a dogfight to stay up. The seeds for the future had been sown.

Chapter Five
2010-2012

After keeping Tranmere up, Les Parry was offered the manager's job on a permanent basis. He had achieved his remit in ensuring the club were still playing in League One for the 2010/11 season, yet nobody was more stunned when a 12-month contract was put on the table.

"I was a little bit surprised," he admits. "Peter Johnson is swayed by the fans. I've got a feeling it was the fans who got John Barnes the sack and not Peter Johnson.

"I don't read any social media whatsoever. I didn't go on the forums, because I didn't see the point in it. Peter did. He must have known that it wouldn't have gone down very well.

"The fact that he still appointed me is quite a big plus. If he'd have had an option though, I don't think he'd have given me another year."

Parry is clearly under no illusion that plenty of supporters would have preferred him to move back to the treatment room after keeping the club up. He had achieved the miracle, but in their eyes, it was time for a 'proper' manager.

"I think the fans were disappointed when I stayed on permanently," he continues. "I'm not stupid or blinkered. I only have to look at things that happen now. Look at Newcastle. They're disappointed with Steve Bruce, because they want a bigger name. Everybody wants a bigger name. I was the smallest name in the whole Football League and Tranmere Rovers had me as their manager.

"The problem with people, not fans, is the negative ones are normally the noisy ones. Even towards the end, when I went, I was still getting a lot of support from a chunk of the fans. Obviously I was getting a lot of negative stuff as well.

"But it was the same in 2010. There would have been some fans who thought 'give him a chance, he did alright last year'. You probably had a few who thought that, a few who thought it was the worst thing that could ever happen to Tranmere Rovers, and a chunk in the middle who thought it wasn't a very good appointment."

The manager was now, for the first time, tasked with building a squad. He let a number of players go, including Craig Curran, Charlie Barnett and Chris Shuker.

The latter is somebody who did not play too much during Parry's reign. A lightning fast winger who started his career at Manchester City, Shuker's effectiveness was diminished by a nasty knee injury he picked up in a game against Carlisle.

He could still have an impact at times, but the ability to breeze past defenders with ease was gone. In one interview, he said: "Physically, I've never had the full extension, so I've never been able to run the same and I lost a lot of power in it."

The man guiding Shuker through all his rehabilitation was Parry, still a physio when he did the damage. The pair built up a strong relationship and the winger's family even received some care under Tranmere's watchful eye.

But once Parry became Rovers manager, things started to deteriorate. Shuker once commented: "I'd tell Les if he was sat here with me now that the way he handled the transition was horrendous. He literally went from a physio, not having a clue about football, to 'I know everything' and telling me and Alan Mahon how to kick a ball and how to take a corner.

"With the greatest of respect, he's an unbelievably clever man in his field, but that wasn't his field. It didn't go down very well and that's not only my opinion. That's the opinion of many, many professionals who were there during his time.

"He wasn't tough to play for, he just wanted to hook it on every time. So we had John Barnes, who was 'let's pass it out' and 'do everything Manchester City style'. Then the other side of it was Les, who was 'don't even look at a man. Hook it on and face the other way. If you're looking towards your own goal, hook it over your shoulder and hope for the best'. They are two ends of the scale.

"I'm a coach now for a college team. I'd teach them to play what you see. If you can play and you have time, go and play, no problem. If you're under pressure and you need to kick it long, do that, no problem. Les was just the opposite to John Barnes. It wasn't my style of football to be honest." .

Parry on the other hand admits to feeling let down by Shuker's attitude during his time in charge. He would make 32 appearances during the 2009/10 season, but only 19 of them were after Barnes' sacking, nine of them from the start.

"Shuker disappointed me a little bit with his attitude," Parry says. "He was one of the ones I called in to tell him that he wouldn't be playing, so he's got reasons for saying that about me.

"He didn't have that many opportunities to listen to what I said because I didn't pick him! But I looked after him really well. I looked after his family and he was one of the ones who was a really bad influence in the dressing room.

"That's why I let him go at the end of the season. But I can understand him saying that and I don't blame him. I wouldn't argue with him. I've no doubt there were other players as well. But there must have been a few who did listen to what we said, and I don't mean I, I mean we, because we did alright.

"My relationship with the players changed when I became manager. I was really friendly with a lot of them, including Shuker. I brought his wife in for treatment and all that.

"The minute you leave players out, that relationship changes completely. It's not just me. It's managers throughout. There are 11 happy players. To everybody else, you haven't got a clue what you're doing. That's football. If you don't pick them, you don't know what you're doing.

"I found that quite difficult at first, but I don't think I changed that much. They soon got used to it being slightly different. I'd seen so many managers faff around with players, telling them fibs and just keeping them happy.

"I wanted to be honest with the players, and I hope that most would say I was really upfront. I used to name the team on a Thursday so I could tell the lads who'd played before that they weren't playing this time.

"Of all the managers I'd seen before, that had never happened. Managers would hide the team. Ronnie wouldn't tell anybody the team. On a Friday, when we were doing shape, he would mess the teams around so nobody knew. Then we'd go to the game, get in the dressing room and he'd walk out and his assistant would tell the lads what the team was.

"I didn't want that really. I think I was honest. There was a difference from being physio, without a doubt. I think I adapted okay and the lads accepted it okay."

With Shuker released, together with Bas Savage, Gareth Edds and Michael Ricketts, and several other players heading back to their parent clubs after loan, Parry had quite a job on his hands to fill the holes in his squad.

Joss Labadie arrived on a permanent deal after his loan spell from West Brom proved to be a successful one, whilst Enoch Showunmi joined on a free transfer from Falkirk. Other signings included French defender Max Blanchard following an impressive trial period, and youngsters Lucas Akins and Adam McGurk.

Meanwhile Dale Jennings would be promoted from the club's academy and had an immediate impact, resulting in his £600,000 transfer to Bayern Munich in the summer of 2011. Loan signings were made throughout the season and included Robbie Weir and Michael Kay, both from Sunderland, Coventry defender Jermaine Grandison and Lateef Elford-Alliyu from West Brom.

Money, however, was always tight, just as it had been the season before when those fans had to raise the funds to bring Andy Robinson back to Prenton Park.

Parry's insight into his transfer dealings reveals just how stretched the budget was. He explains: "At the beginning of the season, you want a squad, so you might need four or five players. You're paying out the least of all of the clubs.

"If I go to a player and say 'I want you to join us, we're willing to give you £1,000 per week', that player will keep me hanging until the last minute in the hope that they can get something better than that.

"So the teams who pay the least are always left until the last minute in filling the places. They get the players that nobody else wants. I know that sounds awful, but it's pretty true.

"I know and I hear our fans with what they say about formations, plan B, fitness and the rest, it's all a load of rubbish, believe me. It's about players. The teams with the better players are the better teams.

"If you look throughout all the league, you do get outliers, I admit that, but generally there is a massive correlation with money and finishing position. Money attracts the better players."

The wages some of those players received were remarkably modest. "Lucas Akins was on £150 a week," Parry reveals. "Adam McGurk was on £150. David Buchanan, who I signed in the summer of 2011 was on £300 a week. Even though he'd played a lot, he couldn't get a club."

Danny Holmes returned to Tranmere just a few weeks before Buchanan's arrival. The defender, a boyhood Rovers fan who had captained the club at schoolboy level, had been released two years earlier by Ronnie Moore.

He spent a couple of seasons playing in the Welsh Premier League with TNS, where he won the title in 2010 and was involved in some high profile European games. But the pull of coming back to Prenton Park was simply too strong for him, even if it meant earning less money.

"I took quite a big pay cut to come back to Tranmere from TNS," he reveals. "I was on close to £500 a week there, which was pretty decent at that age. At Tranmere, it went to £300.

"It just goes to show what budget Les Parry must have been working with. I think it was poor for the league we were in, but to me that shows that he did a really good job. I couldn't speak highly enough of him.

"It was in my contract that if I made so many appearances, my wage got bumped up quite considerably, because I'd be a first team regular. That's what happened in the end.

"The wage didn't matter too much to me though. I only lived two minutes from the ground, so I saved money on petrol and things like that! I just needed to, at that time in my life, prove that I could do it.

"I knew the reward for that would be greater in the long run. Fortunately enough, I had that mentality to go back and prove myself. Les gave me the opportunity and it was fantastic."

Parry really was working on a shoestring. "My approach to it, and I suppose I was a little bit different, was not to negotiate," he continues. "I would just say to players 'this is all I've got. I'm sorry,

I've only got £300, but it's there. By all means go and look elsewhere. What I can promise you is that if anybody comes in for you, I'll release you'. McGurk, Akins and Buchanan were all under that agreement."

Akins in particular is a player some supporters just did not take to. A gangly, perhaps ungainly winger, he joined Tranmere after being released by Scottish side Hamilton.

It took him a while to settle and his goal return was fairly poor, especially for a forward. He ended his first season at Prenton Park with just two strikes to his name, both of them coming against Exeter in late April.

He was involved in nearly every game under Parry though, eventually scoring seven times in 87 appearances before being sold to Stevenage at the start of the 2012/13 season. He has since become a club favourite at Burton, helping them into the Championship for the first time in their history.

"I know the fans didn't like Lucas," says Parry. "That pleases me a little bit. Going back to Chris Malkin, the fans used to give him stick about his finishing. When he left, there were about five or six clubs trying to sign him. Somebody saw in Chris Malkin what our fans didn't see.

"Lucas Akins was the same. We got money for him. But the fans didn't see it. I still see Lucas and he still calls me gaffer. He was a great signing for us, although the fans didn't appreciate him."

As well as building a squad, Parry needed to have a look at his backroom staff. Rovers cult hero Wayne Allison, nicknamed The Chief, had assisted him during the 2009/10 campaign, whilst Shaun Garnett had also stepped up from his position within the Centre of Excellence.

The latter, though, was keen to go back to working in Tranmere's youth system, whilst the budget for the coaching team allowed only for a manager, his assistant and somebody to work with the goalkeepers.

Because Parry had been carrying out physio duties as well as being the boss, he was effectively fulfilling two roles on one wage. Once he was taken on permanently, it limited him to just one outfield coach, as opposed to two, and chairman Peter Johnson wanted him to be assisted by somebody with more experience.

"The Chief was probably one of my worst decisions in football," Parry continues. "I brought him in until the end of the first season and he was fantastic. The three of us, me, Shaun and Wayne, worked really well together.

"Peter Johnson said 'I'm going to offer you the job permanently, but there's no getting away from it, as a manager you're green. You need that credibility as well. Garnett is green and The Chief is green. None of you have got much real experience. If you take the job, I want you to bring somebody in'.

"It meant one of those two had to go. I knew Kevin Summerfield from doing the rounds and watching games. I quite liked him. So I phoned him up to ask him in for a chat.

"He thought I was going to offer him a youth job, but I told him I was looking for a number two with experience. He'd been promoted with Plymouth a few times.

"He agreed to come and it meant either Shaun or Wayne had to go. It couldn't really be Garnett, because he'd been at the club so long. I took the Chief in and I said 'thanks for everything, but I've got to let you go.'

"I didn't blame the chairman. I said that I wanted to bring somebody in with experience. And Wayne was brilliant. How he really felt I don't know, but at the time, he was brilliant, and I still speak to him all the time. We've not fallen out over it!"

The dynamic of the coaching team was an interesting one. Parry also brought John McMahon back to Prenton Park, a highly thought-of coach who had previously worked under Brian Little during his days at Tranmere, as well as enjoying spells with Liverpool and Shrewsbury.

The manager really did only manage. He told Summerfield and McMahon what he wanted of them and just left them to it. It was their job to carry out the day to day duties on the training ground.

"Les knew what he was good at," says Danny Holmes. "He was obviously a really good people person and man manager. You knew what he expected of you. Training was always very organised. Kevin Summerfield and John McMahon had us well drilled.

"The gaffer would only jump into training sessions when he had to. He knew when to say the right thing. If he saw somebody slacking, he'd be on them, because with his physio background he would do that anyway.

"Tactically, Kevin and John knew what he wanted them to do, so he didn't really need to jump in and say anything anyway. If he felt he needed to, he did it at the right time. He knew what he was good at.

"He left Kevin and John to do the main training. He would pop in when he had to. They knew the players and they got the best out of us. Les came from a physio background so he can get labelled with whatever, but he was a decent manager and people don't give him the credit for that."

The only coaching role left to fill was the goalkeeping one. John Achterberg had held the position until moving to Liverpool. Tranmere legend Eric Nixon was desperate for a return to Prenton Park and threw his hat into the ring, but Parry just could not see it working. As such, he plumped for a couple of different options, including little known Australian Simon Miotto.

"Eric Nixon is one of my best friends," continues Parry, "And the goalkeeping position came up a couple of times when I was manager. Nico thought he would get it each time, but I just didn't think we could work together well, even though we were friends and had known each other for years.

"I met him when Simon Miotto got it, and I had to be upfront with him. I said to him: 'the way you are and the way I am, I don't see us working together'. That was one of the hardest things I did as a manager.

"Simon was actually our goalkeeping coach and registered goalkeeper, just in case he had to play. I don't think he'd played at a great level. I ended up sacking him because he was very volatile.

"George Cain was behind the goal in training one day and he would kick balls back into play when they went behind. On one occasion, he hit it back in and it went back to where they were working and Simon ripped a strip off him. After training I had to say to him 'don't ever, ever speak to a member of staff in front of players like that again'.

"He did the same to Tony Warner. The two of them were in the office and had a big ding-dong. I was in the office too and I backed Simon, although I didn't think he was right.

"So I backed him in front of the player, and then when the player went out, I said to Simon 'you were wrong there, don't ever deal with it like that again. Don't let it get out of hand.' He said 'if you feel like that, I'll leave'. I said 'okay, when are you going?' That's how he left."

***

With his new squad, Parry's first full season in charge was not too dissimilar to 2009/10. Tranmere were stronger at the back than under John Barnes, and they lost fewer games, but the football was not particularly appealing to watch.

As a result, attendances started to drop. People were beginning to turn their backs on a team who had little hope of challenging for promotion. Another long season was in the offing.

"I like Les," says Mark Bartley. "I thought he was a really good physio and he is a really good character. But in terms of the entertainment, it wasn't the best football that I've ever seen.

"That was reflected by our attendances, which dropped off. We were fairly stagnant. We didn't progress anywhere. It wasn't pretty to watch; it was just drab. We lost the momentum that we'd had a few years earlier when Ronnie Moore was in charge."

Rovers started the campaign with a 2-1 defeat to Oldham before beating Walsall 1-0 in the League Cup, Ian Goodison scoring the only goal as young 'keeper Joe Collister put in a strong performance.

They had to wait a while for a first win in the league though, drawing plenty of matches before loanee Arnaud Mendy netted in a 1-0 victory over Peterborough at the start of September.

Back to back wins were hard to come by as Tranmere were incredibly inconsistent. They would win one, lose one, draw a couple and so on.

October seemed to be a turning point as they went on a run of five wins in eight, including a stunning 4-2 victory over MK Dons when the young Dale Jennings began to make a name for himself.

The 17-year old had been snapped up by the Rovers Centre of Excellence after being released by Liverpool. He scored a stunning goal in his second appearance, a 1-0 win at Bristol Rovers, but it was his display against Karl Robinson's side that made headlines.

Didi Hamann, a former Liverpool and German midfielder was in the MK Dons side that day, and Jennings turned him, and others, inside out. He scored twice, both of them stunning individual goals, and Hamann was hooked off at half-time.

At the end of that season, he managed to convince his former club Bayern Munich to sign the forward, one of the stranger transfers in football history, although the forward did not last too long in Germany.

Even with the electric excitement of Jennings in the side, Tranmere were never able to pull themselves comfortably clear of the drop zone. They lost four in a row in a fragmented six weeks between the middle of November and New Year's Day, with games falling foul of the weather and postponements caused by the FA Cup. It left them outside of the bottom four only on goal difference with 22 points from 20 games.

That was the story of the season. Tranmere would go on a good run for a few weeks, but a bad run would be just around the corner. One defeat in eight between early January and mid February was followed by seven without a win.

It looked like Rovers might be heading for another final day showdown in terms of beating the drop, or at least taking their quest for safety into the last couple of weeks of the season.

It took a 2-1 win down at Bournemouth to really kick them on, Adam McGurk netting a stunning late winner, his first for the club.

"There was an away game at Wycombe," recalls Bartley. "At around this time, the Trust were starting to build a bigger profile. There was a fan who said he wanted to contribute towards fans going to away games because the attendances down south were quite small.

"I'd never been a fan of going by coach before. I'd always driven and made my own way with friends. But I stewarded a coach and actually quite enjoyed it.

"It was a game down at Bournemouth. We were pretty poor and were losing, but McGurk scored to get that win and it was a really important win."

Tranmere won three of their final six games, registering a 4-0 success over Exeter at Prenton Park and beating Leyton Orient 3-0. It meant they finished in 18th place, nine points clear of the relegation zone and only one win away from the teams in mid-table, something that still frustrates the manager.

"We could have finished higher that season," he groans. "Some of the players we had, like Marlon Broomes, if you go backwards in his career, he had pedigree. At one point he was going to be the next great centre-half.

"You can see why we signed him, but he could pick an injury up as well. He was good at that! A lot of the other players were loan players. Jermaine Grandison came in from Coventry, Michael Kay and Robbie Weir from Sunderland and Scott Wootton from Manchester United.

"I still think it was an achievement to actually stay up that year, but maybe not as big as the year before. We ended up quite a way clear of relegation, but then I made one of my other big mistakes as a manager!

"Towards the end of the season, I let the lads go to Chester races on the Wednesday before the final game. They got smashed. Then we got turned over by Swindon, who had already been relegated. It wasn't a great game.

"We ended up finishing a couple of places above the relegation zone, but if you look at the league, if we'd won, we'd have finished above the likes of Charlton. So that wasn't one of my best decisions!"

***

Les Parry signed a new one year contract at the end of the 2010/11 season, with Peter Johnson keeping faith in the man who had guided them to safety 12 months earlier, followed by a slightly better finish in the table in his first full campaign in charge.

"We've got a better team than this time 12 months ago," said Parry at the time. "We ended the season in a higher position and with more points, which shows we are making progress.

"We're also in a better position to push on next season with the players we've already got at the club and we'll be working hard all summer to bring the right players in to complement those who are here."

And the summer saw Tranmere make some impressive signings. Owain fon Williams, a highly rated Welsh goalkeeper, joined from Rochdale, whilst Weir and Kay made their loan signings permanent.

David Raven, a former Rovers academy player who was snapped up by Liverpool at a young age, made his return to Prenton Park and Martin Devaney, an experienced, quick footed winger signed after a six year stint at Barnsley.

Parry was unable to keep hold of highly rated full-back Aaron Cresswell, though. He joined Ipswich after his contract with Tranmere expired, following the likes of Dale Jennings and Sam Morrow in making their exits.

Danny Holmes returned to Prenton Park that summer too. It was two years on from his release by Tranmere and he could sense a shift in quality.

"When I was there the first time," he says, "Tranmere were challenging around the play-offs. They scraped to survival against Stockport when I wasn't there and when I came back, it was a different atmosphere. They weren't challenging for the top of the league.

"I could tell the quality had changed. The 2009 team contained well established Football League players. In every training session, they demanded high standards. There were leaders, like Antony Kay, Ben

Chorley and Chris Greenacre.

"They're all really vocal in the changing room and they demanded high standards. In this day and age, there aren't as many leaders knocking about but that team was full of winners and that's why Tranmere performed so well.

"I'm not saying the lads from 2011 onwards didn't demand high standards, but you just know that some people have a bit of an aurora around them. They know what to expect and how to deal with themselves away from football. You can tell the difference between players in that aspect.

"I could tell that the ambition of the club had changed as well. I've been a fan and I've seen Tranmere do well. I was training with the first team back in 2009. I was younger then, so maybe I was naive in a sense. I was just turning up to training every day and giving everything that I could.

"When I got into the first team in 2011, I could see a bigger picture. You start to see where you want to go and what you want to challenge for in your career. I think in that aspect, you knew they couldn't kick on and challenge for the league. It was a massive change."

The squad Parry had built looked stronger. Although his budget was not increased from the year before, he had been able to add some quality. They started the campaign with three wins from five.

By the end of October, Tranmere had moved into the play-off places. A brace of goals from Lucas Akins on a cold Tuesday night in Hartlepool earned them a 2-0 win. They were in sixth place after 15 games, losing just four times.

But that's when things started to go wrong for Parry. That victory in the North East was Rovers' fourth in a row in all competitions. A few days later, they travelled to Scunthorpe where, in spite of Mustafa Tiryaki twice putting them ahead, they lost 4-2 and had midfielder Jose Baxter sent off.

"We had a good squad in that season," says Parry. "But that's where the fans got me the sack, really. Up until October, we played a certain way. We were hard to beat. We were organised. We played a 4-3-3 with Akins and McGurk working their socks off to help defensively as well. We ended up in the play-offs and got on the TV and everything, but some fans were still having a real pop at the way we were playing.

"Instead of me thinking 'sod it, I'm sticking to my guns, we've done well doing what we do', I suddenly thought we could play a little bit of football. So I signed Jose Baxter from Everton and we swapped from a 4-3-3 with a sitter in the first three, to a 4-3-3 with a number 10 and we barely won another game!

"That was me giving into a little bit of public pressure. Had I not, we'd have probably won a few more games than we did."

Unfortunately for Parry, the Hartlepool win would be his penultimate one as Tranmere boss. After losing to Scunthorpe, they drew 0-0 at home to Colchester, before losing seven in a row, culminating with a 2-1 defeat at Stevenage.

"I came on as a substitute for my second debut in that match," recalls Danny Holmes, who had been obliged to bide his time to get back into the side following his return. "When I came back to Tranmere, I didn't let my fitness go, so to speak, but at TNS, we were dominating games. It was a different type of game.

"Every training session at Tranmere was really strenuous and tough and it took me a while to get used to that again. I had experienced the pre-seasons under Les before, so I knew what to expect, but it was just getting up to the speed of things.

"In that pre-season as well, I had a bit of a transition because I've got flat feet. I had new inner soles and because Les' pre-seasons are that tough, it literally took the whole skin off the bottom of my foot. It took me a while to recover from that.

"Sometimes you have doubts in your head. You want to hit the ground running but I couldn't do that. It took me a little bit longer, but once I showed what I was about and what I was capable of doing, it was fine.

"At that time, Tranmere were set up defensively and looked to nick a 1-0 win. I'm quite adaptable. I can change formations. But it was getting used to the strenuous training and the players being right on it.

"The way we were set up, we were either going to sneak a win or get beat. It was tough to take, coming from a team who were attacking all the time. I'm a defender. I love defending. But it's hard mentally when you're set up to defend because you know you've got to be on your game in every single match.

"Kevin Summerfield and John McMahon demanded high standards in training, so every session was full on and getting used to that again was tough. I got thrown in at the deep end and had to sink or swim. I knew what to expect from Les and it was just a matter of time until I was able to kick on.

"It was a tough time to be coming into the side, too. I remember coming on at Stevenage and I was up against Luke Freeman, who's now at Sheffield United. I did really well and I made a great block from one of his volleys. I chested it and it flew out. At that point, they knew I could handle the situation."

Holmes became a mainstay of the Tranmere defence for the rest of the season, but the team's form did not improve. There was a rare win over Bury just after Christmas. Joss Labadie and Ash Taylor were the goal scorers in a 2-0 victory, Rovers first in nine matches.

Picking up three points was a relief, but it did little to ease fan pressure. 'Parry Out' banners were unveiled at Prenton Park and the audible anger from the terraces increased game by game. Many fans had seen enough of what was on show. It was understandable, given the results.

"It was very draining," admits Mark Bartley. "It felt to me like we were treading water and just scraping by. You could tell that with the performances and people were very unhappy with how we were playing."

The games rolled by at the start of the year. Three 2-1 defeats on the road in a row, against Sheffield Wednesday, Yeovil and Bournemouth, with three home draws in between. Tranmere simply could not buy a win.

"The problem was," says Parry, "Nobody turned us over. You know if you're getting beat 5-0 every week, you can do something about it. We only lost three games by more than one goal.

"When it's 2-1 or 1-0 or whatever, you're only just about losing. The lads are having a go, so you think 'I'm not changing it, it's hard luck'. But you shouldn't do that. You should wake up and smell something because you do need to change it."

Things were turning toxic and Tranmere were in serious trouble. Their final game in February resulted in a 1-0 defeat to Oldham. It extended their shocking run of form to one win in 19 games in all competitions.

They were just two points above the League One relegation zone, and next up was a trip to Chesterfield, themselves just below the dotted line.

"There was a different atmosphere with the directors before that game," Parry continues. "Lorraine Rogers (a director and former chairman) said to me 'good luck today', but she said it in a way that made me think 'that's odd'.

"I didn't really pick up on the atmosphere from the fans being any worse than the games where they had the 'Parry Out' banner and all that. There were times at home games when they'd unveil that banner, and the crowd would jeer them. So although it was happening, there were other things countering it."

It turned out to be a terrible match. Ian Goodison made a vital clearance off the line in the first half and Nicky Ajose had a shot saved. At the other end Andy Robinson went close. But other than that, there was little separating the two teams.

With 15 minutes left, struggling Chesterfield took the lead. Jordan Bowery got the goal, beating fon Williams after being picked out by Jack Lester. And that sent the away end into overdrive. The percentage of people who wanted a change of manager was increasing rapidly.

"It turned a little bit toxic between the fans," says Mark Bartley. "You'll always get an element of the fans who'll support the manager. That will happen even if you're bottom of the league.

"But others had had enough, and I think I'd got to that point. If I had to lay my cards on the table, I wanted Les out."

Bowery's goal was enough to settle the contest. Tranmere lost 1-0 and sunk closer to the relegation zone. Chesterfield on the other hand managed to haul themselves off the bottom of the table.

"It was a crap game," admits Parry. "Chesterfield were below us. John Sheridan was their manager and Tommy Wright was his assistant.

"I went into the dressing room after the game and said to the lads 'listen, I don't think I'll be here tomorrow, so I just want to say thank you for everything. Managers don't normally get the chance to thank the team, but I've got this opportunity. Every one of you has given me everything you've got, so thanks'.

"It was really quiet. I then went to speak to their manager and said 'thanks for that, you've got me the sack!' We then get on the coach and it's all quiet."

Danny Holmes recalls being startled by what Parry said to the team afterwards. "I thought it was a bit too soon," he says. "How did he know? Maybe he'd had conversations. When he came out with something like that, you knew something wasn't right, but the game had only just finished.

"Honestly, I couldn't feel any pressure on the manager. Les bubbled you away from it all. I had no inkling that he was going to leave. Every session, the way it was set up every day was the same. We had quite a good bond. Nobody was going to stick a knife in his back because we weren't like that. It was a shock when he went."

Parry knew the game was up, though, especially when the chairman called him in for a chat the next day. "We were on the coach," he adds. "We get to within a few miles of Prenton Park and Peter Johnson, who always sat at the front, said 'Les, can I have a word'.

"I go to the front of the coach and he said 'could you do me a favour? Could you come and see me at my house tomorrow at 10am?'

"I get to his house the next morning, go in and I said 'listen, I know you want to give me a pay rise, but I really can't accept it, because we aren't doing very well'. He just laughed and said 'I've got to let you go'.

"He was filling up. I don't think he enjoyed sacking me. But I knew. I got longer than I should have done, I don't think there's any doubt in that. The reason for that is I had a good relationship with Peter Johnson."

Parry had gone. It was a move that needed to happen. Tranmere were sinking closer and closer to the bottom four and given the form they were in, relegation was looking a serious possibility. Negative momentum like that, just one win in 20, is tough to turn around.

"We still had enough time to stay up," says Bartley. "Word went around very quickly. It was quite a relief I think. I felt sorry for him because Les was Tranmere through and through, but something needed to change."

"It was a weird one to take," adds Holmes. "The majority of us were gutted. We had lots of local lads who all got on really well with Les. It was tough to take when he went, but that's football at the end of the day. If you don't get results, those things tend to happen.

"Did we let Les down? I don't know. I felt everybody in that team gave everything that they could, we just didn't have the quality to kick ourselves up the league.

"We were hoping for a 1-0 win and then a draw against the tougher teams, but we didn't have the quality. You couldn't fault any of the lads for their effort and endeavour. We were just going through a sticky patch."

Parry though accepts that his time was up. Rovers looked down and out. They were trying and the dressing room was still behind him, but the performances were poor and they did not look like winning. They needed a spark to get them going again, and it seemed unlikely that he would be the man to provide it. They also needed something that would get the fans back on board.

He confesses: "I should have probably gone, not that much longer before, because we weren't in the drop zone, but maybe five games earlier. I got another month longer than I should have done.

"But things like that don't bother me. I know people don't believe me and some managers won't admit it. But when you get the sack, you've had fans singing 'you don't know what you're doing' or 'you're getting sacked in the morning'. You've had them screaming at you. You know it's coming.

"Nobody gets the sack for doing well. So when it does come, it can be a little bit of a relief. That's how I took it. I shrugged my shoulders.

"It was on Sky Sports, I was breaking news for 15 minutes. Then

Andre Vilas Boas got the bullet from Spurs and custard pied me! My moment of fame went!

"But going back to what Chris Shuker said, I've worked with loads of managers who got the sack. The one thing in football is the next day, there's always a new spring in the lads with banter going on in training.

"If you look on YouTube at a video of Ronnie Moore, who came in for me, he said he had to pull the lads together and lift their heads. They were moping around as if they'd lost somebody. I think that says a million words about whether I've ever played professional football or not."

Chapter Six
Ronnie Returns

Less than 12 hours after Les Parry's departure had been confirmed, there was a new man in charge at Prenton Park. Once again, it was a familiar face, as Ronnie Moore, who had been at the defeat to Chesterfield on the Saturday in a media capacity, returned to the dugout.

It was close to three years since the former Rovers captain, coach and manager had received his shock sacking. In the interim, he had enjoyed a couple of seasons at Rotherham, getting them to the League Two play-off final in 2010, where they lost to Dagenham. He was dismissed a year later after the Millers missed out on a place in the top seven.

"It's great to be back," he said when the appointment was announced. "I can't wait to get started. It's nice to have the opportunity to keep the club in League One. I'm looking forward to being back at Prenton Park, meeting the players and hopefully starting things off with three points against Notts County."

There were still a handful of players at the club from Moore's first stint in charge. One of them was Ian Goodison, and he was over the moon to see his former boss return.

"Once Ronnie came back, I was happy," he says. "Him and Brian Little mean a lot to me in my career at Tranmere. They did a lot for me and helped me a lot. Les was the same, as a physio. He was always there for me. If I needed an idea, I'd go to his office and we'd sit down and talk.

"When Ronnie came back it was amazing for me. I was really excited. He would tell you what he wanted and do his best to get what he wanted. He would try to get the players to do as best as he could. He would get us together and then we'd go out and try and do it.

"As soon as a new manager arrives, the club gets a boost. We had a good run as soon as Ronnie came back. That always happens in football. The players were just so excited.

"He got the squad together and he got us to play his way. We were playing proper football. He got us going the right way at the time. We just did what we had to do. We got our heads down and played for him and the supporters, because once the supporters are behind you 100%, you get the result."

One of the players was a little bit apprehensive about Moore's return, though. Danny Holmes had been released by the manager during his previous stint with the club.

"I had a sleepless night when that got announced," he jokes. "Don't get me wrong, I do think he's a good manager. He's proved that in his time. But as an individual, I didn't like him. I'd say hello to him and he'd ignore me at times.

"He didn't say anything to me about releasing me when he came back in, but I didn't expect him to anyway. Even if he had said nice things, I was still going to prove a point, which I think I did. He wasn't the type of manager to throw an arm around you. He was old school. He'd rollick you and then expect you to react to that.

"When he came back, given he'd released me once before, I thought he'd do it again. He ended up giving me a two year contract, which I was shocked about! I was playing really well at the time, but I always felt if I had one bad game, he would drop me, which he did on a couple of occasions.

"He brought in a few loan players, but they often got injured or sent off in their first game, and I'd get back in, which was karma! I honestly do think he's a good manager, but the way he portrayed himself with certain players was poor, and I was one of those players."

***

Moore took over a Tranmere side who needed a lift. His first game was at home to Notts County the day after he took charge and he made two changes from the defeat to Chesterfield, with Robbie Weir and Lucas Akins replacing Martin Devaney and Adam McGurk.

However, it looked like the change of manager had had no impact whatsoever when the visitors took the lead after just five minutes. Damion Stewart got the goal, prodding home from inside the six yard box following a goalmouth scramble.

Rovers tried to rally, but Keith Curle's side, chasing a fifth successive win, looked most likely to score next, with Jon Harley and Jonathan Forte both coming close before the break.

Tranmere looked to be heading for another defeat until John Welsh equalised from a corner in the 90th minute, sending Prenton Park wild. This was the spark that they needed. Their season had been kick-started.

"I took the corner that led to the goal," laughs Danny Holmes. "I'd never taken a corner for Tranmere in my life! I have no idea why I ended up on it. I think it was a last ditch thing, maybe, where I'd tried to take somebody on and get a cross in and the ball went out.

"I'm quite good on set pieces, to be fair. People maybe don't believe me. One of my strengths is one v one, so from corners I'd stay back for that situation. The feeling in the changing room after that was great, you could tell it was a big moment."

Ronnie Moore was over the moon. "The spirit, determination and commitment from the players was brilliant," he said afterwards. "Overall in the second half, there was only one winner.

"Notts County have had some tremendous results and that was the first goal they've conceded in six games. I think we deserved more than what we got, but, if we keep working hard, maybe we can find something for someone to put the ball in the net."

Les Parry, a Tranmere man through and through, was keeping his ears open for how his team did. "It was a late equaliser and that was the moment I thought, personally I'd had to go, it needed a spark.

"Ronnie happened to be that spark. I didn't have any thought at all about getting relegated. I knew that once I went, the lads would get something. That goal from Welsh was the spark that got them through to the end of the season."

From then onwards, Tranmere's form improved dramatically. They had been just a point above the relegation zone after the game, but won four of their next five, beating the likes of Preston at home and Rochdale away to move well clear of danger.

The returning manager had guided the team to safety, but Holmes does not give him too much credit. "I don't think he really did that much," he insists. "Training was the same. The camaraderie and togetherness was the same.

"Because we had such a long run of bad results, it was just a case of turning the tide. That Notts County result was the one that fired us up. You could tell, coming in after the game, how important it was, with the fans as well as the players.

"It's all about momentum, negative and positive, and that's the same in life as it is in football. If you keep working hard, you might get the bad times, but the good ones will come back. We just had to give 100% and that Notts County result turned it around for us.

"I didn't fear relegation under Les. We had a great bond as a team. I loved going into training every day and the other players did as well. There was a great craic between us all. We used to train properly.

"Most of the time, especially when we suffered the relegations later on, you could tell in training that people weren't arsed. With Les, everybody cared. It was a tough one to take.

"Everything was spot on in training under Ronnie. But when you go to the relegation seasons in later years, you could tell the difference from when Les was there, even though we weren't doing so well then either."

Tranmere would finish the season in twelfth place, 13 points clear of the relegation zone. It was a strong recovery given where they were when Parry left at the beginning of March.

Moore was in charge for the last 13 games, picking up 22 points thanks to six wins and four draws. He had completely changed the momentum of the club and, having signed a short term deal until the end of the season when he initially arrived, was rewarded with a new contract as permanent manager.

***

That summer saw a flurry of transfer activity at Prenton Park as the new manager got his chance to shape the squad. He allowed a number of Les Parry's signings to leave, including Robbie Weir and Enoch Showunmi, whilst he was left disappointed at Preston pinching John Welsh and David Buchanan.

Defender Dave Raven and midfielder Joss Labadie were both released after their contracts expired, Moore not convinced they had done enough to take the club forward, whilst Lucas Akins was sold to Stevenage on the eve of the new season.

With so much of his wage budget freed up, the boss made some thoroughly impressive additions. One of them was highly rated Everton youngster James Wallace, who was offered the title of club captain in a bid to convince him to turn his loan move into a permanent one.

Joe Thompson arrived from Rochdale, with Akins' departure paying his transfer fee, whilst free transfers included Abdulai Baggie, Paul Black, the returning Danny Harrison and Jean-Louis Akpa Akpro.

Meanwhile Jake Cassidy, who had been on loan from Wolves towards the end of the season, re-signed until January, and Liam Palmer and Ben Gibson also joined on temporary deals from Sheffield Wednesday and Middlesbrough respectively.

The strong additions included players with pedigree and experience and some who boasted bags of potential. When the squad reconvened for pre-season training, Danny Holmes remembers being impressed with what he saw.

"We needed some attacking players," he says, "But you didn't expect them to score as many goals that the likes of Jake Cassidy and Jean-Louis Akpa Akpro did. When we came in for pre-season, you could tell we had some really good players, even if they weren't well known.

"The back four was great. Ben Gibson had a top debut at Chesterfield and was a massive part of our team. He was a natural left footer playing as the left centre-half, which was vital to the way we were playing. He wasn't shy vocally either, even at a young age.

"Then there was Ian Goodison, and he's just Ian Goodison! He'd perform whatever game it was! It was great to see Zoumana Bakayogo kick on as well, because he's a great character. He's a real confidence player. When he got his tail up, he was brilliant. He had an unbelievable season.

"We were a solid back four. You knew what you were going to get from us, with the exception of Zoum and his mazy runs! We could perform because we knew we had a solid base."

Tranmere took everybody by surprise when they started like a runaway train. They registered nine wins in their opening 12 matches, soaring to the top of the table and scoring plenty of goals in the process.

Opponents were swept aside. Andy Robinson scored one of the finest hat-tricks you are likely to see in a 3-0 win at Carlisle, Colchester were battered 4-0 and Holmes himself got a rare goal in a 5-2 victory down at Crawley.

"I didn't expect us to make the start that we did," Holmes continues. "How could you, given the season before? The previous season is always a good benchmark of where you could go. But to be fair to Ronnie, he made some really good signings.

"So for us to make that start was a surprise at first, but once we knew we were capable of doing it, it was like a snowball effect. You couldn't stop us. We had an unbelievable bond. That's the best team I've ever played in, both with togetherness and ability.

"It was a fantastic time. You used to love going into training, but even away from training, you'd have a great craic. It was the only team where we did stuff away from football. We had a really good bond."

Even the manager was surprised at how well his team were doing. Ronnie Moore would often express that he simply wanted to get to the cherished 50 point mark, the number that was usually enough to avoid relegation.

"We don't talk about promotion," he said after that win at Crawley. "I want 30 more points. We've got 20 now and the other 30 will give us 50 which means we'll be playing in this league next year."

"Managers will say stuff like that to protect themselves and their team," reflects Holmes. "Looking at it, we probably were punching above ourselves, so that's understandable.

"But we were battering teams. We knew we were a good team. Managers are just protecting themselves and the club but I'd probably say the opposite."

"We were top of the league at Christmas," adds Shaun Garnett, "But we didn't say 'right, we could go for promotion here'. We were still thinking about avoiding relegation. As a whole at the club, we took our eye off things and the consequences came."

Some fans argued Tranmere were setting themselves up for a collapse. In their opinion, they should have had more belief in their ability to maintain a promotion charge given the stunning start to the season.

By the middle of October, they had opened up a seven point gap at the top of the table, with Holmes again on target as they came from 2-0 down to beat Yeovil 3-2 at Prenton Park.

A week later, Rovers suffered their first defeat of the season down at Bournemouth. The match was Eddie Howe's first in charge after returning from Burnley, and the Dean Court side almost literally kicked the visitors off the park in securing a 3-1 victory.

But then things started to collapse. Akpa Akpro had already picked up an injury by this point, fracturing a metatarsal in a win at Notts County, whilst Baggie and Gibson were other long term casualties.

In December, James Wallace picked up a knee problem that would keep him out for nearly a year, whilst Palmer was recalled by Sheffield Wednesday until he had put pen to paper on a new contract.

The straw that broke the camel's back was Cassidy, who was was on 11 goals by the time his initial loan from Wolves came to an end in early January.

Tranmere wanted to extend the deal, but Dean Saunders had just taken charge at Molineux after leaving Rovers' promotion rivals Doncaster to take up the post. In order to help his former club, he refused to let the striker remain at Prenton Park.

"That's where it all went wrong," continues Holmes, "with all those players becoming unavailable. At that point, we were in a tremendous position. Their replacements weren't as strong.

"That's just a fact and something that happens in football. Our first XI was a really strong team and if anybody got injured, which they did, it was going to have an effect on us."

A 5-0 defeat at Swindon before Christmas was a sign of what lay ahead for Tranmere. They then lost by the same scoreline to Derby in the FA Cup third round in early January.

In between, they notched up three successive League One victories. However, following a 2-1 win at Brentford in January, things started to go downhill pretty quickly. Adam McGurk's late goal earned the three points at Griffin Park, but the match is perhaps most memorable to Rovers fans because of what happened afterwards.

The club had unofficially adopted a new anthem that season, "Forever In Blue Jeans" by Neil Diamond. 'Money talks, but it don't sing and dance, and it don't walk' are the opening lyrics. And that's how the players viewed themselves.

They knew the budget was low. They were getting paid nowhere near as much as some of their counterparts at Sheffield United, Bournemouth or Preston, yet each of those teams, and 20 others, were looking up the table at them.

Following the Brentford game, a video of the team singing the 1979 hit appeared on social media. Owain fon Williams was the man behind the camera. The main protagonist in front of it was the larger than life Andy Robinson, a home favourite belting out the lyrics as if he had penned them himself.

The song even started getting played before matches at Prenton Park. It all coincided with the downfall that was just around the corner. Fans, even to this day, will tell you it was a curse.

"The video may have come out after that Brentford game,"

continues Holmes. "But that singing and everything, honestly, we did it after every match.

"They tried to put a song on the PA system, Forever In Blue Jeans, when we came out. That was our song. When people got the gist of what was going on, perhaps they thought that was the starting point.

"We'd had a great win down at Brentford and we were having a singalong on the bus, then the video comes out, so it does look that way, like it was the starting point. But we did it after every game."

Rovers were still top of the table at that point. They had climbed the mountain. With 17 games to go, they were in pole position to return to the Championship for the first time in over a decade.

They had also set themselves up for an almighty fall. The loss of so many influential players from the squad began to take a heavy toll. Ronnie Moore's side would manage only three more victories over the remainder of the season.

They tried to reinforce the squad with the limited funds available. Loanees Michael O'Halloran and Mama Sidibe came in from Bolton and Stoke, whilst David Amoo joined on a free transfer from Preston.

Other arrivals later in the season included Sean McGinty, the final player to leave Manchester United under Alex Ferguson, and Donervon Daniels. But in truth, none of them improved the starting XI and they would only make a handful of appearances.

"You can see the drop-off in quality with the new signings," adds Holmes. "With no disrespect to some of them, they couldn't fit in with our team bond and what we had going on, so they ended up being more individualistic about it.

"Nathan Ecclestone was with us earlier in the season and he is one who was definitely like that. He came from Liverpool and you could see from the way he was on social media that he wasn't as down to earth as the lads who were there.

"We didn't treat him any differently or single him out, but you either get on with somebody or you don't. That's the way it is.

"I think we should have thrown a little bit more money at it to get one or two players who could have got us over the line. I just think we needed somebody to come in who'd been there and done it, even if it was just one or two players. It didn't have to be a massive overhaul.

"With Peter Johnson looking to sell (the club), he didn't want to put any more money into it and that's completely understandable. You can't knock him for what he did because he saved Tranmere from extinction.

"I think the hierarchy at the club wanted us to go up, yes. But when it came to money, definitely not. If they had put just a little bit more in, I totally believe we would have got promoted.

"In that same season, Yeovil did exactly the same, except they maintained their team and added one or two in January. They managed to get into the Championship. It was so similar to us, except they strengthened. It just goes to show.

"I know money talks and you don't want to waste money in certain areas, especially if you're looking to sell the club. But the gold that was at the end of the tunnel was massive. Just a little bit of money here or there could have made a massive difference."

Moore himself referenced the budget towards the end of the season when he addressed a six match run without scoring, five of them which Rovers lost 1-0.

"We had a little bit of joy with Cassidy and he's been a massive miss for us," he said. "Mama gives his all and holds it up well, but is he a 20-goal-a-season man? I would hazard a guess to say no.

"You've got to be scoring goals. Getting that first goal is so important in games. We need a poacher but they don't come cheap and they're very difficult to find."

Tranmere lost their next four after winning at Brentford. By the start of February, they had been knocked off top spot, but that was far from the end of the slide. Come March, they were even out of the play-offs.

Amazingly, after amassing 50 points by New Year's Day, a period which included 14 wins, they added only 17 more points over the remainder of the season, finishing way down the table in 11th place. It was a staggering fall from grace.

"To not get promoted was shocking because we were playing good football," admits Ian Goodison. "We were so disappointed. With the squad that we had and the players that we had, we thought we were untouchable at times.

"We thought we could beat every team. The squad was so together. We worked hard and we thought we were going to make it all the way to the Championship."

"At one point, you were questioning how it had come to that," adds Holmes. "Even when we were in the play-offs, it was like 'how are we in the play-offs when we've been top for six months?' It was a tough one to take.

"Finishing outside the play-offs wasn't a disaster, because before the season started, you'd most probably have taken that position. But once you're top and in the play-offs for so long, not to get there was a massive blow.

"It was a massive missed opportunity. If we'd kicked on and got into the Championship, the gates that you'd get and the teams you'd play against would have been such a massive thing. We could have added to the team again.

"Once we didn't reach that goal, with it being so close, that's when the standards seemed to come down and down, as a club as a whole. It was just left to us to go out and perform. Nothing else was getting looked after. It was really tough."

A year later, Tranmere would return to Griffin Park to take on Brentford once again. Both teams were still in League One, although Rovers' fortunes had changed dramatically.

The fixture brought back painful memories. The previous trip to this particular corner of London had been their pinnacle 12 months earlier. Now they could not be further away from the promotion challenge.

Ahead of the game, Nick Hilton, long-time Rovers correspondent for the Liverpool Echo, penned his usual preview, except on this occasion it contained one stand out line that would strike a real chord.

"They finished 11th," he wrote of 2012/13, charting the fall from grace that came after that Brentford win, "still punching above their weight but well short of the impossible dream of promotion, or even a play-off spot.

"There was, by some accounts, a measure of relief in the boardroom that Tranmere did not have to follow through on preparing a budget for playing in the Championship in 2013/14. A daunting scenario could have faced the club that was sustaining significant losses on day to day operations, in spite of the success on the field."

Perhaps promotion was not so keenly sought, after all.

Chapter Seven
Relegation Number One

Momentum, in football, is huge. When a team gets on a winning run, like Tranmere had at the start of the 2012/13 campaign, they can become an unstoppable force. Confidence inhabits every touch and there is an inner belief that, no matter what the scenario, the team will be victorious.

The opposite can also be true. A losing streak can be difficult to arrest. The ball seems to constantly bounce in the wrong direction, a freak injury to a key man is more likely to happen and as confidence ebbs, players may not take the risks required to win.

Rovers ended the 2012/13 season with a run of five straight defeats, followed by a 0-0 draw with Bournemouth. They did not score a single goal in their last six matches.

Inevitably, there was concern that the alarming fall-off in form from that campaign could carry into the following season, regardless of the changes that were made to the squad.

Ronnie Moore made some impressive signings, including the arrival of Ryan Lowe, a prolific lower league striker from MK Dons and Tom Hateley, a versatile defensive minded player who had been with Motherwell.

Meanwhile Jason Koumas, one of the most gifted footballers to pull on a Tranmere shirt and who had earned the club a £2 million-plus transfer fee when he moved to West Brom in 2002, returned to Prenton Park. It was two years since he had walked away from the professional game at the end of a spell with Wigan.

The midfielder, a former Welsh international, was determined to prove he could still cut it and wanted a chance to play in front of his young son. It was a popular signing, albeit a risky one as well, given he had so much work to do on his fitness.

Some duds came in as well, though. Stephen Foster, a centre-back from Barnsley, was one of the flagship arrivals of the summer, but his best days were long behind him and his body was failing him.

Indeed, he would manage only five appearances before having his two year contract cancelled at the end of August, with Moore saying in a brief statement: "After discussing things with Stephen it was agreed that it was in the best interests of both parties if we part company. I wish him the best of luck in his future."

Akpo Sodje and Evan Horwood were amongst the other arrivals, although neither had much of an impact during their time at Tranmere. Chris Atkinson joined on loan from Huddersfield.

He was far from the only temporary signing that season. Fourteen of them came in in total, from every corner of the country. Many were quickly forgotten, so brief was their time at Prenton Park.

Among them were goalkeeper Brad Watkins, who joined from Aston Villa but did not make a single appearance, and defender Ryan Edwards, whose sole game was a 5-0 defeat to Peterborough in the FA Cup.

"At the time, the fashionable thing to do seemed to be to look at loan players," recalls Shaun Garnett. "That means they're not your players and they come to the club knowing they won't be here long term.

"It didn't help. Neither, further down the line, did the constant changing of managers. Each one would bring his own players in, and then we'd have another one, who'd want his own DNA and philosophy. It had a knock on effect.

"Every time something happened like that, it chipped away at the club. It was just making the holes bigger and bigger.

"It really is such a misty period. Every season seems to be the same. It was always a case of 'this is what you've got, these are the only players you can bring in and you've got to make the most of them'."

There was some consistency in the squad. Danny Holmes had penned a new two and a half year deal midway through the 2012/13 season, therefore keeping him at Prenton Park until 2015.

Yet his position would be constantly challenged as Moore brought in a plethora of players in his right-back spot. Hateley was one of them, although he left at the start of 2014, while Andrai Jones, Jon Otsemobor and Matthew Pennington all joined on loan.

The club had become a revolving door. There were times when the media would turn up for a pre-match press conference and not recognise the player presented to them for interview duties.

"The club lost its identity, 100%," says Holmes. "When you're there at the time, even I'm guilty of it, you're always positive and think everything is alright. Looking back on it now, it was a shambles, both in the way it was run and the number of players who came in.

"We completely lost our identity. I used to watch from the stands. I'd worked my way into the team and I was   thinking 'what the hell am I doing here?'

"You'd go into training and there would be scuffles between teammates. When we were top of the league, you'd have scuffles in training, but after the session, it would be squashed, no problem. Later on, there was an edgy feeling around the place. People would get stuck in and there'd be scuffles. The club just lost its way."

At the end of September, one loan player did arrive at Tranmere who would be sticking around. Liam Ridehalgh joined from Huddersfield, making the move a permanent one at Christmas. By the time the 2018/19 season came around, he was the club's longest serving player.

"I wanted to play League One football," he reveals. "I had been out on loan before, but those clubs had been in League Two and with me going there and getting promoted twice, I felt I wanted to play in League One.

"My agent rang me and said 'Tranmere want to sign you' and I just felt it was the right time to leave Huddersfield, because I wasn't getting a look in there, rightly or wrongly. I just wasn't getting any games. I think it was the next step in my career to push on.

"I had been on loan quite a few times, but I wanted somewhere to call home. That was important to me and Tranmere were offering that."

By the time Ridehalgh joined, Tranmere were already in trouble. They had registered just one league victory, 1-0 at Oldham courtesy of an injury time penalty from Ryan Lowe, and were in the middle of a run of seven games without a win.

"I wasn't expecting a relegation battle when I signed," insists Ridehalgh, despite the fact Rovers sat in 19th place in the table. "Obviously I did come when the team was struggling, but it was still early on because I initially signed at the end of September.

"I thought that they were a big club and a good club. I didn't think we'd be anywhere near the bottom four come the end of the season. We had good players and we had experienced players too. Ian Goodison especially helped me settle in."

Less than a month later, another intriguing signing arrived. Steve Jennings had joined Motherwell after leaving Tranmere in 2009. He had since moved to Coventry, but his time with the Sky Blues had reached its conclusion when his contract was terminated.

Like Ridehalgh, the midfielder, who had been used to better times during his first stint at Prenton Park, was sure the club would pull well clear of trouble by the end of the campaign. Yet when he signed in mid-October, on the back of a 4-0 home thrashing to Leyton Orient, Rovers were in the relegation zone with just eight points from 12 games.

"I had just been paid up by Coventry and I was going in and around a few places," he explains. "I had a chance to go down south and there were one or two other options too, but I just felt something when I spoke to Ronnie on the phone.

"He explained the situation, and I sort of knew what it was anyway. It was a no brainer coming in for two months, and don't get me wrong, it was two months where you were putting your body on the line.

"I didn't know we were in a relegation fight when I arrived. I know we were down there, but that was after only around 12 matches. There was still plenty left to fight for. Looking around the team, I think that's why I did come back."

Tranmere, at the time, were still cash strapped, to the point where, off microphone, Ronnie Moore predicted after one press conference that relegation at some stage was inevitable due to the lack of investment at the club.

He managed to convince Jennings to sign a contract until January in which he basically worked without payment. There was no weekly wage, only a match appearance fee.

"Ronnie Moore and John McMahon were still at the helm and they were two faces I knew quite well," Jennings continues. "The place hadn't changed too much from when I left in 2009, if I'm totally honest.

"You still got changed at the ground, jumped in your car and travelled to Raby to train. The majority of the faces behind the scenes were still there, such as the office staff.

"Yes, the players had changed on the pitch. You've gone from a promotion challenging team to basically trying to avoid relegation, and that mood had changed.

"But even when I came back, we had characters such as Andy Robinson, Jason Koumas, Ryan Lowe, myself, James Wallace and a young Max Power. We had those big characters. We just didn't have the right fit on the pitch, as it proved."

Whilst Jennings talks of the attraction of coming in to work with a familiar boss, Danny Holmes believes Moore was a different manager to the one who arrived back at Prenton Park in March 2012.

At that time, Moore had been out of work for a period and was also keen to prove a point about his sacking by Peter Johnson in the summer of 2009. Holmes, though, questions his passion.

He explains: "When he did come back in, after Les was sacked, I saw a slight change from the Ronnie Moore in 2009. He seemed to be more positive and I think it's because he was trying to prove a point.

"Then towards the end of his second spell, I felt he didn't care as much. At first, he'd be at training all the time and he was a positive figure around the club. Near the end, he didn't turn up to some training sessions. You'd be wondering what was going on.

"There was one pre-season training session and it was a red hot day. We'd get changed in the Kop and then go down to Raby. We were doing all of our running and Ronnie wasn't there, even though it was one of the first days of training. As we were walking back through the ground, I saw him sunbathing. You can't be doing that!

"Sometimes, I thought he was 100% in, sometimes he wasn't, but that's just my opinion."

Ridehalgh, on the other hand, had Moore as his manager for the first time. "He was very old school in his ways," he says. "I think the game has progressed a lot since then.

"We have a lot of GPS data and fitness coaches and other stuff on that side, plus you've got to look after yourself a lot more now. We're only talking six or seven years ago, but it has progressed. You've got to be a lot fitter and I believe you've got to be mentally a lot tougher too."

Despite all the new signings, Tranmere's form was abysmal. They still only had three league wins to their name by the end of November, but thankfully, at that point they finally began to pick up.

A 5-1 hammering of Coventry was notable for James Wallace making his long-awaited return from the knee injury picked up against Colchester in the FA Cup a year earlier. He scored after coming on as a substitute, much to the delight of everybody associated with the club. There was also a 2-1 home victory against Colchester, in which Ryan Lowe netted a brace, and that left Rovers in 19th place in the table, three points above the relegation zone.

They had still not registered back to back wins, though, a sign of a team who are struggling for consistency. Holmes reckons it showed they were still feeling the effects of what had happened the previous season.

"Looking at it now, there was definitely a hangover," he admits. "The players who were still there wanted to kick on and have exactly the same start. But the players who came in had a different mindset.

"As the years went by, people were just coming for the money and to maintain being a footballer. In 2012, the team was passionate about doing well for Tranmere. You could tell that, in the end, there were only about four lads who truly cared. You're fighting a losing battle straight away. It was horrible."

Ian Goodison agrees. "I think there was a hangover, most likely, going into the next season," he says. "From being all the way at the top, we went all the way to bottom. Coaches were bringing in new players. Players were going in and out. That can make a big change."

Given the quality of the players available, Rovers should have been winning more games. Lowe, in particular, was having a splendid debut campaign with the club, with 14 goals to his name by the end of the calendar year.

It had been many years since Rovers boasted a striker who was quite so prolific in front of goal. Nobody had reached the 20 strikes in a season mark since Simon Haworth a decade earlier. At the start of 2014, Lowe was well on course to equal the Welshman's efforts.

Yet despite Lowe's marksmanship, Rovers were failing to win games. In the opinion of Shaun Garnett, that tells its own story. "Having somebody like Ryan scoring goals but not getting results, that was probably frustrating for the majority of the players and the coaching staff," he says.

"Could we have done more with him? In the last few games of the season, we were creating nothing for Ryan. You always say your most successful season is one where you have a goalscorer. We had one in that year and possibly didn't make the most of Ryan."

***

As well as struggling with on the field, Tranmere were marred by what was happening off it. They hit the headlines on three occasions, all of them for the wrong reasons.

Firstly, Joe Thompson was diagnosed with cancer. The winger, an integral part of Ronnie Moore's squad in the previous season, had struggled with tiredness through the summer, causing him to miss some of the friendly matches in preparation for the new campaign. After undergoing a series of tests, it was discovered he had a form of cancer known as nodular sclerosis Hodgkin lymphoma.

"Joe is a fantastic young man," said Moore in a statement. "He will be missed around Prenton Park while he has treatment. He has the full support of all the coaching staff and his team-mates and we will do everything we can to help him make a full recovery."

"It was very upsetting for all of us, as well as Joe himself," says Ridehalgh. "I actually didn't really know him that well. I had only been here about a week before he received the news and then he wasn't in. But it wasn't nice to hear."

A few weeks after the news surrounding Thompson emerged, Tranmere were rattled by another headline. Legendary defender Ian Goodison, who in October had made his 400th appearance for the club, was arrested, as was his teammate Akpo Sodje and four other men, as part of a National Crime Agency investigation into spot-fixing in football.

Rovers passed little comment on the situation, other than a press release that confirmed: "Tranmere Rovers are aware of reports in today's media regarding Ian Goodison. As this is an ongoing investigation the club has no further comment at this time."

Both Goodison and Sodje were cleared to carry on playing after being released on bail, although the latter barely made another appearance as his Football League career reached its conclusion. Goodison, on the other hand, was too important to leave out.

"I don't think what was going on away from the playing side of things helped," says Shaun Garnett as he recalls the situation. "Sometimes in football, you have to pin your shoulders back and get on with it. You can't let it impact on your business. But it did, it had to have done."

Both players were re-arrested in April 2014 after the National Crime Agency revealed they had uncovered "new evidence". Goodison always denied any involvement and the Crown Prosecution Service announced the case had been dropped in January 2015.

The period of time, however, is still etched in his memory. "I was going back and forth with the police," he recalls. "They'd come and pick me up out of bed when I was sleeping. I had to take the train.

"I remember one night, they let me out and I had to get back for the next morning because the team were travelling to a game. So I got a bus from London. It took 6 hours to get to Liverpool. I got there in the morning and got a taxi to Tranmere and got ready to catch the bus. When I arrived at Tranmere, I was told I wasn't in the squad.

"I was busting my arse to get back just to get a point for the team, then when I get there, I'm told I'm not in the squad. I'd go back home. I would sit on the bench when there was a squad game in training or I'd be training by myself. It was very disappointing.

"I still had life in me. I was better than who was playing. They weren't winning many games. The players were telling me to go and talk to the manager, who by this point was John McMahon, to tell him I wanted to play for him, but he knew me.

"Once I pulled on the shirt, it didn't matter who was in charge. I was playing for Tranmere Rovers Football Club. I always put my 100% in, because it was the club who were going to go down, and I didn't want it on my resume that I'd been relegated with Tranmere."

Regrettably, that would not be the only scandal involving Tranmere during the 2013/14 season, as Ronnie Moore was charged with a breach of betting offences in the final few months of the campaign.

The manager was first quizzed by the Football Association in mid-February, with the news emerging the day before Rovers travelled to Bristol City for an important game in League One. They were two points above the relegation zone at the time. It was bound to have an affect.

A few days later, on the eve of another away game at Crawley, Moore was suspended by the club. Assistant John McMahon was put in charge of first team affairs on a temporary basis, pending the outcome of the enquiry into the manager's conduct.

"When Ronnie left, it had a huge effect on me," continues Goodison. "He's like a dad to me. We were so close. He would come to me before the game and say 'listen, we need three points today. Anything you have to do to get the three points, do it.' I would say 'okay, I'll make sure we get it'. We talked about a lot of stuff.

"When he left, it was the turning point for me. Everything was going wrong for me. I wasn't playing. I was sitting on the bench and it was because of politics with John McMahon.

"Ronnie and me were so close. I think John McMahon thought I wasn't going to play for him. The players we had in defence, I know I was older, but none of them were better than me. I could still do a better job than them.

"I was put in a for a couple of games and I produced for them, but John McMahon wouldn't play me. I don't know the reason why, but I think it's because Ronnie and I were so close. Once Ronnie went, everything went down hill.

"That was the point when I knew we wouldn't stay up. With the players in the dressing room, it was a case of 'there's no way we're going down', but you can't be disappointed if we go down.

"The fans are travelling and saving their money to come and support us. They're taking trains all over the country and it's very disappointing for them. We had to sit together and discuss it, the players and coaches, because the fans didn't deserve to go down. I don't think the players did either. We gave our hearts but weren't getting results."

"I felt we were beginning to pick up a little bit until Ronnie Moore left," adds Ridehalgh. "I thought we were in a good place as a squad. The manager then leaves, he gets put on gardening leave, and John McMahon takes over.

"To be fair it was a difficult task for John to take over on his own. He had the help of Shaun Garnett, but it really did affect us. He was on a bit of a hiding to nothing. It really was a tough job for him."

"It did affect the dressing room, I'm not going to lie," admits Steve Jennings, who knew the manager better than nearly anybody in there. "Ronnie's a big character. He doesn't do a lot of coaching on the field, but he earns his money on a Saturday. He's always been like that. We lost him with 15 games to go and it did have an affect.

"However, we did have John McMahon who was more than comfortable in taking the role. You sort of see him every day anyway. Although it was a bad thing, losing Ronnie Moore, whatever the circumstances, John McMahon came in and took the role upon himself."

New chief executive Jeremy Butler had taken the decision to suspend Moore. He had been part of a bid from property developer Michael Wilde, the former Southampton chairman, to buy the club.

The move had come close, but at the eleventh hour, Peter Johnson pulled out of the deal. He then installed Butler as his right hand man at Tranmere, tasked with running day to day operations and finding another potential buyer.

A 2-2 draw at Bristol City just a day after the news surrounding Moore emerged had shown yet more shoots of improvement for Rovers. They were still very much in danger, though, and Shaun Garnett reckons if they had been higher up the table, there is no way the manager would have been put on gardening leave.

"I'm not too sure they'd have suspended him if we had been at the top of the league," he says, brow furrowed at the memory of another painful moment in the club's history. "It's like any club though; the senior management have reasons for doing things, but Ronnie was an experienced manager.

"To put him on gardening leave at that time of the season and replace him would be hard. Yes, John McMahon is a very good coach and given time I think he would have turned it around. But a lot of pressure was put on him when there was already a very experienced manager there.

"I feel very sorry for John, because he was a very good coach. He was given the opportunity to manage Tranmere Rovers, which is great for his CV, but his hands were tied slightly.

"He had to work with what he had. He possibly could have done with bringing one or two new faces in, but wasn't able to. Again, at that time, without being too controversial, we didn't have Tranmere players. We had journeymen. They had no part of Tranmere, and that didn't help either."

Moore was eventually charged with 'multiple breaches of betting regulations' by the Football Association on March 31st. He was given until April 8th to respond, at which point he admitted his wrongdoing.

A day later, he was sacked by Rovers, who were outside the relegation zone on goal difference. It was a sorry end to a long relationship with a club where he is still held by many in very high regard, not just for what he achieved as a manager, but in his playing and coaching days as well.

In May 2014, he was given a personal hearing by the Football Association, where he was handed a one month suspended ban and fined £2,000.

His crime had been to place 95 bets on matches, including one game involving Tranmere, a fixture which they won against Colchester. In England, all club employees, whether playing or non-playing staff, are banned from placing any football related wager, regardless of whether it involves their club.

"The only thing I'm guilty of really is I'm embarrassed," Moore said at the time, "because as the manager of Tranmere Rovers I should have known, so I hold my hands up, it was my fault. The last three months have been hell. I have been abused and accused of this, that and the other."

The hearing cleared the manager of any integrity issues, with his son Ian Thomas-Moore taking to Twitter to say: "For the record: £1100 was his outlay of bets in three years, he won £900! Not one was on Tranmere to lose, it's a family account. FACT." He later added: "Just the way of the world, people judge before knowing the facts. Glad it's all out now, he can concentrate on getting back into management."

Ronnie Moore did not respond to an approach for comment for this book.

***

At such a crucial time in the season, it was just the kind of upheaval and uncertainty Rovers did not need. Especially the players. Their manager had gone and, for the third time in four years, the club were heading for a relegation showdown in the final weeks of the campaign.

John McMahon had not enjoyed a particularly successful start to his tenure. They recorded sporadic victories, against Coventry and Notts County, which were followed by a clutch of defeats.

At the start of April Tranmere finally put together back to back league victories for the first time since January 2013, with Jean-Louis Akpa Akpro and Ryan Lowe scoring in a 2-1 win at Colchester, before a late strike from Junior Brown secured a vital three points in a 2-1 defeat of Shrewsbury.

At that point, with five games to go in the season, Rovers sat in 19th place in League One. They were three points clear of danger, and had played a match fewer than several of the sides around them.

That is when disaster struck. Tranmere just hit the buffers. They ran out of form and they ran out of goals, failing to score in their next four matches. Three of them, all away from home, ended in miserable 2-0 defeats, at Crawley, Gillingham and Leyton Orient, whilst at Prenton Park, they managed a 0-0 draw against Sheffield United.

"I still look back now at that game against Sheffield United," admits Steven Jennings. "We were clear of the relegation zone and we drew 0-0. We had a couple of chances to win it, but didn't. If we had, I think we'd have ended up safe, but we didn't. Then the heartbreak came."

The draw against the Blades meant Rovers were still above the bottom four, even if only by a point. Staying up was still very much in their hands. They did not have to rely on other teams slipping up, they just had to equal or better the results of those below them.

Unfortunately, that proved easier said than done. The loss at Gillingham on Good Friday had been poor, but the penultimate game of the season against Leyton Orient was even worse.

Tranmere were proving completely toothless. Jake Cassidy had come back to the club for his third loan spell, but returned just one goal from 19 appearances. He was hauled off at half-time, as was fellow striker Akpa Akpro as McMahon desperately tried to turn around a one goal deficit.

However, former (and future) Rovers striker Chris Dagnall settled the game when he made it 2-0 late on, leaving the visitors in disarray. Results elsewhere, with Crewe drawing at Bristol City and Notts County beating Swindon, meant the Wirral side had dropped into the relegation zone with just one game left to play.

Speaking afterwards, McMahon lay the blame at the feet of his players, saying: "It's just galling really, that we've suffered another defeat. From what I think and from what I've seen through my rose coloured glasses, it was a good performance.

"I thought that in the second half we absolutely dominated the game. But I can't legislate for mistakes like that. I can set teams up. I can look at systems and shapes. What I can't do is go out there and stop silly mistakes from happening.

"We haven't dealt with a lot of things throughout the season, and that's why we're in the position we're in. We can play all the attractive football you like and create chances, which I thought we did, but when you can't do the simple things well defensively, you're going to suffer."

A week later, Tranmere took on Bradford City at Prenton Park in a do or die clash. Their League One status was, yet again, on the line. However, on this occasion, unlike against Stockport four years earlier, they required a victory and help from elsewhere, in the form of a defeat for one of Notts County or Crewe, to have a chance of staying up.

McMahon tried a number of tricks to motivate the players, and one of them came with a very personal touch. He attempted to pull on their heartstrings and give them some extra gusto as they crossed the white line.

"John had spoken to everybody's family behind the scenes," recalls Steven Jennings. "He got them to post a little message on a video, clipped it together and showed it to us in the changing rooms.

"We had our families and kids wishing us good luck. It was quite emotional to be honest. I had my mum, dad, sister and a couple of my little nieces wishing me good luck. It was powerful. You've just got to use that to fuel the fire in your belly and go out there and do as well as you can."

"I was only young, so it didn't really involve me," adds Ridehalgh. "But the senior players had their family on the screen saying 'good luck', which was emotional. We had to depend on other results, but if we did win, there was a possibility of staying up, which was always in our head."

McMahon's presentation seemed to have worked a treat when, after just seven minutes, on-loan Everton defender Matthew Pennington found himself in the penalty area and curled a magnificent shot into the back of the net to put the hosts 1-0 up. In real time, it lifted them out of the relegation zone given the other games were still 0-0.

Over 10,000 fans had packed into Prenton Park for the occasion, perhaps from a morbid fascination about what could unfold should things go wrong. But with the goal, the ground erupted.

"It just goes to show the support is there when you need them," adds Jennings, whilst Ridehalgh quips "at that point, I can remember thinking 'we're going to do it'."

His optimism, however, would not last. News soon filtered through of Crewe taking the lead against Preston before, for the eighth time in the campaign, Tranmere were reduced to ten men.

Brown was the man to see red, and rightly so. Only half an hour had passed when the on-loan Fleetwood winger lunged in rashly on Mark Yeates and was given his marching orders immediately.

Rovers now had it all to do. They might have been 1-0 to the good, but they faced an hour of action with only ten men and still needed results elsewhere to go in their favour. Even the most positive of supporter was struggling to see how they could get out of jail this time.

Their hopes of staying up received a boost when Adam Lockwood put Oldham 1-0 up against Notts Country with 68 minutes played at Boundary Park, once again lifting Tranmere out of the bottom four.

But County responded from the penalty spot through Alan Sheehan. A point was all the Magpies needed and that scoreline remained at 1-1, whilst Crewe added a second against Preston through Mathias Pogba, brother of French World Cup winner Paul.

As it stood, Tranmere were back in the relegation zone and their afternoon completely collapsed when Bradford scored two late goals at Prenton Park, through Jon Stead and Aaron McLean.

The Bantams held on for a 2-1 victory. Rovers, after a 13 year stint in League One, were sent tumbling through its trap door, failing to register a single win in their last five matches.

Perhaps they could take some solace from the fact that the result at Prenton Park that day was immaterial. Crewe and Notts County did enough elsewhere to be sure of their own survival. The damage, from a Tranmere sense, had already been done.

"The dressing room afterwards was awful," says Ridehalgh, whose first season with the club had ended in relegation. "I can remember driving home feeling very lonely. I had never experienced anything like that before in my career. It really wasn't good."

"Maybe some of us were too pumped up," recalls Jennings. "With Junior getting sent off, you've got to use that fuel to get you through it, not to make a daft tackle.

"I feel sorry for John McMahon. Everybody was playing for him. There wasn't one person out there not playing for him. He's got a lot to offer the football game, but he hasn't had too many chances at the top level.

"It's just football. If the ball bounces well for you on a Saturday, you do well. If it doesn't, you don't do well. There's nothing you can do."

Shaun Garnett, meanwhile, had stepped up to help out on McMahon's coaching team after Moore's departure. He had experienced plenty of highs during his long association with the club, but not once had he suffered a relegation.

"The Bradford game was always going to be a big ask," he reflects. "We had only ever mended holes without fixing things, and that day summed the club up. We went 1-0 up and all got carried away with it, but it was a stop gap; it was only a goal.

"We think we've done it, but they score twice, we end up getting beat and getting relegated. I think that summed up the mood of the place really.

"It was a big step up for John McMahon. The situation with Ronnie could have been handled better, and I mean that from a club point of view and the FA.

"I think it shook the club and it made it hard for John to pick up the pieces. He had Ronnie's players, he had to patch the side up and get a few results to keep us in the league. In the end, it wasn't to be."

He starts gazing through the fixture list, looking at the results towards the end of the campaign. His eyes go a bit hazy, trying to recall some of the matches, but there is nothing there.

"You forget how bad it was," he adds. "You get involved in it at the time, but if you took yourself out of it, you'd probably see the problem. You're engrossed in what's going on in the club.

"We only scored one goal in the last five games! But again, if I was being brutally honest, and you don't like to admit it, I could see the club going down. I thought it might need to go down to rattle a few bones and bring a little bit of stability to the club.

"Am I surprised it took as long as until 2013/14 to go down? Yes, probably. We were never fixing things, we were only mending them. We weren't getting to the root of the problem. It was always going to happen.

"We had a few scares with relegation and got away with it, and then we had that fantastic first part of the season in 2012/13 when everybody sort of got a little bit carried away, and I'm talking about the staff, management and business side of the club, not the fans. We got wrapped up in it.

"But it was going to come, it really was. We couldn't carry on the way we were, unless we had some massive investment. I really do think that relegation was inevitable. I thought it might have been what we needed.

"As a club, and I was part of it, I thought it might be a wake up call that could stop the rot. You felt the rot had set in. There was lots of negative talk around the club. There was uncertainty over who was going to own the club and the future was uncertain. In the end, it took its toll and affected everyone."

The Bradford game proved to be Ian Goodison's final one in a Tranmere shirt. Having initially been brought in by Brian Little in 2004, he was released after over ten years of service, amassing 410 appearances. He truly was a popular player during his time at Prenton Park.

Fans of a certain generation will describe him as the greatest defender they have seen play for the club, and that is a fair assessment of somebody who is rightly described as a Tranmere legend.

"The 2013/14 season was my biggest disappointment at Tranmere Rovers," he says. "The ship was floating all over the sea. It was never steady, for about two years. The ship was all over the place.

"We were trying everything to get it right. We would have team meetings, go walking, go bowling and everything but it just wasn't happening. We couldn't escape.

"The Bradford day was the worst day of my football career, you have to say that. It wasn't about me though. It was about the fans. They go to work, spend their money, buy petrol to go to the games and stuff.

"It means more to the fans, so it's sometimes not about the players. The Tranmere fans are die hards. Sometimes they go to the game but they are struggling to get back on the train! They didn't deserve it.

"I was released afterwards and I gutted. I was trying to get one more season but I think because of my age and with the spot fixing stuff, they didn't keep me. I went back to Jamaica and played for two seasons so I could still play.

"A year later, I returned for my testimonial and it was very emotional. I did everything for Tranmere for ten years and I knew I was departing for the last time, so it was very emotional, having all the fans and players there. I know players come and go but it was very emotional for me.

"Tranmere mean a lot to me because they put food on the table for my kids. It was a job, at the end of the day, and they provided for me and my family. I don't know if all players see it like that, but that's how I see it. They provided for me and did their most to keep me at the club.

"Peter Johnson, Lorraine Rogers before him, I thank them for having me for ten years. I appreciate it. When Brian Little brought me in, Lorraine was there and Peter Johnson came back and I respect them both. They put food on the table for my kids and family and accepted me at their club. I hope they thought I did a good job.

"These days, the club looks very different to when I was there. Since I left, the standard has gone up. Outside the football ground, they have the pictures. There's the walkway with the names on as well.

"I appreciate it so much that there's a picture of me, right by the traffic lights. It means a lot to me. I was so excited when I saw it. I appreciate that people considered putting me up there. There are other past players too and it's very nice.

"For a normal person like me, from Jamaica, a ten hour flight away, to have that does mean a lot to me. I'm from a normal ghetto community, but I'm at a football club in England. Kids can grow up and ask who is that? People have to explain it's me and that means a lot to me."

Chapter Eight
Another Change Of Manager

For the first time since 1988/89, Tranmere were facing up to a season in the fourth tier of English football. They had been on an alarming slump since Peter Johnson slashed the budget in 2009 and there were genuine fears that a second successive relegation could become a reality.

It had, after all, happened before. Stockport County, another financially troubled club, had gone down twice in a row from 2009/10 to 2010/11, whilst Luton actually suffered relegation heartache three years running, dropping from The Championship to The National League in the mid-2000s.

Rovers knew the path that lay ahead. They had to find a way to arrest the negative momentum that had swallowed up the club over a significant period of time. Before progressing, they had to consolidate.

That meant they were faced with making one of the most important managerial appointments in their history. If the wrong guy came in, then dropping into the National League for the first time was a realistic possibility.

Jeremy Butler was the man charged with finding a replacement for Ronnie Moore. Butler was a decorated former journalist who had worked on Michael Wilde's attempt to buy Tranmere. Had Wilde's proposed takeover been successful, the pair would have appointed as boss Albert Ferrer, an ex-Barcelona and Chelsea defender who had represented Spain on 36 occasions and cut his teeth with Dutch club Vitesse.

John McMahon was on the shortlist Butler was drawing up. He went as far as producing a dossier on where Tranmere were failing and what they needed to implement if they were to get back into the League One and, as a secondary target, the Championship.

Former Arsenal and Ipswich striker Chris Kiwomya was also interviewed for the post. He had been in charge of Notts County the previous year, but his reign at Meadow Lane lasted just 34 games after he picked up just nine wins.

There were plenty of other interested individuals as well, some of them high-profile names, but Butler went very much for an outside-of-the-box appointment with a lower league player turned coach who had never managed a first team match.

That man was Rob Edwards, a former Wales international who could count Bristol City, Preston and Blackpool amongst his former clubs. His career started with Carlisle.

The defender had hung up his playing boots three years earlier after a five year stint at Exeter where he was a popular character. He became part of manager Paul Tisdale's backroom staff at St James' Park and was beginning to make a name for himself in the coaching arena.

But could he cut it as a manager? "He was a lovely guy with the potential to be very good", recalls Shaun Garnett, who had gone back to leading the club's academy after helping John McMahon at the back end of the previous campaign. "But to get him in at a club who'd just been relegated wasn't the right choice."

On May 27th 2014, Edwards was confirmed as the new Tranmere boss. His appointment took fans by surprise, and they were soon split into a number of camps. A handful were intrigued to see how this green, exciting young coach could do. Others wanted a bigger, more experienced name. And then there were those who were unconvinced, but willing to give him a chance and liked the idea of a fresh start.

"I've worked hard for this chance and feel I've been ready to manage for some time," Edwards said at his press conference. "I'm ready to put into practice the skills I've learned from 25 years in the game that has seen me work with, and learn from, some superb managers and excellent players.

"I believe I can develop a team at Tranmere Rovers that the whole of the Wirral can be proud of. My aim is to make sure we are challenging at the top end of the table, as well as setting up a structure to produce more home grown players."

Butler added: "Our aim was to find a young, hungry manager with the drive to lead Tranmere Rovers forward. We want a manager capable of winning promotion but also one able to improve our current bright young talents, as well as putting in place a pathway to bring through more players from our academy."

The squad were just as surprised as the supporters by Edwards' arrival. His name had come completely out of the blue. There were no rumours or speculation, even in an age of growing social media use.

"I remember watching Sky Sports news and Rob Edwards was announced as the new manager," says Liam Ridehalgh, one of only ten first team players who remained at Prenton Park from the previous campaign.

"We didn't get a message from the club! It's probably changed in this day and age. Social media is massive now, much bigger than it was back then. I wasn't really on any platform other than Facebook anyway, which is just for personal news, not footballing stuff. So it was Sky Sports News with the yellow ticker! But I remember looking at it and I felt positive."

Upon Edwards' appointment, John McMahon reverted to his role as assistant manager, whilst Shaun Garnett returned to working as the head of the club's academy. The job now was to build a first team squad.

The new boss also brought Matt Gill with him to Prenton Park as a player/coach. The 33-year old had spent a large chunk of his career at Peterborough and Exeter, where he played alongside Edwards.

Come the start of the season, McMahon was pushed aside as Alex Russell, a Crosby born former midfielder who counted Rochdale, Torquay and, again, Exeter amongst his former clubs, was signed as first team coach.

***

Edwards did not have much of a budget to work with as Tranmere manager. He also had Butler and Operations Director Mick Horton working above him identifying new signings.

The day after Tranmere's relegation from League One, Butler had penned an open letter to the club's fans about his plans for the future, and the ambition of winning promotion back to the third tier.

He criticised the existing recruitment policy, citing that previous managers had been too keen on signing players at the wrong end of their career, instead of those with a future sell-on value.

That meant Horton had been tasked with devising a profiling system in order to identify any potential new faces. The intention was to bring in the 'right' players and ensure the new manager was not as reliant on so many loan signings to prop up the squad.

"As we build the squad," Butler wrote, "We will be aware of the number of players we need that can cover certain positions so we can work within our tight budgets. We should never be overstocked in one area and short of cover in another again.

"Now this work has been done we are focusing on the players we believe match our criteria. We are building up a database of not just one target but four or five that fit the bill.

"Budget restrictions may mean we are unable to afford our first choice but we now have a definitive list of the options. We will not need to rush in a gamble signing on deadline day any more."

Such a system saw some intriguing players come in. Eliot Richards was one of them, a young striker who progressed through the youth ranks at Bristol Rovers, then left after their relegation to the National League.

Butler built excitement over one arrival by announcing "we have a new striker in the building" on Twitter. Supporters were then a little underwhelmed when they discovered it was Kayode Odejayi, who had spent years in the Football League with Barnsley, Colchester and Rotherham, but had never been prolific. His best days were behind him.

Other signings included Marcus Holness, a defender brought in as the new club captain, midfielder Marc Laird and Michael Ihiekwe, a centre-back who had started his career at Liverpool but had just been released by Wolves.

The new player profiling system also saw some hugely dependable figures leave Prenton Park. Ryan Lowe, attracting interest from former club Bury, wanted a new contract with Tranmere.

He had finished the previous season with 19 league goals, easily the club's top scorer, and thought he deserved a 12 month extension on the two year deal he signed in 2013. Butler disagreed. The striker was sent packing.

Steven Jennings was another shown the exit, as he can explain. "I left because of circumstances out of my reach. Jeremy Butler came in upstairs and for some reason he stamped his authority. He didn't want a certain age of player, or somebody earning X amount per week.

"One by one, he forced a few of us out. It was out of my control. He said 'this is what we're offering players of your age' and it was less than what I signed for in January. It wasn't just me. You're talking between £500 and £700 a week less for some players.

"It was all down to age, not how good you were. Ryan left and signed for Bury on a two year contract and got promoted. For some reason, Jeremy had it in for players who were over 30 and wanted them out. Ryan went there, I went to Port Vale."

It was a policy that Shaun Garnett did not agree with. He wanted to see change at Prenton Park; he knew that it was desperately needed. But this, in his opinion, was not the right path to take.

"If I'm being honest with you, I didn't particularly like Jeremy Butler, both personally and in terms of football," he says. "His knowledge of football was very limited. Business wise, I'm in no position to mark him on that, but I didn't think he was the right choice for Tranmere Rovers at that time. He wasn't what we needed.

"Some fans have described Butler as somebody who played Football Manager with Tranmere. I'd have to agree with that. I think he's come into it and tried to run us as if we're a Premier League club, but we weren't.

"We'd just been relegated out of League One. There was a lot happening within the club that he couldn't fix and I felt it was a little bit head in the sand. That's only my opinion, but I just didn't share his views.

"He came in with several generic policies that you pick up from other managers. He sat in on a lot of Alex Ferguson's press conferences, and other managers, and if you're in their position and you can back it up, that's fine.

"If the market you're shopping in means you need to pick up one or two 31 or 32 year olds who've only got a season left in them, you've got to do it and see where it takes you. With him coming out with these big, bold statements, I don't think it helped in terms of our recruitment.

"Just look at Ryan Lowe. He'd scored 19 goals. We'd just been relegated and were favourites to be promoted, or at least be up there, because of who we are as a club, but we let our centre forward go."

The blueprint devised by Butler and Horton had legs. They knew that Tranmere needed a change of direction if they were to start competing on the pitch again, because things had been going the wrong way for some time. Their idea was to source players who had future sell on value for the club, and could therefore make some much needed money.

It was a similar policy to one Les Parry had aired a handful of years earlier, expressing that he did not necessarily want players who wanted to play for Tranmere, but instead those who saw their future at a much higher level.

If you could convince them to sign for a couple of years, though, they would be helping the club by putting in performances on the pitch before moving up the pyramid. When Parry had suggested such a scheme, it was met with disdain from some supporters.

Likewise with Butler and Horton, a section of the fanbase were sceptical. Unfortunately, at that time, Rovers were in no position to devise such a policy. They needed quality and experience, and a lack of both would prove to be the club's downfall.

Chapter Nine
Deep Trouble

Expectations at the start of the 2014/15 season were mixed. Having suffered the relegation, some fans were happy to have a year of consolidation, just making sure they stopped the rot and were ready to kick on towards promotion 12 months later.

Others thought it was vital Tranmere got back into League One as quickly as possible, and as a relatively big team dropping into a division that contained the likes of Accrington, York and Morecambe, they believed Rovers should be challenging from the off.

"I knew 2014/15 would be tough," says Shaun Garnett. "It was a new era and it was do or die for me, a little bit. I never thought we'd get relegated, though. Never, ever. I just thought it might be tough because there were so many new things happening in the club."

Handling those differing expectations was always going to be a big ask. No matter how unrealistic, some people believed the new manager should have his side in the top seven, and if performances did not hit the heights they believed possible, the fans would make their feelings known.

Edwards' first game in charge was at home to York, and he immediately found out what an uphill task he was facing. Rovers were poor, and their blushes were only spared late on by midfielder James Rowe, who netted an equaliser deep into second half injury time to rescue a 1-1 draw. A crowd of 6,287 were in attendance and some of those booed at full-time. The tone for the season had been set.

"When you look at the team that started against York," continues

Garnett, "you think where did it go wrong? You look at the likes of Marcus Holness, a Steady Eddie, Danny Holmes would die for the club, Max Power who went on to play in the Championship, Jake Kirby who I always thought was a gifted player. It's some side. Owain Fon Williams has represented Wales.

"James Rowe scored, I had honestly forgotten about him, and Eliot Richards. Because of the turnover of players, you forget who was there and how many were there."

It already looked like an uncertain start for the new manager, and he would have been having even more doubts about his future two days later when Peter Johnson finally managed to sell Tranmere, nearly three decades after he first bought the club.

Former Rovers midfielder Mark Palios, once the head of the FA and a specialist in turning around failing businesses, had taken the reins, alongside his wife Nicola. Was Edwards the man he believed capable of taking the club forward?

Although it took until early August to complete the deal to buy Johnson's shares, the pair had been involved in negotiations for some time. Mark Palios has revealed the advice he gave to the club when they were searching for Ronnie Moore's successor.

"I specifically said to them that they shouldn't get an inexperienced manager at this stage because there was a massive negative momentum in the club," Palios says.

"As an assistant manager, you've never been sitting there with people shouting your name in terms of getting out. They don't shout at the assistant manager, they shout at the manager.

"When you have dropped a player, you walk past him in the corridor and you can't avoid him if you're the manager. You've dropped him. It's your decision. If you're the assistant manager, you can put your arm around him and say 'come on, keep your head up'. It was a totally different scenario and I think it was an added variable."

Edwards tried hard to win the fans over. He attended question and answer sessions at Prenton Park and went at lengths in press conferences to explain what he was trying to implement on the pitch.

His philosophy was more akin to the style of football John Barnes had played, keeping hold of possession and trying to unlock a defence through patience and ability, rather than the kick and rush of Les Parry or the more attacking, aggressive, sometimes long-ball brand favoured by Ronnie Moore.

He wanted his players to pass the ball, instead of hoofing it forward at the first opportunity. They should be comfortable in possession and have the ability to pick their way through even the most sturdy backline.

It was a system designed to bring the best out of Jason Koumas, comfortably the most talented member of the squad, even if his fitness let him down at times. Max Power, an up and coming midfielder who had progressed through the club's academy would benefit from it, too, but there were flaws.

In spite of having a variety of attacking options, which on top of Richards and Kayode Odejayi included Abdulai Baggie and a young Cole Stockton, they simply were not scoring enough goals. That often meant that conceding one goal could prove fatal.

That was the case in the League Cup, where Tranmere were beaten 1-0 by Championship side Nottingham Forest. A few days later future Rovers striker Andy Mangan scored for Shrewsbury as they netted twice in injury time to come from behind and win 2-1 at the New Meadow.

And that was the other problem. The team was fragile. They could be leading in matches, but you could never be confident they would hold out for the three points, regardless of how well they were playing.

Edwards' fourth game yielded his first win, a 2-0 victory down at Wycombe courtesy of goals from Stockton and Power. But their inability to hold on to a lead was again on show in two of the next three fixtures. They slipped from 2-0 up to lose 3-2 to Cheltenham and then surrendered a 2-1 advantage with 20 minutes remaining at Accrington to suffer another 3-2 defeat.

At that point Tranmere had picked up seven points from the opening six games and sat comfortably in mid-table, well clear of the relegation spaces occupied by Oxford and Exeter.

They drew their next two games 0-0, against Newport and Hartlepool, after which things went down hill pretty quickly. A 2-1 defeat at home to Exeter signalled what was to come, before David Amoo haunted his former club by scoring Carlisle's only goal in a 1-0 win at Brunton Park. The supporters were beginning to turn.

"I'm not enjoying that the fans think I'm hopeless and don't like me, but that's how it is," said Edwards afterwards. "I've got to get on with it. I understand what the job is and I'm determined to turn it around.

"As I look over and see the fans with a nice, big 'Edwards out' banner, I think it probably tells the players where we all are at the moment."

The pressure was well and truly on. Garnett admits he could see from some way out that a change might be made sooner rather than later, because it was vital the team's struggles did not become terminal.

"I thought Rob Edwards' days were numbered unless he started getting results," he adds. "He's a very good coach and a nice guy, but it was a big ask to come from Exeter to Tranmere.

"With no disrespect to them, the pressure is not the same. Mark Palios didn't want to change for the sake of changing, but he wanted results to improve. He wanted to find a little bit of stability on the pitch."

By the time Tranmere rocked up to Gigg Lane to take on Bury on October 4th, it looked like the writing could already be on the wall. They were sliding down the table and had failed to score in four successive games.

A fifth was about to follow. Rovers lost 2-0, conceding twice from set-pieces, a problem they persistently suffered from in the Edwards era. There were long periods of the game in which they impressed, but at no point did it look like they were going to pick up a rare win as they managed just two shots on target over the 90 minutes.

Once again, the fans let the manager know how they felt, with many of the 900 travelling supporters booing and chanting for a change in the dugout both before and after the final whistle.

Edwards addressed the issue in his post match interview, admitting: "There's obviously a few mumbles and grumbles. I understand that. The support was fantastic; I'm delighted that they turned up. They're sticking with the team.

"We all have to stick together to pull this round and get this club to where it should be. Looking at the table, it's difficult, I won't lie. We need to start winning football matches sooner rather than later. I have just got to try and lift them up.

"I've been in this situation before as a player and it can be ruthless. Nobody feels sorry for you. I understand it's about hard work and I'm hoping it will turn around. I feel for the players at the moment.

"They need a break, we all need a break. They're doing everything they can, so if we can get a break on Tuesday night it'll help morale."

Fortunately for Edwards, that break did come on the Tuesday night, as Rovers picked up a third win of the season, albeit on penalties in the Johnstone's Paint Trophy.

Again, though, the hosts made life hard for themselves, leading before the break through Max Power only for Brad Potts to equalise late on and force a shoot-out.

There were some positive signs in the performance, but the pressure in a cup tie is simply not the same. What mattered more was a home clash with Plymouth four days later, where defeat could leave Tranmere bottom of the Football League.

"I knew this job was going to be really hard," Edwards admitted ahead of the game as he assessed the realities of the task he had taken on and how successful he was in implementing his blueprint. "But it has still surprised me, the challenges that we have faced.

"I've been in this game long enough to know how difficult it can be. You've got to dig in and keep working. I knew what the job was, and I knew that it would be tough for whoever came in here. But it's not a case of me thinking 'corr, what have I done?'

"If I walked away in a week, or a year or 10 years, I know I would be walking away from a great club. Someone will be lucky enough to get this club moving forwards again, and I'm determined that it's going to be me."

The challenge facing Edwards looked even harder after half an hour as Reuben Reid put Plymouth 1-0 up. It was a well worked goal, with the visitors displaying patience in their build up before Kelvin Mellor whipped in a dangerous cross that was expertly headed home.

Tranmere never recovered. "They looked less like a team than a bunch of strangers during this home defeat," wrote Nick Hilton in his scathing post match report for the Liverpool Echo.

Edwards, in his own assessment, admitted he needed to be harsher on his squad, detailing: "When I came in and assessed the players here, I thought I would have to go steady because I saw some fragile people looking at the floor.

"I have been nice sometimes and at times told them where I think they are going wrong. But if I could change things, I might not have been as concerned about how they felt, because they are not changing.

"If players can't survive with the toughness and brutality of football then they won't be successful. That may be one mistake I have made and I will assess myself for sure."

The defeat had seen Tranmere sink to the bottom of the Football League. They had picked up just two points from their last seven games, but the manager did not appear to fear for his future.

He continued: "Do I still want the job? Yes. Am I still proud to be manager of this club? Yes. I've told the players the future of this club is at stake. People's futures are at stake. They need to sharpen up, otherwise it isn't going to work. I'm not going to give up. I'm a fighter. I'm more of a fighter than a couple of players who are playing for me."

Two days later, Edwards was sacked. His time at Tranmere had lasted just 12 league games, with only two of those ending in victory. They had accumulated only nine points and been beaten on eight occasions in all competitions.

"Rob is a decent man who has worked very hard over the past few months for the football club," said Mark Palios in a statement. "However, with the club currently sitting at the bottom of League Two for the first time in 32 years, it was decided this was the right time to make the break."

Reflecting now, the chairman adds: "All I would say is that Rob came in at the wrong time in his career for the situation that we had. By the time we got to October and we were rock bottom of the league, decisions had to be made.

"If you're bottom of the league in October and you've kept cash back for the transfer window, you have to decide whether he's the guy to spend the money. He came into a fairly intense situation here. He's a good coach but it's more the psychological issue. Can he take the pressure? Can he win over the fans?"

Mark Bartley adds: "He was a very nice guy and I'm sure he was very keen, but he was out of his depth. He would have been really good as an assistant. He'd done really well as a number two at Exeter.

"But he didn't have any contacts up here. We needed somebody with experience who was going to get us back up. Not an experiment."

A week after his departure, Edwards broke his silence on his sacking. He defended the blueprint he was working towards, and believes the constraints he had placed upon him made success difficult to achieve.

"In May," he said, "I agreed with the club a philosophy trying to move Tranmere forward giving the young home-grown players an opportunity to develop. Very early on I realised that it was going to take longer than the new owner and most of the fans were prepared to give a first time manager.

"The recruitment in the summer was done under tight budget constraints which unfortunately didn't enable us to sign a proven goalscorer and as it turned out this was a major weakness in the team.

"As the pressure to get a result increased the players' performance suffered but I believe the team and individuals were developing and as the scorelines showed we weren't far away."

Upon leaving Tranmere, Edwards joined Cheltenham as their assistant manager, and has since held spells with Southampton and in the Wales youth team set-up.

Chapter Ten
Micky Adams Arrives

Tranmere were bottom of the Football League. It was, once again, a defining moment in their history. Even more than with the appointment of Rob Edwards, they could not afford the next managerial selection to be a bad one. The stakes were too high.

A few names were touted to come in. One of them was Dave Jones, the former Southampton and Wolves boss. Mark Palios had asked the experienced Jones to give Edwards a bit of advice towards the end of his reign.

Experience was indeed the key attribute needed at this point. Somebody who had been there, done it and worn the t-shirt. And the man who appeared to fit the bill perfectly was Micky Adams.

Then aged 52, the ex-Leeds and Coventry defender had enjoyed a long and successful career in management, having started young as a player-boss at Fulham, a role he also briefly held at Swansea and Brentford.

He led Fulham to promotion in 1997, a feat he repeated at Brighton four years later, both from the fourth tier. He was soon moving up the divisions, and in 2003 he guided Leicester back in to the Premier League.

A decade later, having hit a few bumps, he picked up his fourth promotion after dropping back down to League Two to take Port Vale up. It was an impressive CV, and, crucially, he had never been relegated.

A month before Tranmere fired Edwards, Adams was sacked by Port Vale. They had lost six games in a row and were showing little sign of any improvement. Now he had enjoyed a short rest and Mark Palios was quick to snap him up.

The appointment was confirmed on Thursday October 16th 2014, just three days after Rovers had given their previous manager the boot. It was a swift turnaround, but it needed to be given the situation.

"In our present position we felt it was important to appoint an experienced manager with good connections and a track record of success in League Two," said Palios in a statement.

"Micky has an impressive win ratio, which he has sustained over a long career and often in circumstances where he has had to operate in difficult situations or with limited budgets. His success is no flash in the pan.

"We have acted quickly to fill the post so he has as much time as possible to lift us up the table and to identify his targets to strengthen the squad in the transfer window."

Adams himself added: "The immediate task is to get the club off the foot of the table. There's a lot of hard work ahead but it's a challenge I'm relishing.

"Tranmere are a good club with a proud history and one which shouldn't be near the bottom of the division. In the weeks and months ahead I'll be doing everything I can to drive the club forward and to a much healthier position."

Adams looked like just the kind of person Tranmere needed to turn their fortunes around. Few people, among fans or football insiders, saw his appointment as anything other than a sensible move by the club.

"People kept ringing me up and saying 'fantastic appointment' when we did it," recalls Mark Palios. "He was around and he had a track record that was second to none, and he'd done it in all divisions."

"I thought Micky Adams looked like a really sound appointment," says Shaun Garnett. "I got on really well with him, having come across him as a player. I'd always known him as a hard man.

"He worked his players hard and he was very disciplined and regimental in a 4-4-2, be that at Fulham, Brighton or wherever. I was fairly impressed with his signing. I thought it was exactly what we needed. He was a big name, an experienced manager and he had a good track record. You were thinking 'let's see what happens here'."

Liam Ridehalgh was out injured at the time, but he adds: "I had played against Micky Adams' sides before so I knew of him as a manager. He was at Port Vale and was quite a strong character there. I knew about that because of word of mouth."

***

Like Rob Edwards, and John McMahon before him, Adams was faced with an almighty task. Not only was he taking over a club in 24th place in the table, but they were suffering from a severe lack of confidence and were extremely goal-shy.

He watched from the stands for the first game after his arrival, so quick was the turnaround between his appointment and the trip to Oxford. Assistant manager Matt Gill was put in caretaker charge and Rovers lost 2-0.

Adams did not respond to a request for an interview for this book, but in his autobiography, 'My Life In Football' he recalls the troubles he saw out on the pitch at the Kassam Stadium.

"They had this system but it seemed muddled to me," he writes. "I couldn't work out if they were trying to pass it or hustle. So I went down at half-time to introduce myself and tried to get them going."

Adams also discusses his decision to take the reins at Prenton Park, and goes as far as admitting that simply taking charge at Tranmere was a big mistake, one that he should not have made.

"On the face of it," he says, "they didn't have much going for them. Yet, even though they were bottom of League Two, I did think they were a big club for that level. But it was arrogance to think I could turn around a club that had been relegated twice in two seasons [sic; they had suffered just the one relegation].

"They were bottom of the table. Why would I touch it? I shake my head now. I have to apologise to the Tranmere fans. What the fuck was I doing there? Was I thinking straight?"

Adams had an impact early on. He dipped straight into the transfer market, signing striker Armand Gnanduillet on loan from Chesterfield, and he scored twice as Rovers picked up an impressive 2-2 draw in his second fixture down at Wimbledon.

"That was my comeback game," says Liam Ridehalgh. "I was injured at the start of the season. I did my ankle ligaments away at Rhyl in a pre-season friendly. It was disappointing as it meant I never played a first team game under Rob Edwards.

"At Wimbledon, I skied one over the stand behind the goal. The only thing is it was a cross and not a shot! I don't think anybody has ever skied the ball over the stand before with a cross!

"It's difficult when a new manager comes in because we're basically all starting afresh. He's got his ideas. He brings the players he wants. I can't remember the exact stat, but in that season the number of players we used was the most I've ever experienced."

Ridehalgh need not have worried too much about his position at first. Adams described the Tranmere squad as completely imbalanced, because the defender was the only left-footed player he had available.

He would soon add more depth to the side, including a familiar face in Steve Jennings, who returned for his third spell at Prenton Park.

"Micky Adams had to put an arm around me, to be honest," the midfielder admits. "I'd done well at Port Vale in pre-season, but he had four centre-midfielders and said he could only pick two, so two of you will be a bit disappointed.

"I was on the bench for about eight games, then he got the sack and came to Tranmere. He rang me and said 'I need you here' and apologised for not giving me a chance at Port Vale.

"He asked me to come back and it was a no brainer. I came back in early November and we weren't in great shape. It just didn't hit off for Micky, or for myself really. I didn't hit the ground running and the amount of players we had coming in and out wasn't too healthy. You need a bit of a balance."

The draw at Wimbledon was one of three in a row, sandwiched in between a goalless stalemate with Mansfield at Prenton Park and a 2-2 result against Stevenage in which Michael Ihiekwe scored an own goal before netting a 90th minute equaliser.

At last, things were picking up, and consecutive wins followed, although they were both in the cup. Firstly Max Power was on target from the penalty spot in a 1-0 victory over Bristol Rovers before a come-from-behind 2-1 win at Bury.

Adams, however, was already making his enemies at Prenton Park. The players were not particularly keen on some of his training methods, despite the results that they might have been producing.

"He was very strict," says Ridehalgh. "I wouldn't say he was very approachable. Obviously I was a lot younger then and I don't know if I'd feel the same now, but he had that element of fear about him. You couldn't really approach him.

"Football is a results business and later on we weren't getting results, so obviously that was affecting the way he was. It was a real difficult time. I look back now and I can remember thinking that."

Footballers are creatures of habit. They enjoy routine. At Tranmere, the routine was to train on a Monday and Tuesday, followed by a day off on a Wednesday. They would then be back at Raby on Thursday and Friday preparing for the game on Saturday. But Adams did not like that, and as such he wanted to make a slight adjustment.

"He tried to change the day off to a Thursday instead of a Wednesday," says Garnett, "But players are very much stuck in their ways. I think Micky, because the reserves were on a Wednesday, wanted to move it, but it didn't go down well.

"However, I don't think he was the kind of guy who'd explain why he'd done it. He'd just say 'that's it, take it or leave it', but if you give the players a reason why, be it for recovery or being sharper on the Friday, they'd buy into it.

"I personally don't have a problem with this, because players are getting paid and they should do what he asked, but I think it was his training methods. His mentality was that you work hard and you play hard.

"Tuesday was a running session. On a Thursday, if you weren't training right, you'd do more running. So a lot of the lads felt a bit leggy come Saturday. It was all because the training was shite and it wasn't good enough."

Garnett was also worried about getting some of his young prospects into Adams' team. His job was to continue the conveyor belt of talent from the academy into the senior side.

He had a few young lads with plenty of ability. Defender Evan Gumbs was one of them, and he would make his debut as a substitute at Luton just before Christmas. Utility player Mitch Duggan was also coming through, alongside goalkeeper Luke Pilling and midfielder Ben Jago. But was the pathway there?

"Micky was quite aggressive to deal with," Garnett continues. "I

118

don't know whether there was a long term plan or he just had a short term plan to keep us in the league, but he just let me get on with things.

"I realised it was always going to be hard to get kids into his teams. I'd looked at his teams and his career as a manager and, don't get me wrong, at Leicester and Brighton he'd brought kids through, but it was hard to get games under him.

"But, again, in the short time he was there, I got on okay with him. I knew Alan Rogers (Adams' right hand man) really well from my playing days, so that was my connection to Micky. It was fine."

Steve Jennings recalls a conversation he had with the manager about taking over as captain. Marcus Holness had been wearing the armband after his arrival in the summer, but his form was not great and Adams had attempted to address Tranmere's fragilities at the back by bringing in a number of central-defenders, including Josh Thompson and Will Aimson.

"Micky Adams had been there, done it and worn the t-shirt," says Jennings. "He could do no wrong and say no wrong. If you had something to say to him, he'd reply 'I've got two t-shirts here'.

"I didn't really have any major fall outs with him myself, because I pin a lot of pressure upon myself. You need to. You can't look for excuses. Players in this day and age and forever always try and find the excuse.

"From my personal point of view, the only thing he pulled me in over was about dropping Marcus Holness. He wanted me to be captain until the end of the year, which should have been a very, very good thing, but under the circumstances and with the turnover of players coming through the door, I was on a hiding to nothing."

***

As well as building a team, Micky Adams started to shape his coaching staff. Alex Russell left the club soon after Edwards departed, and, despite what he offered in central midfield, assistant boss Matt Gill was pushed out of the door too.

Adams did not work with a designated Number 2 but he did bring in a couple of coaches. One of them was Alan Rogers, an ex-Tranmere defender who had transferred to Nottingham Forest for big money during the 1990s but had returned to Prenton Park during the summer to work with the youngsters in the academy.

There was another familiar face in the dugout, too. Former Rovers winger Chris Shuker joined as part of the coaching staff, having previously crossed paths with Adams at Port Vale.

But writing in his autobiography, the manager admits it was a big mistake to bring in somebody with so little experience. "He had not long retired and had never coached at any level," he says. "Maybe his personality didn't help. He wouldn't say boo to a goose. He was quiet and I needed someone to get my juices going."

And here comes one of the more bizarre stories in Tranmere's history. Shuker's playing days had come to an end because of a knee problem that had blighted his final years.

But he had rested up after retirement, and once he returned to Rovers, he started joining in with some of the training sessions and found the injury, to an extent, had eased. Adams was impressed with what he saw.

"We came in during October," Shuker said in one interview. "I had been doing a bit of personal training at the time, so I was in quite good shape really.

"I joined in a few sessions because numbers were down and I was doing okay. One day, Micky came up to me and asked me: 'if I have to, could I sign you again? I could do with your quality.'

"My main aim was to go in there and help the club. Did I feel I could help it enough being on the sidelines, or did I feel I could help it more on the pitch? When he offered me that, I thought I could genuinely help the team, whether I got stick or not. I was big enough and strong enough mentally to deal with that. As long as I help the team, that's all that matters."

On Boxing Day, seven months after his retirement, Shuker made his return to first team football. He came on as a substitute as Tranmere were beaten 2-0 down at Burton, where Liam Ridehalgh was sent off in the first half.

Two days later, they were taking on Northampton at Prenton Park. They had only won two league games under Adams at this point, and incredibly, Shuker found himself in the starting line up.

"The manager asked for our teams," Shuker continues, "And I put myself in the team. So he gets the team, gets my sheet and says 'You're starting yourself?' I just said 'I know!' He then responds 'why?' I explained that it was because I thought I could help the team and I was putting in the team that I thought could win the game. He said 'okay' and he went with it."

Tranmere beat Northampton 2-1, with Kayode Odejayi and Jake Kirby on target. It lifted them out of the relegation zone at last, above Dagenham, who sat in 23rd place, on goal difference.

Shuker would only make one further appearance, and it did not come until Rovers faced the Cobblers again in March, a fixture they lost 1-0 at Sixfields.

Chapter Eleven
The Bombed Squad

When a new manager takes charge of a club it can become a time of uncertainty for the players. New signings are inevitable. He will, naturally, want to bring in people he can trust, perhaps those he has come across earlier on in his career.

In turn, those already at the club can be pushed out of the frame, even some who have been having an impact before the change of boss. If your face does not fit, you will either be put on the transfer list or discarded from first team duty.

This was certainly the case under Micky Adams, who made his enemies. Eliot Richards, Abdulai Baggie and James Rowe were quickly pushed out of the picture. They were asked not to train with the first team, and therefore had to make do with keeping fit in the gym or joining the under-18 squad.

"The new lads came in and made us a big squad," says Shaun Garnett, who was in charge of the youth team. "That resulted in the 'bombed squad'. Micky felt those players were harmful to the atmosphere to the first team.

"So I had four or five professionals training with me every day and they were great. I had no issue with them. The only time I had an issue was when I had to come in on a Saturday afternoon because Micky wanted them to train and he had them training at 3pm on a Saturday. That was a bit of a nightmare."

It was a less than healthy situation which became worse when Adams brought in a fourth signing, Iain Hume, who was quickly exiled to the youth squad

The Canadian international is a Tranmere cult hero. He made his debut as a teenager back in April 2000 and would go on to feature in some of the club's most memorable matches around the turn of the century, including the 3-0 demolition of Everton at Goodison in the FA Cup. By 2005, when he departed for Leicester, he had amassed just shy of 180 first team appearances and netted 37 goals.

After spells with Barnsley, Preston, Doncaster and Fleetwood and a stint in the newly formed Indian Super League, Hume found himself out of contract and looking for a club. Tranmere needed a striker as they desperately attempted to stave off relegation to the National League. It looked like the perfect fit.

"It was supposed to be a fairytale, my return, but it turned into a nightmare," Hume admits. "I said to my wife afterwards that I should never have come back. Not then, anyway. As much as I was happy that it happened at that time, it turned out to be one of my biggest mistakes.

"I was away for four months in India, and when I got back just before Christmas, my agent told me there were a couple of teams interested, including Plymouth and Portsmouth. They were offering a little bit more money but they were down south and I was looking for something a little bit more local.

"He also told me he spoke to Tranmere and asked me what I thought and it was a no brainer. At the time, I was living in a rental house, because we'd just had a fire, literally just up the road from Tranmere on Storeton Road. I went in and it was the opportunity to play back here after nearly a decade away. I was playing at home again.

"I sat down with my agent and Micky Adams and had a conversation and I had a little feeling that it might have been a transfer pushed by the fans and perhaps the chairman as well.

"So I said to Micky 'If I'm a player you want, brilliant, I'm ready to go. I need to get fit because I haven't played for a month.' He told me I was definitely a player he wanted because he'd known me for years, managed against me and thought I was a good addition to the squad because they were in trouble and I could help.

"I'd always wanted to come back. I started my career at Tranmere and they gave me everything. I live right up the road too. I could get on my push bike and not pedal to get to Prenton Park. It really was an ideal return. I thought it was a big roundabout and I'd come back and be living at home. But it was a nightmare."

So where did it all go so wrong? Hume made his debut in a 2-0 defeat at home to Swindon, coming on as a substitute for the final half hour. After another appearance from the bench three days later against Newport, he was handed his first start as Tranmere travelled to York on Valentine's Day. There proved to be no love in the air at Bootham Crescent.

Rovers were wretched. They again lost 2-0, but it could have been so much worse. Pass after pass went astray, defensively they looked all over the place and, with six new faces in the starting line up, Hume included, it looked as if the team did not know each other.

"It was one of the worst games of football I've been involved in," Hume continued. "I was terrible and if anybody who was on the field says they weren't, they're lying through their teeth. It was an unhappy dressing room after the game."

The striker had already displayed his emotions when being hauled off after 67 minutes, slamming the dugout in anger at how he had played. He knew he was out of shape and needed to get fit quickly if he was going to have any kind of impact.

"I was frustrated with myself," he admits. "I walked into the changing rooms afterwards and apologised because I was horrendous. I was unfit, but that's no excuse. I couldn't trap a bag of sand, I couldn't beat people, I just couldn't do anything.

"People have bad games technically. It happens. There are only a few games in my career that I can look back at and think 'what on earth was going on?' We had one against Brentford when I was at Preston. We got beat 3-0 at home and I got taken off after about an hour and I volleyed the water bottles. That was at me. Not at anybody else.

"I won't argue publicly with staff, because it's not good for people to see, but I just couldn't hold myself in. I volleyed the water bottles and it went all over our bench, their bench, the ambulance staff, the fourth official. I sat down and put my head down.

"York was another one of them. The pitch was horrendous. It was like a bog down the side. Me and Danny Holmes were struggling to run up and down and I just couldn't finish a pass or do anything. It got to a point where I was happy he took me off, but raging with myself because I'm trying to get myself back.

"I sat down with the club and said 'listen, I'm out of shape, give me a couple of weeks' hard training'. I spoke to the fitness coach and told him to batter me after training and see how close he could get me to match fitness."

The damage, however, had already been done. Hume was dropped for Tranmere's next game, a 2-1 win over Shrewsbury, who at that point were managed by a certain Micky Mellon. It would prove to be their penultimate victory of the campaign.

Despite the poor form, Hume would not start another first team fixture until Micky Adams' final match in charge. He had been banished, spare a handful of substitute appearances. He had to watch from afar as the walls came tumbling down.

"After York, we had the Sunday off, trained on the Monday and Tuesday and had the day off on Wednesday," he recalls. "I came in on the Thursday and Alan Rogers told me the gaffer wanted to see me. I hadn't even put my bag down.

"I went up to see him and next thing I know, he says: 'you're right, I don't want you here. I didn't sign you'. This is after telling me to my face that he wanted me as a player. He said: 'You're not involved anymore. If you want to come in and train, then get changed in the match day dressing room'.

"This was before Solar Campus, it was when everybody got changed in The Kop. I asked him where it had come from and he said: 'I know you've been saying this and that' and it baffled me a little bit. The wording that he used was from a conversation that was held in our card school, which was disappointing.

"I went in, picked up my bag, all the lads were there, I said 'see you later' and they were asking questions about what was going on. I just said 'I'm not involved anymore'.

"As I was walking out, I went the other way past his office and spoke to Shaun Garnett to ask him if I could train with the kids. If I couldn't work with the first team, I wanted to train with the kids and do what I can. Garno was thrilled. He said: 'I don't understand what's going on and don't want to know, but come and train with me every morning'.

"I did that for the next two months. I cycled up to Raby to watch the youth team matches and would go to Total Fitness after training because for one reason or another, whether he was told to or not, I didn't have one training session with the fitness coach after I asked him to batter me.

"So I took it upon myself to train every day with Garno and help Sam Ilesamni and Tolani Omatola, two young strikers. Ben Jago was there as well. I was just trying to help them out a bit.

"I looked after myself and played in a few reserve games and it got to a point where I was scoring two or three a game. Garno was saying to me: 'You shouldn't be here. Have you spoken to him?' But it wasn't up to me to go and speak to him. It was up to him to accept that I was getting fit and working hard.

"I don't know whether Garno had words, or the chairman, or somebody else involved in the club, but one morning, with the first team still struggling, I came into training and got a phone call asking me to go and see the gaffer again.

"I went in and he said 'I misread you. I expected you to be a complete so and so, because I told you you weren't wanted'. But it was still my career. He was misreading the person massively.

"If he knew anything about me, he'd know I always work as hard as I can. So he said 'yeah, I didn't expect it. I thought you'd be a complete so and so'. I said: 'that's where you got it wrong, along with other things'. Anyway, he invited me to come back and train with the squad and that was it. I was back in."

Hume would make a further nine appearances for Tranmere after that York game, the majority of them from the bench. Adams is far from complimentary about him in his autobiography.

"I have to hold my hands up," he writes. "He was the worst signing I've ever made, anywhere. He'd been playing in India and to say he had developed a problem with his eating habits was an under-statement.

"He was fat and unfit, yet believed himself to be far better than he was. It's a deadly combination. And when your team is struggling, it's not what you want."

Hume, then, had been cast aside, barely involved in a team that was lacking in passion, something he says he would have shown by the bucket load. But what became of the other players who had been banished from the first team?

Eliot Richards' final game for the club came in a 1-0 defeat to Bristol Rovers in the FA Cup, with Adams commenting afterwards that he would need to work extremely hard to get into his first team plans. By February, he had moved on to Cheltenham, where Rob Edwards, the man who brought him to Prenton Park, was now an assistant manager.

James Rowe and Abdulai Baggie meanwhile were both released by mutual consent in February, their final outings for the club coming a month earlier in a 6-2 FA Cup defeat to Swansea.

Hume recalls: "It was an interesting time. It was upsetting, but that's football. I've been quite fortunate. I've come across two of the maddest, worst, strangest managers I could have come across, through my eyes, in England, with Micky Adams and Graham Westley.

"I thought it was going to be this whole swan song, coming back and helping the club get out of their relegation troubles. It was tough to be a part of. The downs well outweighed the ups and the positive parts.

"The only way I could say it was positive was that I was at home and I could pull on the shirt again. Football is a horrible game."

Chapter Twelve
The 51

Tranmere lost their identity during the 2014/15 season. Prenton Park had become a revolving door for not just managers and loan players, but free transfers as well. Each new boss brought with him a collection of fresh faces, and it became more and more difficult to keep track with who was on the pitch.

Micky Adams was the worst offender. Player after player after player, week after week after week. Having arrived in October, he quickly started to put his stamp on the squad, including a manic January that saw a total of seven new arrivals.

"I kept £300,000 back for January," reveals Mark Palios. "My view was that we needed to get better quality in. Unfortunately, and I say it with hindsight, you shop in the window at that time, or late in the window, and we were desperate, which makes it worse.

"You can't attract players to the club if you're in danger of going out of the league. We tended to pick up poor quality for what we paid."

It completely derailed the squad. They did not know who they were going to be playing with from game to game. Even after a victory, the starting XI would be changed.

"There was no continuity," says Liam Ridehalgh. "When you're using that many players, you don't know what team is playing. It's an absolute mix and match. Every week, you feel like you're playing a trial game.

"If you look back over the years, our successful ones, we've had four, five or six stable players in the back four. Under Micky Adams, I reckon there was a different back four every week!

"There were times when somebody would walk past me and I couldn't remember their name. There were new faces every week. He wanted to put his stamp on things, which I understand. But I think there were far too many of them.

"I think it's worse as a defender. You build relationships, and I know you do that all over the pitch, but as a back four, you work as a unit, rather than a front two or a midfield two. You work a lot on that back four through the week. Chopping and changing didn't help."

Ridehalgh was one of those who found himself out of the team because of Adams' signings. Lee Molyneux and Rob Taylor were just a couple of the January arrivals, both of them left-backs.

Iain Hume came in too, right at the back of the month, as well as centre-backs Josh Thompson and Adam Dugdale, all three on permanent transfers until the end of the season. Meanwhile there were a further two incoming loan players, winger Jennison Myrie-Williams and striker Rory Donnelly.

Such a busy month disrupted the team heavily. Tranmere had been on an upward curve before the new year, impressively beating Portsmouth 3-1, their first league win under Adams, as well as registering valuable victories against Dagenham and Northampton.

But following the January arrivals, things imploded in dramatic fashion. After beating Exeter 2-1 down at St James' Park at the end of the month, they went on a three match winless run, with a draw at Newport sandwiched between defeats to Carlisle and the aforementioned York game.

Rory Donnelly and Danny Holmes then scored in a 2-1 victory over Micky Mellon's promotion chasing Shrewsbury, but this would prove to be their final Football League win at Prenton Park for over four years.

Five defeats in a row followed, including a shambolic performance at Cheltenham, who were also embroiled in the relegation battle.

"We started poorly;" said Adams afterwards. "We didn't get anywhere near them in the first 20 minutes, which is unbelievable really. We got exactly what we deserved: nothing.

"In these games, the first goal is all important and the first goal gave them a massive lift. It deflated us somewhat. But we can't take anything away from Cheltenham. They've stuck to their game plan and deserved their win."

The loss at Whaddon Road came just days after Tranmere had surrendered a 2-0 lead at Portsmouth, conceding three times in the last 14 minutes in a 3-2 defeat. They were also beaten by Wycombe, Dagenham and Northampton.

Steven Jennings recalls: "They say 'don't change a winning side'. But if we won a game, there'd be three or four changes the next week, be it down to people being injured or being a bit stiff and needing more time.

"The bodies who were coming in, it was one or two a week, even if they were only on trial to do a week or two of training. I can remember, off the top of my head, five or six lads who came in for a week or two and never signed.

"You were seeing new faces in training every week. It's not healthy. You need faces who you know you can trust on the ball. We weren't getting any of that.

"You can make a lot of excuses for everyone, but the amount of loan players that came in was a lot. To get a loan player right at any level, you're probably working at a 70:30 basis, with 30% working and 70% not."

By the time George Green made the switch to Prenton Park in late March, joining on loan from Everton, Adams had made a remarkable 20 signings in little over five months. Fourteen of them were on temporary deals. Regardless of the quality of the arrivals, it was a recipe for disaster.

Shaun Garnett admits he lost track of all the players coming in. "There were days at the training ground," he says, "where people would walk past me and I'd think 'who are you?'

"You'd only find out of a morning, because as youth coach, Alan Rogers or Chris Shuker would come to me and ask for another kit for somebody who was coming in. I'd ask 'who's he?' It would be another loanee.

"It was every other day that they'd need kit. There was no continuity within the footballing side of things. If we didn't win a game, we'd just change the team, and that's not always the answer.

"The number of players the club used that season tells its own story. We could come up with loads of excuses as to why the relegation happened, but to go through a season using 50 odd players, how do you get familiar with that as a back four? How do you get used to a system when you're constantly changing the system? It's hard for the players."

In total, Tranmere used 51 players in their match day squad in the 2014/15 season. A handful of those, such as youngsters Liam Davies and Sam Ramsbottom were unused substitutes. But a glance at the rest of the squad list uncovers some instantly forgettable names.

Guy Madjo is one, a Cameroon born striker who was found guilty of sexually assaulting a woman in his home in 2016. He made three appearances for Rovers, all of them as a substitute, and looked like he had won a competition to be there.

Jordan Hugill came in on loan from Preston in February. The striker scored once in his six appearances for the club, in a 2-1 defeat at home to Wycombe, but struggled at Prenton Park, largely due to being played out of position as a wide man in the front three.

He returned to Deepdale after just a month, and was promptly sent on another temporary deal, to Tranmere's relegation rivals Hartlepool, for whom he scored four times in eight games to help keep them in the Football League. Less than three years later, West Ham splashed out £8m to buy him.

Calaum Jahraldo-Martin, Danny Johnson and Harrison McGahey had equally poor loan spells, whilst Will Aimson, arguably the most promising of all of Adams' signings, saw his time at Prenton Park cruelly cut short by a broken leg after he collided with teammate Danny Holmes.

**

It was not just the volume of players that were arriving at Prenton Park that was the problem. It was also their character and ambition as well. When a player signs for a club on loan or a short term deal, it can be difficult to develop an affiliation with the side. A number of players looked like they did not know each other while on the pitch. How much they truly cared about the plight of the club is questionable.

"If you're coming into a relegation battle, people don't want a relegation on their CV," says Steve Jennings. "They'd rather say they're injured and find an excuse not to play. It's tough.

"With players coming in and out, we didn't have a settled side at any point. The writing was on the wall a long, long way out, even though it took until the Plymouth game for it to actually happen.

"Lads lost faith in the manager or whatever, but we had a lot of weak characters around. In football you can't be weak, you've got to be strong.
"I do my talking on the pitch, if and when I can, whether I was captain or not. If somebody wasn't pulling their weight, I'd take it personally, because as well as playing for yourself, you're playing for your team.

"If somebody isn't doing it for the team, it's going to affect you as well. There were numerous times where I had to speak to somebody on the pitch, and if it meant speaking to them in training too, it wasn't a problem. Morale was quite low anyway, but it was quite hard to pick the odd one or two up."

There was a frustration that several of the players Adams had brought in, and was persisting with despite poor performances on the pitch, kept their place at the expense of people who really did care about Tranmere.

Danny Holmes, for example, is a Rovers fan through and through. He graduated through the club's academy and had he not made it as a professional footballer, you can guarantee that he would have been on the terraces every week cheering his side on.

Iain Hume, regardless of his fitness issues, has the club deeply embedded in his heart. The same goes for Jason Koumas, who could run a game from midfield, but Adams simply did not fancy him.

"He had seen his best days," writes Adams of Koumas in his autobiography, "and that's being kind to him. He was always injured and did very little training before he announced he should be joining the squad. That didn't sit kindly with me."

"You're fighting relegation," says a clearly exasperated Hume. "You're in a dogfight. And I'm not saying 'I'm better than him', but you want somebody who's going to show a bit.

"Danny Holmes is a Tranmere lad through and through. He's got no choice. He lives up the road! You want somebody in the dogfight, I'm sorry, but there you go.

"Jason Koumas started at the club when he was about 11 or 12. He came through the system. Okay, Jason is not exactly the one person you want to put into war with you, but you want somebody to pull that bit of magic.

"You've got ten guys behind him who are willing to do that work for him. If you're playing somebody ahead of him who is athletic and does nothing, why not take that risk and put in somebody who is going to win you a game?

"Jason was training every day but not getting a sniff. He'd come on and play and take the mick for ten minutes, but because he wasn't fit and he wasn't playing reserve games, as good as he was, he could only do it in glimpses.

"It was just a frustrating time because the club was struggling massively. We were bringing in loans left, right and centre and they weren't doing it. Then you had players who were dying to play for the club and they weren't allowed to do it.

"A lot of players were brought in who had no desire to play for the club. It was just a case of coming in, getting a couple of games and then moving on again. It was a tough one to take because you had players who had deep feelings for the club who weren't involved.

"Adams brought in that many of his boys and there was no team spirit. There just wasn't. People were there for three or four months and they lived down in Stoke or Birmingham. They were just jumping in their car and going. It didn't matter to some people. I won't name names, because individually they were good guys, but I wouldn't back them to go to war with me, and that's what we needed at the time."

Koumas was one of those who really struggled under the Adams regime. He scored early on in the manager's tenure, a stunning strike from outside the box to earn an FA Cup replay against Oxford.

Another impressive display came as an early substitute for the injured Marc Laird against Accrington in January. The midfielder came on in the ninth minute and he absolutely ran the show as Rovers romped to a 3-0 win, their biggest victory under Adams.

He found himself back on the bench a week later when Hartlepool visited Prenton Park. Indeed, his appearances were few and far between, as he started just three games following the manager's arrival.

When asked by the media why the former Wales international was not being used, Adams would often snap.

***

With so many new players coming into the club, there was bound to be disruption within the dressing room. Cliques formed between the different groups; those signed by Adams, those who were at Prenton Park before his arrival, and those who had seen their noses put out of joint.

That is not a recipe for success. At a time when Tranmere needed everybody pulling in the same direction, the squad was fractured. And Adams appeared to have no control over it whatsoever.

"I always just kind of get on with things," says Liam Ridehalgh. "Whatever happens, I never change the way I go about things. I always train hard, get on with it and then go home, basically.

"I think that I've always done that. I can never regret anything, because I come in and work hard. It's always put me in good stead.

"But I think it's very fair to say that Micky lost the dressing room, apart from the ones he signed. He brought in quite a few and they were a team in themselves."

"He did lose a few there," adds Steve Jennings. "But to be honest, even if you do lose faith in the manager, it still shouldn't harm your performance on a Saturday. You need to be playing for yourself as well as the manager.

"He probably did lose the odd few for whatever reasons he had in his own head, but I still think the lads have got to be a bit more professional and play for themselves and for the badge."

Having been banished to train with the under-18s, Iain Hume was not a part of the first team squad at the time. Despite that, he could see the problems that were forming, even if it mystifies him as to how it could happen.

"I don't know how he could lose the dressing room, because they were all his players," he says, exasperated. "It wasn't a good dressing room. There were good guys individually, but you had to be careful with what you said, which is something that no football club likes.

"Your dressing room is your dressing room. You go in there and you joke around and you get pranks. Whatever happens in there, stays in there. I figured it out when I got pushed to the side: you couldn't trust anybody. Even guys I'd known for 15 years.

"You were questioned by people in conversation and you'd give an honest, direct answer. Then you'd find that your answer was getting back to people. How can you trust that?

"It got to a point where, whether he'd lost the dressing room or the dressing room had lost each other, it just wasn't a great place to be around. As good as the guys where individually, I just don't think it was a very trustworthy dressing room."

Shaun Garnett was another looking on from afar, as well as getting the stories fed back to him by the senior players involved with his youth team.

He had been part of some of the great Tranmere sides of the past, teams who had been promoted and battled for a place in the Premier League. He was also in and around the club, although still only very young, when they nearly dropped out of the Football League in 1987. But even during that period, things were never this bad.

"John King was a big believer in the changing room being right," says Shaun Garnett. "So was John Aldridge. For successful managers, it's all about the changing room, and Micky Adams lost it.

"January had ruffled a few feathers and didn't get the expected response. There were cliques evolving with the new players and the old players and the chemistry wasn't right.

"That's the most toxic season and dressing room I can remember. Even the season in which Tranmere stayed in the league in 1987, it was never toxic. It was never that bad. There was never the same doom and gloom.

"I've been involved in football for 33 years, since I left school when I was 16, and that's got to be the worst experience I've had in professional football, both from a personal and footballing point of view.

"I would say, just when they needed the players to step up to the mark, they didn't do it because they weren't good enough. League tables don't lie. We got relegated.

"I just think the way Micky went about it, the players didn't respond to it. They weren't having it. They downed tools a little bit and it created a problem, because I felt we had two camps. We had the lads in the first team and the reserves, the bombed squad.

"I actually think the partnership between Tranmere Rovers and Micky Adams had a lot of potential, but in the end it seemed to break both parties. We suffered with the relegation and Micky Adams has never really come back into management."

Chairman Mark Palios was the man who funded the January transfers. He knew the squad needed work doing to it if the club was going to stay up, and had held that £300,000 back. How much does he think it affected the squad?

"I didn't really get the vibe back to me that he'd lost the dressing room," he says. "I can understand it; I'd speculate from the outside looking in that we'd made so many changes and they hadn't gelled.

"Footballers are, by and large, quite selfish. They've been the apple of their father's eye since they were a kid and the apple of their teacher's eye. Fans want to know them and speak to them and so forth.

"It tends to develop people who are fairly brittle in terms of criticism. That's a generalisation, but it's one that I'm reasonably comfortable with. That's why you lose a dressing room.

"At the end of the day, the manager will go. There's a certain England international who's had quite a few managers. I always laugh, because every time he gets a new one, it's a case of 'the king is dead, long live the king'. He's publicly out spouting about how great the new manager is. You have to understand that.

"I think that probably the combination of poor results and a massive change in the dressing room over the year just made it difficult to get that consistency."

Chapter Thirteen
Oxford and Plymouth

Tranmere would land just one more victory after that 2-1 win against Shrewsbury, and it did not come until the middle of March when they finally ended a run of five defeats in a row.

Dan Gardner, on loan from from Chesterfield and one of Micky Adams' more successful signings, inspired the side to a 2-1 win at Cambridge. Unfortunately, he would pick up an injury and only managed four appearances for the club, scoring twice.

The win at The Abbey Stadium was immediately followed by another shambolic display as Rovers were hammered 4-1 by Burton at Prenton Park. With just eight games to go, they were outside the relegation zone only by virtue of goal difference.

The arrival of George Green, on loan from Everton, sparked a bit of new life into the team. He scored an absolute screamer on debut in a 1-1 draw with Wimbledon, before Tranmere picked up another point, this time down at Stevenage in a 2-2 draw.

But that, in terms of points picked up, would be that, for Rovers. They were on 39 for the campaign, and, even with six games left, would not add to their tally.

Three 1-0 defeats in a row followed, at home to Luton and on the road at Southend and Mansfield. The pressure was seriously mounting on Adams ahead of the visit of Oxford as, with three games to play, they sat at the bottom of the Football League, two points from safety.

Mark Palios, though, had been receiving questions about sacking the boss for some time. "We got to within ten games to go and it's a stick or twist decision," he reveals. "At that point in time, I genuinely believed that it was a black and white decision; do you back Micky Adams or not?

"You put the question with hindsight, but hindsight makes it an unfair question. The real question is, if based with the information you've got at the time, would you make the same decision? I would say yes. I'm not certain that a new manager coming in at that point with that group of players would have made that much of a difference.

"Whilst I've been here, I've often tried to go for stability, because I believe there's currently too much pressure for change from social media. People are entitled to their opinion but it doesn't really help. It's more about them than the club.

"For me, stability is massively important. You know from having been a player that you need to knuckle down, get back to basics, get a result and build on that. There wasn't a particular moment when I knew we'd get relegated, but you knew it was becoming a distinct possibility."

Even in such a tough position in the table, though, the players were refusing to give up hope on Tranmere managing to keep their heads above water.

"I've never had that attitude or mentality in my head," says Steve Jennings on whether the writing was on the wall. "You have to have a winning mentality at any level. If you have ten games left and you need to win them all, that's the mentality you have to have. So there was no moment where I knew we were going to go."

Iain Hume agrees, adding: "There was never a point when I thought we'd go down, because I didn't want to admit that staying up wasn't possible.

"I've been involved in relegation scraps before. We had one with Preston where we had an unbelievable team on paper. The same with Leicester, where I think we were second bottom with eight or nine games to go and managed to win a few. We were well out of it come the end of the season."

The Oxford match, even if the players did not want to admit to it, was another one of those do or die clashes. Tranmere's remaining games were against teams fighting for promotion, so if they were likely to pick up a win anywhere, this was the most promising fixture.

And they started brightly. Hume made his first start since February and had an early chance, whilst Jennison Myrie-Williams dragged one shot wide and George Green forced a save from Jamie Ashdown with a long range free kick.

But as the goalscoring opportunities came and went, the tension increased around Prenton Park. The fans were getting nervous, and so were the players, especially as at half-time it was still 0-0.

That, unfortunately, was as good as it got for the hosts as Oxford ran away with the contest after the break. Kemar Roofe got the first, heading home when left criminally unmarked near the penalty spot, before Danny Rose doubled the lead from close range two minutes later.

In next to no time, Tranmere were 2-0 down and Prenton Park turned toxic like never before. "The last few games were like the final curtain on that chapter," says Mark Bartley. "I can remember in one of Adams' final games, I was sat a couple of rows behind Mark Palios, who I felt sorry for.

"He'd come in as a chairman and didn't want the reputation of getting rid of a manager every ten minutes. We'd already sacked one that season. You don't want to start sacking them every month.

"But a fan stood up behind the bench, right behind Micky Adams and he turned around and shouted 'Palios, why is this man still in charge of our club? This is a disgrace.' I've never seen anything like it'. I could see Mark looking down and it was terrible. The manager must have heard it and it just summed everything up."

That fan was not the only one. When Oxford netted their third, Roofe grabbing his second after again being left unmarked in the box, there was a mass exodus as hundreds of fans headed for the exits.

Plenty of those in the Paddock however diverted their route out of the ground so that they could have their own pop at the manager. One was even escorted from the ground by a steward after a particularly over-zealous response, although he was given a standing ovation by the Kop for the protest.

Tranmere had been wretched. Their chances of staying up were slipping away and everybody knew it. With two games to go, they were two points from safety.

Alan Rogers was put on post match media duty and he was furious. "I'm dumfounded by the second half performance," he blasted. "We huffed and puffed in the first half but never really looked like scoring.

"In the second half, we couldn't have had a worse start. We conceded, but then you've got to have a bit of mental strength about you and make sure you're tight for the next ten minutes and try and get back in the game. But to concede a second after a minute, it's not acceptable and it's not good enough.

"The players have got to start taking some responsibility. It's okay everyone pointing fingers at the manager. But I was a player. Stand up and be counted. Defend set-pieces, defend crosses.

"It's an easy option to point fingers at the manager but these players have got to look at themselves. Have they done enough? The answer is no, they haven't.

"I started my career out of this club. It's a great club with great supporters. What they're seeing isn't good enough. But do we keep on pointing the finger at the gaffer? Well, no you can't. Sometimes as a player you've got to stand up and be counted and the players haven't today."

Rogers denied he was standing in for Adams in the post match press conference because the manager was soon to be leaving his position. But the media knew that his race was run, for they had seen his demeanour.

Press conferences after a match at Prenton Park take place in the tunnel area. On this occasion, they had to walk past the dressing room and the physio room to where the interview would take place.

The door to the latter had been left ajar. Inside, Adams could be spotted sat alone, head bowed. He knew his time was up.

Adams, however, describes those post-match minutes differently in his autobiography: "When we got back into the changing rooms, I could hear a crescendo of noise. 'We want Adams out' was the gist of it.

"I went to do the press and the chanting kept going. The fans were demonstrating against me and, as the players were leaving, they were throwing eggs at them."

Shaun Garnett recalls: "He (Adams) came in after the game and told us he was done and that he was going to speak to Mark Palios. Alan Rogers wanted him to stay on, but he said he'd had enough. That was when I thought 'we're fucked. We're going to struggle now. It was a sad day."

The ugly scenes Adams describes led to the gates to the car park being locked to prevent protesting supporters from getting near to the players' entrance as they continued to vent their feelings.

"We had to stay in the changing room for a good hour afterwards," says Liam Ridehalgh. "The fans, understandably, weren't happy.

There were rumours that Micky Adams' car got egged on the way out. That was the point when I knew we were done."

"The fans were banging on the windows," adds Steve Jennings. "Looking back, they were well within their rights to, for what was getting served up. Even if you're not playing well, you've got to run hard for 90 minutes. There were people not running hard for 45 minutes, never mind 90.

"The stuff that was getting served up, the fans had a right to have a go. Whether you take it that far and are waiting outside, I don't know.

"We were fighting to stay in the Football League, which is unheard of for Tranmere, never mind League One or the Championship, but fans had every right to have a go and they've never been shy in letting you know when you're not pulling your weight. I think every football club has that."

***

Micky Adams' departure was confirmed the following morning. With two games to go and Tranmere bottom of the Football League he had resigned.

"I don't know if I was bottling it," he continues in his book. "I probably was. We only had two games left, but we [Adams and Mark Palios] agreed that to give us the best opportunity of winning at Plymouth the next weekend, it would be best if I stood down."

First team coach Alan Rogers was put in charge for the remaining fixtures, assisted by Shaun Garnett. The latter, though, remains frustrated that Adams decided to stand down when he did.

"I don't know the reason why or when Micky made that decision," he says, "But he left it late. If he was going to do it, he should have done it sooner to give somebody else a chance. The Oxford game left us very little time to turn it around.

"That was the game when I thought it had gone too far. Could Micky have not seen this sooner and said with six games to go 'I can't fix this'? It could have given Alan Rogers a chance to fix it or we could have brought somebody in with six games to go.

"I don't know the answers and it's probably wishful thinking on my part, the inevitable was going to happen. Can we win at Plymouth? Can we beat Bury? They're going for promotion, Plymouth were challenging for the play-offs. We couldn't have had two worse games to be honest."

Iain Hume is also highly critical of the manager for deciding to leave when he did. He accuses Adams of stepping down purely to protect his managerial reputation.

"He's bad mouthed me in his autobiography, which made me laugh," he says. "He singled my name out and everything about his time at Tranmere. This is somebody who didn't know me well enough and then had the audacity to call me out when he'd just walked away from a job so he didn't have a relegation on his CV.

"It's double standards there. You're so eager to hammer somebody for something that for the majority of the time was out of their control, but then ran away with his tail between his legs.

"I'll be honest, he should have walked earlier. You either go six games earlier or you stay to the end. You take it on the chin, we're going down. I'm sorry, don't run away.

"I think there's no hiding it, I don't like him. For some reason, he doesn't like me, so the feeling is mutual. It was just a hard place to be around at the time. It was hard to accept.

"He should have walked six games earlier. If he had, Shaun Garnett and Alan Rogers can take over and have a chance to change it. Okay, we wouldn't have won all the games, but we might have won three or four, or lost just one, and we'd have had a hell of a chance.

"You'd also have a chance to trial and error with what you want for a couple of games. You could say: 'you are the 15 or 16 players that we're going to be playing with, you guys are going to keep us up'. You'd get that belief within the squad.

"But they were given two games. How do you change a negative and losing mentality in two games? We had to win them both and by clear margins. How do you leave a situation like that? Just stay. If you're going to walk, do it at the end of the season.

"I thought it was cowardice to leave in the way he did, just so he didn't have a relegation on his CV. But I hope he knows it will show up on his CV with the percentage of wins and losses, regardless of whether it says relegation. He was at the helm.

"Alan Rogers took over and he said 'let's prove him wrong. Prove to him that he made a mistake'. But it was already far too late for him to have any impact.

***

So with two games left, Tranmere had to pick themselves up, dust themselves down and try and save their League Two status.

"We have a difficult job now," said Alan Rogers ahead of the trip to Plymouth, where defeat could spell the end of the club's 94 year stint in the Football League. "We want to do a solid week of training, get the basics right, tweak a few things and win the game.

"Hopefully, if we can perform a minor miracle, the club can stay in the League and we can build on it. We will be looking to do some things differently. Shaun and I were in early on Monday, looking at ways to get the best out of the players we have here.

"We think we can come up with a cunning plan. We are confident we can go to Plymouth and give ourselves a fighting chance."

Part of that cunning plan was just to get the players smiling again. It had been a tough season, especially for those to whom the club meant so much. The enjoyment had almost been sapped out of football by this point, and that needed to change for the game at Home Park.

"It was doom and gloom in training ahead of the game," admits Steve Jennings. "So Shaun and Alan just tried to make it as enjoyable as possible. We just played small sided games all week, just to get the enjoyment back into playing football. We didn't work on the tactics at all until the Friday when we travelled down there and worked on them for the whole day."

It seemed to have worked at first. Although Reuben Reid gave Plymouth the lead, Tranmere's traveling support, desperate to see their side pull a rabbit out of the hat, were sent wild when Max Power equalised just after the half hour mark.

"We travelled down to Plymouth on the Friday and we were full of excitement and belief," says Garnett. "We still thought we could do it. As a footballer, you've got to. Looking at the side that went to Plymouth, it still had the potential to win a game, but then it all fell apart.

"Max's goal came from a set piece that we'd used in the youth team. It was great, but from a personal point of view, I probably got a little bit carried away. I was inexperienced. Maybe we all did.

"Plymouth get the goals to go 3-1 up and you knew the clock was ticking away. I don't think it sunk in until we got in the changing room after the game, but you knew it was coming to an end.

"The harsh reality was we'd gone out of the Football League. I'd been here in 1987 when we survived it and it was a fantastic occasion. This went the other way. I didn't think I'd experience it and it was tough."

Kayode Odejayi did pull one back for Tranmere in the 89th minute, but it proved to be nothing more than a consolation as Plymouth eventually won 3-2.

And then the news filtered through that Hartlepool had beaten Exeter 2-1. Jordan Hugill, on loan at Prenton Park earlier that season, scored one of the goals. Cruelly, the Monkey Hangers were also managed by ex-Rovers boss Ronnie Moore and had been 10 points from safety at the start of January, not long after he took charge.

Their win confirmed that they would be staying in the Football League. Tranmere were down and out. The National League was calling.

"We were grown men crying," Garnett continues. "We knew there was no second chance. We didn't have another game to put it right. We were down and relegated. We were in the National League.

"If I'm looking at the team from that day, the two big stand outs are Steven Jennings and Max Power. They really felt it. They'd both been at the club since they were kids.

"Jennings had seen good times with the club and had enjoyed a good career. But this was Max's second relegation in two years, so it was a tough one for him."

"It was devastating," adds Hume, who came on as a substitute. "Nobody wants a relegation on their CV. I've been through a few through. I got relegated with Preston and Leicester.

"You could see it on the players' faces after the game, with the likes of Max Power and Danny Holmes. They were devastated. Shaun Garnett was broken. He'd been involved with the club for that long.

"For myself, I know I hadn't been involved with the team for a while but it still hurt. You had fans coming down to watch the game hoping there would be a miracle. Tranmere were in the League for so long, and then all of a sudden, it was 'crap, what are we going to do? I don't want to be here anymore'.

"I imagine that's what the majority of fans were like. They didn't want to go and watch Non League football. As hard as it would be for the vast majority of them to admit it, they didn't want to support a Non League team, as much as they love Tranmere, because they'd never witnessed it or been involved in it.

"Then they get over it and are thinking they'll go straight back up, and it doesn't happen. Their love and loyalty is tested again. It's always hard, especially with the younger fans, to get them on board here because you have the guys over the water."

Jennings meanwhile recalls the devastation of the long journey back from Home Park, situated 300 miles and a minimum of five hours from Birkenhead by car. There can have been no worse a place to be traveling back from.

"Because Alan Rogers and Shaun Garnett weren't held responsible in any way," he says, "You just had to stop off, get some lager in and try your best to not think about it.

"I'd like to think nobody spoke a word to each other. We couldn't put our heads up and look at each other. You could actually see that to one or two, it did matter. There were tears. The others were playing on their phones straight away and getting on with their everyday life. You could see it didn't mean a lot to them.

"We definitely had chances to get out of it. I know I took a lot of stick myself, but there were a few players there who literally weren't pulling their own weight. We signed a few dodgy players. I'm not going to name names, but there were some bad signings.

"The burden of being captain was huge, and the pressure of it was huge. I could put my finger on about three or four names who were putting a shift in week in, week out. The rest were passengers, if not worse.

"You could see, going into the last five or six games, the players who cared about what happened to the club. Those ones have gone on to make good careers for themselves. The rest of them, I don't think you've heard of them play any type of real football."

"It was just about licking your wounds and going home," Garnett adds. "The coach was quiet. Players are players and they probably had more answers than the coaching staff. Players are very much like that. As a coaching staff, we were gutted."

Liam Ridehalgh had the odd situation of not being involved in the game and having to follow his team's fate from afar. "I didn't even travel to Plymouth," he says. "Me and Marcus Holness met up in Manchester on the Saturday and watched Sky Sports News, but we already had that feeling that we were relegated. It wasn't good.

"It's difficult when you're not involved and you're not able to help. In one respect, it's easy because you know there's nothing you can do about it, but you want to help and make a positive impact. It just wasn't meant to be."

Mark Palios had already come to terms with being relegated before the game was played. He admits: "The dye was cast after that Oxford game. I sat there all week thinking about how to deal with it.

"What you've got to do is to retain your credibility but say things that keep everybody's heads up. You've got to get that balance right as chairman. If you're trying to lead anybody, you will have bad times, but you keep people's heads up. It was quite difficult.

"I remember sitting down and I like alliteration. When I said 'It's devastating today but not disastrous tomorrow', I'd sat there thinking about that right through the week. I needed something that encapsulated it right away and I was trying to find the adjective. It is devastating. But how do you say that? 'But it's not disastrous'.

"Alan Rogers and Shaun Garnett had taken over and it was just unfair, so I went into the dressing room and there were a few lads who were in tears. It's not a good place to be when you've been relegated.

"So I went up to take the media; it wasn't Alan and Shaun's bag, they weren't responsible for it. It was my job to stand up and take it. It was relatively easy to do. I've got a bit of experience.

"People started to ask me about Micky Adams and that, but it wasn't right to talk about employees, so I didn't. 'You wouldn't like me to talk about you in terms of what you did wrong and what you did right. We just sort of learn from it, thank everybody for their efforts and move on and deal with it'. That's what we did."

A week later, Tranmere played their final game in League Two for three years. They lost 1-0 at Prenton Park to Bury, who, as a result, were promoted to League One.

Part Two

The Turnaround

Chapter Fourteen
New Owners

Tranmere's stories of financial hardship go back a lot further than the period covered in this book. For decades, they have existed in the shadow of Liverpool and Everton, the top flight giants on the other side of the Mersey.

During the 1980s, the club was close to meeting its demise. Faced with mounting debt, they staved off insolvency thanks to a loan from Wirral Borough Council and fundraising friendly fixtures against teams such as Manchester United and Wolves.

In 1984, American attorney Bruce Osterman purchased the club. It made them the first team in England to have a foreign owner, but the relationship was a disaster from start to finish.

The San Fransisco based lawyer was ambitious. He wanted to take the club through the leagues and invested a tidy sum in an attempt to get them out of the old Fourth Division. He also fancied himself as a bit of a player and at times trained with the first team as he tried to improve his goalkeeping skills.

Unfortunately, Osterman soon fell out with the manager Bryan Hamilton and on field, performances were poor. That had an affect on the attendances, which were perilously low to start with. Rovers were failing as a business. As the money ran out, the owner began looking at which assets he could sell to keep the club afloat.

Just three years after the American's arrival, Tranmere went into administration. This was long before the days of 10 point deductions and other such sanctions from the football authorities. But it was also a time when going into administration seriously threatened the existence of a club, unlike the current era where a solution is often just around the corner.

With Rovers in turmoil, and with their Football League status at stake, local businessman Peter Johnson was approached for help in preventing the club from going under. He was seduced by the idea of owning the team, and went ahead with the purchase of a controlling stake.

The new owner had much deeper pockets than Osterman, which helped in a swift turnaround of the club's fortunes on and off the field. Johnny King was appointed as manager and Tranmere staved off the immediate threat of relegation on the final day of the 1986/87 season thanks to a narrow and famous 1-0 win over Exeter.

From then on, the direction of travel was always upwards. In the words of King, Tranmere went on 'a trip to the moon'. They won two promotions and reached Wembley five times, qualifying for two play-off finals, two Leyland DAF Trophy finals and the Mercantile Credit Football League Centenary Tournament.

"I thoroughly enjoyed my time at Tranmere," says Johnson in a rare interview. "I'm very pleased with the success I had, and of the team we built. We had Pat Nevin, Eric Nixon and John Aldridge amongst others.

"We were so close to going into the Premiership. Plus we had a very good manager in Johnny King; he was a very good choice.

"Johnny didn't make decisions quickly! But most of them were right. He was an incredible manager for what he did at Tranmere. One might say a lot of people could have produced those performances with the players that he had. That's not to criticise his player management though, as that was very good.

"He was a man of habit. Before we went to Wembley, the first time, we went into his room and cracked a bottle of scotch before getting back on the team coach and going down to London. He insisted on doing that each time we went! He was a sound man.

"It seemed easier in those days. I would say it's more difficult now.

When I came in, I am afraid to say I did believe that we could have the success we did. I don't go into anything to lose! But it did seem easier in those days than today.

"We were going to Wembley. We went four times in two years. If silverware and visits to Wembley are a measure of success, then we were very successful. We went up into the old Second Division, which was quite important. We stayed there for ten years. What was interesting was that we had young supporters who had never known Tranmere to be out of the Second Division."

The success Johnson enjoyed as Rovers' owner was unprecedented. From a club apparently stumbling toward relegation, they turned their fortunes around. They got to within touching distance of the top flight, three times in a row qualifying for the play-offs, only to fall at the semi-final stage on each occasion.

The owner, however, had left Prenton Park by the time the glory years reached their conclusion. In 1994, he had purchased Merseyside rivals Everton. Frank Corfe, who had served as Johnson's chief executive at Prenton Park, became Tranmere chairman. But with Johnson's financial support no longer on tap, the club's prospects of gaining promotion diminished.

"I have one regret," Johnson admits of his time at Prenton Park. "It's well documented where I went to for a few years.

"I think if I hadn't gone there, Tranmere might well have got into the Premiership. I don't think we'd have lasted long there, but just to get there would have been fantastic. We were very close to getting into there with the three play-offs. With hindsight, I know what we should have done."

By 1999, Johnson had washed his hands of Everton. He came back across the Mersey, taking a controlling role of his stake at Prenton Park while naming businesswoman Lorraine Rogers as chairman.

Money, by this point, was much tighter. Rovers had to sell popular home-grown players Kenny Irons and John McGreal in order to pay their way. Even so, success continued, to a degree.

Manager John Aldridge guided Tranmere to their first major final, the 2000 Worthington Cup final at Wembley, in which they were beaten 2-1 by Premier League side Leicester City.

They also reached back to back FA Cup quarter-finals in 1999/2000 and 2000/01. It is this competition which provides some of Johnson's most cherished memories during his time with the club.

"The match that stands out the most is the FA Cup replay against Southampton," he says. "We were 3-0 down at half-time and I was in the boardroom. I said to Tony Adams, who was one of the directors, 'Tony, I don't want to go back out there. We're 3-0 down. Where we do we go from here?'

"He said 'Don't worry Peter. You'll be back in here at full-time and we'll have won 4-3!' He couldn't have known that it would be 4-3, but it came true!

"The Everton away match, winning 3-0, was very interesting too. I didn't go to the game. I went to the south of France to watch it. Near the end, when we were 3-0 up, I sent the waiter around to ask everybody in the restaurant if they'd have a drink.

"These Frenchman must have been wondering why they were getting a drink from the Englishman who only just knew them! They'd have been thinking 'what's he doing?' It was unbelievable!

"In terms of my favourite player, when you've got a player who scores 40 goals a season, he's got to be near the top! John King and myself went to Real Sociedad to talk to John Aldridge and I couldn't believe we were going to sign him.

"I didn't believe it was going to go through because at the time, Blackburn were interested and they were in the First Division. Everton and Oldham wanted him too. But all John wanted was to play locally and train locally.

"He came to us and in his first game, we played away at Brighton. Their fans were singing 'what a waste of money'. Bang, bang. 2-0. They'd just come out of the First Division and we'd just come up from the Third Division."

In spite of the success in the cup competitions around 2000 and 2001, Tranmere were struggling in the league. They were relegated from the Championship soon after Aldridge resigned in March 2001. At this point Johnson began to think about selling his shares in the club.

It would, however, take a decade for him to relinquish control. That was not down to a lack of interest, but instead due to his insistence on finding the right person to sell the controlling shares to. He had built a legacy at Tranmere, and he did not want to see it destroyed by making the wrong call in his final choice.

Chester City owner Stephen Vaughan was one potential buyer. He would oversee Chester's downfall at the end of the decade as they went into voluntary administration and tumbled out of the Football League. Johnson decided not to sell.

American investors Club 9 wanted to purchase 90% of the club's shares. Negotiations were prolonged before Johnson pulled the plug, announcing in July 2011 "we have been unable to reach agreement".

There were others, including property developer Michael Wilde, who spent six months trying to strike a deal with the Rovers owner. As discussions moved towards a conclusion, Johnson signalled that a sale was imminent. He would, however, make a late u-turn.

"I was always keen to find the right buyer," says Johnson. "We had worked hard to achieve the success we had. We didn't want to see it disappear. There are so many stories (about clubs) in the lower leagues of football where assets disappear. It was important that the right people went into it (Tranmere).

"There are always people looking for football clubs, but they don't always have the money to pay for the football club or buy the football club. There was a trickle of interest during the time that it was up for sale."

One party who did have Rovers' best interest at heart was the Tranmere Supporters Trust. They launched an ambitious plan to purchase Johnson's shares, but could not raise the target set for them by the chairman.

Mark Bartley, who was vice chairman of the Trust at the time, has had a period to reflect and says: "With a few years of experience looking at other clubs, I don't know whether it would have been the best thing for us.

"At that point, we were wanting to approach Mark Palios as being the chief executive if we got the club. We weren't going to run it, we would just own it. We tried, unsuccessfully, to get in touch with him several times."

The Trust fell some way short in their attempts to buy the club. Their target had been £250,000, and although there was some interest, it was not enough to convince Johnson to sell.

***

It would take until August 2014 for Peter Johnson to finally find somebody who he trusted to begin the rebuilding job at Tranmere. A former Rovers player, who had also worked in finance and had a spell as chief executive of the Football Association, had entered negotiations. The familiar face was Mark Palios, who was anxious to prevent the club slipping into the oblivion of the National League.

Says Johnson: "When Mark Palios and his wife Nicola showed an interest, I thought 'this is the man for us'. I suppose they were the first serious buyers. I am very pleased with the success that they're now achieving.

"Mark understands football and that was important. He played nearly 300 times for the club and he knows the administration of football through being the chief executive of the Football Association. So he's played the game and he's been in the administration side. He was ideal."

It took some time for the two parties to strike a deal though. Mark and Nicola Palios showed an initial interest in May 2014. They knew the troubles the club were facing, and were listening to the radio in France as they and learned of the relegation to League Two.

It took until the start of the following campaign for a deal to be completed. There were financial issues to sort out, whilst Johnson and Palios were both keen to do due diligence.

"There are two things in this that every bloke should realise," jokes Palios. "First of all, make it your wife's idea. Secondly, ask one of your good mates, who you know is going to give you the right answer. So I rang Ray Stubbs and said 'is this totally wild?' He responded 'no, you've got to do it, it'll be fantastic!' So having got that, I then rang Peter.

"I was slightly embarrassed. I called him out of the blue and said 'you've been relegated and I think you'll go down and liquidation is on the cards'. He said 'no, no, no. It's not going to happen'. It may not have done in fairness to him, he may well have funded the club beyond. I half expected him to bat me away."

Money was one of the big issues. Mark and Nicola Palios had accumulated their own personal wealth over their years in business, but was it enough to fund a football club?

Johnson, on the other hand, was owed a significant sum himself. He estimates that he had invested around £5m into the club over the years, some of it for the purchase of players and a portion for other transactions. When previous buyers had come sniffing, he had wanted reimbursing to the same value. That would not have to be a factor if he sold to Palios.

"My £5m built the new ground," says Johnson. "After the Hillsborough disaster, the Taylor Report ruled that we needed all seater stands. We were soon into that position.

"But I don't think getting back the money was important. The important thing was that it was in the right hands. I wrote off £5m. There were people that offered more money than Mark, but I was wary.

"He is a competent man. I'm very comfortable with him. I'm very pleased to see that the club has managed to get back into League One. I'm impressed with the job he's done."

Palios says he was straight up with Johnson from the off. He admitted he would not be ploughing millions into the club. Instead, he had a plan that would enable Rovers to grow while living within their means. He believed he had the ability to turn Tranmere around.

"I said to Peter that we weren't going to put in stacks," he reveals. "We would put in X amount and we just needed to restructure a little bit. Peter didn't dismiss it, and I was quite surprised.

"Over a period of time, he said he was getting his figures together for the next season and the discussions started from there. I just said send me the figures down and we'll start to talk about it, which we did over the summer.

"I was quite clear that we needed to create that breathing space. I remember lying in bed one night thinking 'I can't do this in a year, it's going to take at least two years' because we were getting closer and closer and they were building a squad.

"I had views on that squad. I did a bit of due diligence on them and I knew we were going to struggle, even in League Two having just got relegated. They appointed the staff over the course of the close season.

"We were in Cuba and negotiations were hampered by the fact that in Cuba, you can probably use Google about once, and then they close you down! We had really difficult communications and at one stage, I thought the thing was potentially off because there was nothing happening!

"When we came back, I had literally said to Peter just before the first game of the season 'it either happens or it doesn't' and Peter said 'come up' and that's when I really knew we were going to do the deal."

Johnson left the club almost where they were when he arrived in 1987. They were back in the basement division of the Football League and hope was dwindling. But the memories in-between will last a lifetime.

He likes to return to Prenton Park whenever he wishes. He has the title of club president and has reflected on the legacy he left at Prenton Park.

"The thing I'm most proud of at Tranmere is getting the regular gates of 6,000 or 7,000," he says. "When I went there, the gates were as low as 1,300. We then got it up to 1,800 and when we touched regular 6,000 to 8,000, it was very pleasing.

"I'm proud of my home town. I'm very proud of what we did at Tranmere. What I've done in business and what I did at Tranmere is all part of the same trend. I think it's just what I do! I still enjoy my visits to the club.

"The club are part of the community, that's what they mean to me. They have a part to play. We were getting up towards 9 or 10,000 gates in the second division. It was a job worth doing.

"It's interesting how it affected people. When I went back onto the pitch to show the new Essar sponsored shirt, as I was walking off, a young boy put his hand out so that he could touch me. He said 'you're a legend'. I don't think I'd ever been called a legend in my life before! But it was quite touching. I'm not sure if he knew what he meant!"

Chapter Fifteen
Mark and Nicola Palios

On 11th August 2014, Mark and Nicola Palios were confirmed as the new owners of Tranmere Rovers Football Club. The former was almost brought to tears at the press conference to announce the purchase, emotional at the task that lay ahead of him.

Peter Johnson described them as "a safe pair of hands". An exciting future was anticipated. But why come back into football now? Palios had been out of the game for over a decade since leaving the FA. Life would have been much easier by staying in semi-retirement.

"I wouldn't have done it anywhere else," he explains. "I was asked to go and look at and get involved in various clubs, but I just didn't have the heart to do it. This was something that needed doing.

"With all honesty, since I retired from working in the city in 2010, I'd done quite a bit in sport in terms of cricket and judo and nothing had been quite as fulfilling as a project like this, which was close to my heart.

"I was born in Wavertree and came over to the Wirral when I was 6. The lads used to disappear off on a Friday night and watch the Rovers play, so it was always there and a big part of what I understood.

"I didn't actually start playing football until I was 14. By the time I was 16, I was playing for Tranmere. It gave me, as a kid, a massive amount. I had been in care. My parents weren't around for a long period during my childhood. The only two stable things in my life were my school, St Anselm's, and sport. Tranmere have always featured large in my life. As a 16-year old in those circumstances, it gives you a lot of confidence and helps you moving forward.

"I was just fortunate that I was okay at school and I was okay at sport. The club tried to sign me professionally, but I guess it was the Greek immigrant that was drilled into you by your father - if you're going to university, you go to university.

"So I said I'd go to university and when I was there and things got serious about potentially becoming a professional, the club let me play. When I finished, I was full time, but they let me go on to study accountancy.

"We all underestimated what that meant. The club thought it was just like being at university again with loads of free time and loads of opportunity. Training as a chartered accountant is slightly different because you're working in an office and then you've got to study as well as doing your training in the evening and keeping yourself fit. But the club were good. We worked on it and it just continued on.

"I left and went to Crewe but still trained at Tranmere with the amateurs on a Tuesday and Thursday night, and then I came back to Tranmere for a second period. It was so embedded in my later teenage years and right through my 20s and 30s that it was something that was there and a big part of my life.

"And then of course it then features because you go into the office and you're an oddball because you're a professional footballer. Going down to Cambridge, where I was for six years, it was just odd, because they didn't know who Tranmere Rovers were.

"By the time I came back in 2014, I had left the whole professional football arena completely, so I lost a bit of touch with Tranmere per se. I had a few mates who I was still in touch with and I was always interested in their results, but it wasn't until I came back one day in 2014 to see Dave Philpotts and the club was in a real parlous state.

"It was in such a state that it wasn't the club I knew. There had been years when Peter had tried to leave, so it's quite understandable that there wasn't the investment in the club that there should have been, and you could see that and sense that when you walked around.

"They were having their perennial struggle against relegation out of League One at the time and there were the allegations of spot fixing against players, which will have killed Tranmere fans and the spirit around the club.

"Ronnie Moore was also sacked for betting. I know Ronnie. You can take your view as to whether that was a serious betting offence, or whether it was just opportunism by the club, but it was all pretty negative.

"We came away from the club, Nicky and I, and I said 'it's in a really bad state'. We were in France on the way back when we got relegated in 2014 and I turned to Nicky and said 'that's it, they'll go down and they'll go down again. I think it'll go into administration. It could be the end of the club.'

"Nicky knew what I did for a living. She said 'well fix it. Do something about it'. I said 'I will, if you will' because I knew I'd get fairly embroiled in it. For me, the return to the club was almost squaring the circle. It needed a turn round and that's sort of what I'd started doing when I was here at the club as a player.

"It was one of those things; it was a great project to do, it was a way of giving something back. If you were to say to me would I have expected it to be like it is, I would have said yes, but it's much more emotional than I would have guessed."

The arrival of Mark and Nicola Palios was like a breath of fresh air. Tranmere had become a crumbling club. With fans sapped of hope, the way forward looked bleak. Suddenly, there was light at the end of the tunnel.

"The takeover was, on a scale of 1 to 10, a ten in terms of how much it was needed," explains Shaun Garnett. "We needed somebody to direct the club. We needed somebody to get hold of the club.

"It was in a bad place. We needed somebody who wanted to do right, both as a business, which Mark has done, but also as a football club, because you can't have one without the other.

"It's no good them coming in and throwing loads of money at Tranmere Rovers. We'd just be in the same position as we were when we came out of the Championship. It needed management. It needed somebody to come in and say, and this is a bit crude, but 'this club's fucked. It's going nowhere.'

"Unless we stopped the rot, it was going to sink. I really believe that. Without Mark or Nicola or somebody else, the club could have ended up as another Stockport - down in the National League North.

"The management off the field had been a major part of the downfall. I also think the reduced budget was hard. You suddenly had to change where you went shopping for players. They were the two big things for me.

"You were noticing it by the purse strings being pulled. You were looking to cut back on everything, and if you do that, the consequences are what happened to Tranmere Rovers. It's happened to other clubs as well."

"It was imperative that Mark Palios took over when he did," adds Mark Bartley. "I quite like Peter Johnson, and when I see him, we chat about football, but he'd got to a stage where he needed to move on.

"He didn't really want to be in charge anymore and you could tell that from the club. If the owners don't want to be there, nobody else does. That's understandable. He'd done it for so long and put so much money in, and he was continuing to have to put money in. I can't blame him. At that stage of his life, he wanted to take a more backseat role than what he was.

"The result was that there was no direction. We were like a

rudderless ship and the fans had just had enough. We were treading water, trying to survive with no direction. The whole club felt like that. What happened on the pitch was a symptom of what was happening in the boardroom.

"There was one change in the running of the club. The Trust got told by Peter Johnson that Tranmere had a new chief executive, called Jeremy Butler, so we arranged to meet him. We took him one of the maroon scarfs as a welcome.

"The meeting got off to a horrendous start though. We had just launched our bid to try and buy a stake in the club, so we had a brochure that listed some benefits, such as share certificates and giving question and answer sessions with the players.

"Mick Horton, who was there too, started going off on us. He said he had to seek legal advice about posts we'd put on the Cowsheds regarding the question and answer sessions.

"He said 'you're not allowed to do that without getting club consent and I've wasted £800 on legal advice'. That was the kind of middle management in place at the time.

"Jeremy Butler came in and he wasn't the same as Mick Horton. He was trying to be fairly neutral. But I don't know what his purpose was, other than to try and get the club sold.

"I don't think he had any idea on how to manage the club from a chief executive point of view. One thing that stands out was when he teased about some exciting news being announced, and it was the Main Stand getting painted. That signifies that era to me. It just worsened the mood.

"I thought there was a fairly toxic middle to senior management team. The people who you deal with on a day to day basis, people like Christine Roberts, they were fine and we still get on very well with them.

"But there was a level of senior management - not the owner, Peter

Johnson - who saw it as a threat when the Trust offered ideas. They thought fan involvement would undermine their work.

"We tried to help boost season tickets by getting the orange and maroon shirts and scarfs made up. Unfortunately the sizing of the shirts came up a little bit tight! Everybody was complaining about them being a snug fit! But we did that off the Trust's own back and it did help.

"When our gates were going down, it at least kept them where they were. It had a positive outcome because we had quite a few people saying 'I wasn't going to renew, to be honest, but I quite like that scarf and shirt so I'll give it another go'.

"It was quite hard work though. There were certain individuals at the club who didn't want fan involvement at the time. They tried to make things very awkward, which was frustrating, because we were giving things away for free to try and help somebody's business and help them in their job.

"It was very draining when you find that you're spending lots of time doing things such as the scarfs and shirts. The fans were very appreciative, but the people at the club saw you more as a headache.

"They're there trying to make life awkward for you. They don't see any benefit or role for supporters in that circumstance. I think it goes without saying that something was amiss, because none of those people are there now.

"Mark and Nicola Palios came in and they were different. They were more highly involved and more attentive to detail. We absolutely needed that. We needed somebody to come in and start brushing aside the culture that was there, start involving fans and make wholesale changes. I think that's been done. They couldn't do it immediately, but it has been done.

"They became involved with the fans very early. It was quite refreshing that they saw fan potential from a very early stage. They said to us 'you've got the supporters' trust and you've got money, which is great. We'll liaise with you and we'll bring you in'."

Palios admits creating that bond with the Trust was an important one. As much as they were there to challenge the club, they were also there to support it, something the new owner quickly recognised.

"My experience with the FA," he adds, "was that every club was fighting with its trust and its community. It was more a feature of individuals, both in the clubs and in the trusts themselves, when at the end of the day, they both ostensibly had the same objective: to enhance and further the cause of the club. That had been the same here.

"When I came here, maybe it was down to the individuals we were fortunate to find in their chairman Ben Harrison and Mark Randles, but we started to develop a good working relationship with them.

"One of the things I was really pleased to do was to turn the director's car park into a fanzone. It was symbolic as much as anything else. It made a massive statement. It was also fulfilling what we wanted to do, which was working with the fans.

"I don't go to the games as a fan. I don't pay my money week in, week out. I can't tell a fan how to be a fan, but the fans can effectively advise us as to what the fans want. It was a massive easy way of communicating both ways with the fans.

"The Trust came on board right away and Ben Harrison has done a great job. That's why, when Mark Randles took over as chair of the Trust, we kept Ben as an associate director. That relationship was the first one. I was always aware though that the Trust wasn't truly representative of the whole body of fans. That's why I wanted an official supporters club.

"It was during that first season that we made a connection with the fans and that surprised me. I thought they'd say 'you've come in and you've taken us out of the league for the first time in our history'.

"But there was a moment just before we went down at Plymouth. We saw the fans and I went and sat back down next to Nicky and said 'we're going to be fine with those fans. They'll be great.'

"It was one of the bigger moments, and it was a positive, not a negative. When I drove back from Plymouth that day, my phone ran out of battery because of the texts I got from people right across the game because of the affection for the club."

Chapter Sixteen
The Turnaround

Mark Palios knew he had a huge job on his hands to make Tranmere a stable club. The process, though, was always going to be a gradual one as Rovers had been blighted by problems, on and off the pitch, for a number of years.

The decline, although appearing steep, had been a long time coming. When it eventually hit, it hit hard. By 2015, they had fallen into the National League for the first time in their history and it looked, to some, like oblivion.

Kieran Maguire is a Football Finance expert at the University of Liverpool. He has years of experience in looking into how clubs are operated, and recently took some time to delve into Tranmere's difficulties. What he found rings true for many other teams.

"Turnover in 2013 was just £3.5m," he explains. "The debt stood at just under £6.9m. When Mark Palios first came in, the club clearly had financial issues.

"He sat down with the major creditors, such as Peter Johnson, and said 'Peter, I'm a chartered accountant, I'm a turnaround specialist, I can do this'. I think he's sold him the vision of how they're going to go about that and it's proved to be successful."

Mark and Nicola Palios came in at a time when it was arguably too late to halt the slide. With hindsight, they might have made some different decisions. But what was most important was stopping the fire-fighting that was taking place. They needed to get to the root cause of each problem.

"When I came here, I had one, two three," says Mark Palios. "That's the way I do turnaround anyway, you won't find it written in a book.

You create a breathing space, extract the organic potential and then you can say 'this isn't a busted flush' and people are prepared to invest money in it.

"What was quite strange, and people wouldn't realise this unless they're working in turnaround, but in turnaround, you tend to be industry agnostic. You're more situation specific. You deal with the problems rather than a particular industry.

"But this was probably the one industry I knew from top to bottom with my background and of course I've completed my education over the last five years by actually having to run a lower league club.

"I think the conditions are extreme, too, because I think the conditions that we have now are probably the worst I've seen for running a lower league club since the mid 1980s."

The fact that Palios had prior knowledge is a key one for Maguire, who has dealt first hand with the Rovers owner. He believes it stands Mark and Nicola in better stead than some of their counterparts across the Football League.

"I think having somebody who understands money so well is absolutely critical," he says. "I've had some involvement over the course of the last 12 to 18 months advising potential buyers of football clubs and trying to give them a guide price of how much to pay.

"That's geeky stuff as far as I'm concerned, but what they don't understand is that if you are in the Championship, you might be close to the Premier League, but the clubs in the second tier lost nearly £580m between them last year. That's over half a billion, and around £20m each, but some are far in excess of that.

"There are far too many people associated with football who take off their business and finance heads once they get involved. They get seduced, a bit like Medusa. You have the siren call with the glamour of the Premier League and if you are in the Championship, you're hosting big clubs like Leeds, Derby and Nottingham Forest.

"Some owners think they need to try and compete with them. Don't try. Just accept they're living in a different environment to you and focus on yourself. Mark Palios has been able to do that.

"I've met a few owners, but I've never met one quite like Mark Palios. The one I'd say he is most similar to is Andy Holt at Accrington Stanley. If you talk to either fan group, they will both say the same thing - they're honest, transparent, committed and see themselves as custodians of the club, not owners.

"They are trying to create a legacy and they are very community focused. But Mark's level of passion and intensity in terms of the financial side of things is amazing.

"Andy is a brilliant bloke and he's also running his own business, so he's got to split his time. But I get the impression from Mark Palios that he has total dedication towards the club, even in the light of his own personal circumstances. He's had health issues to deal with. It's unparalleled."

***

The morning after Tranmere's relegation from the Football League, Mark Palios sat up in bed. He could not sleep. Thoughts of how to return the club to the 92 were racing around his head. It needed to be done, and fast.

It was still dark outside, after all, it was 5am. But the chairman reached for a pen and a scrap bit of paper, on which he scribbled down his blueprint for promotion.

He has recently uncovered that business plan. It outlines his strategy for getting the club back on their feet again. On the other side of that same piece of paper, in the same handwriting, is his cancer treatment.

He lifts it off his desk and starts reading through it. Bullet point number one targets a return to the Football League by 2016/17. "We were a year behind that" he says, recalling Rovers' play-off final defeat to Forest Green.

"Next comes 'Maximise the organic potential of the club without major investment whilst identifying projects that will increase non-match-day income'. That was so we could support a top third playing budget and better than average football systems.

"Thirdly, 'Talent identification, analysis, evidence based training and Continuous Professional Development for the players.' I'm getting into that, because the right time is to do that now.

"Point four: 'Redefine a development club, focus on developing players aged 18-22 into League players, explore the options at The Campus from a category three academy.'

"Five: 'Redefine community club by expanding the concept of Tranmere Rovers as a more effective local delivery vehicle for national public sector investment, broadening the Tranmere Rovers footprint on the Wirral and contributing to the finances.

"Six: 'Change the demographic of the fanbase through the focus on ages 5-12', which is SWA2, 'establish a Tranmere brand image as The Family Club, which is linked into the community, listens to its fans, does the right thing, has an aggressive playing style, is innovative and with affordable live football.

"Then you get on to achieving the second phase of financing, which we did last summer, and initiating projects, which is what we're doing now. For the playing side of things: 'Progressively build a top team', that's the staff in the business, 'and after Solar Campus, further restructuring of the balance sheet and get equity investment in.'

"That was all written at 5am the day after we went down. It hasn't all gone exactly as it was, but we're pretty much there in what we were striving to achieve."

***

So how have the Palios' been able to turn things around? Kieron Maguire insists it is no fluke. The chairman is fully immersed in the day to day running at Prenton Park, more so than many of his counterparts in the Football League.

"I get the impression Mark Palios thinks about his running of the club 24/7," he says. "He showed me his white board and all the plans; short term, medium term and long term. It's very strategic in nature, whereas I think in respect of many other clubs, and there are plenty of well run ones in the North West, such as Rochdale, Preston, Burnley and Accrington, it is beyond who we are going to sign in the next transfer window.

"That's the focus sometimes. Can we survive there? Can we get ourselves a new centre forward or centre half in the next window and use that as a means to get promoted.

"I think what is interesting about Tranmere is that they flipped the situation. It's not a case of the business running the club. It's the success of the business giving the resources to the football side of the operation to be able to compete more, whereas for most clubs, the football side of the business is run crazily and you're constantly firefighting.

"You're spending most of your time trying to fend off predators, placate bank managers and so on. That's not the case with Tranmere. The creditors get paid on time, the bank are perfectly relaxed in terms of their relationship with the club, and that allows everybody to focus on taking it to wherever the next step is going to be."

Maguire has, in a nutshell, described exactly how Palios believes a football club should run. He wants Tranmere to be a business that is not overly reliant on how things are going on the pitch. He has brought in numerous financial arms that support the day to day operation as well as the playing budget, as opposed to cash being solely generated by the first team's performance.

"What they're trying to do is to increase the proportion of total revenue that comes from non-football streams," Maguire continues. "By footballing streams, I mean match day and broadcasting.

"So he uses the alternative sources of income to pollinate the football club. Then it becomes a virtuous circle; if the club becomes more successful on the pitch, you're going to have more people interested in getting involved with programmes and things which Tranmere have to offer the broader community. Everybody wins."

Palios explains: "It's absolutely about having a club that is fed by these businesses, not propped up by them. That's what self-sustainable is to me. It's even more important at the moment as there's a question mark around television money.

"The TV money funds the payments that we get. The central funding dropped when we went into Non League. It's improved now, but in those days it was less. It dropped right off to just the little bit that we got off the National League. That is what you rely on at this point in time.

"What I'm trying to do is build up the other off-field businesses so it replaces it as best I can. If I get a hotel and a 3G pitch and £750,000 spent on the Recreational Centre, which is going to happen, if we get Beechwood as a sports centre that we can run as another unit, you're starting to build something that will be producing money that other clubs aren't getting, clubs like Rochdale, who we are competing against.

"So irrespective of whether the television monies come or go, you're future proofing against that and you're doing what I'm trying to do, build these football agnostic businesses in the club. They're related, but they're agnostic."

Some of the decisions Palios made could be described as gambles. Money was put to one side to dress up the crumbling suites in the Main Stand, while projects in China have also been funded.

At times, some supporters have grumbled that it would have been better to spend that cash on the first team squad, making sure they could get out of the National League as quickly as possible.

Tranmere lost £2m according to their accounts for 2018. But Maguire believes the age old saying 'you've got to speculate to accumulate' could not be more fitting to describe their circumstances.

"They have invested in the playing squad, but not only in the playing squad," he explains. "When your income is less than £5m, and you're losing £2m, that's pretty significant.

"Losing money is one thing, but being unable to pay your bills is the key thing in football. So I would never get too hung up about profits and losses, to be perfectly frank, because they're abstract accounting nonsense. It's all to do with cash.

"What Tranmere are very good at doing is managing their cash. Whilst they have money going out, and they are losing money, they said 'how are we going to fund these losses?' They've done that through injections of shares, interest free loans and things of that nature which don't have nasty repayment dates or repayment terms.

"If you compare Tranmere to Bury, Bury were losing roughly the same amount of money. Perhaps a little bit more, maybe £50,000 a week as opposed to £40,000. The difference is they went and borrowed money from a loan company who are charging 138% interest per year. That's nuts.

"What you've got to do is make smart business decisions, and I think this is where having somebody who comes from a finance background is beneficial to the club.

"They won't make decisions which are very short term in nature and are not in the long term interest of the club. The present owners want to set up a legacy in the form of Tranmere Rovers Football Club and the approach that they're taking, which is fairly unique within the 92, although I think some clubs are beginning to cotton on that they need to do things of a similar nature.

"They are trying to use the additional funds which are being generated from these items. Mark Palios' aim is to have a competitive budget in the lower half of the Championship. You can't do that on the crowds Tranmere are getting at present.

"They've been very smart in taking advantage of government grants to get central funding, EU funding, things of that nature, and that's smart business, more than anything else.

"They also generated an extra £500,000 by issuing new shares in that financial year and that brought in cash, and that's quite good in the sense that it's free. They borrowed £400,000 in the year and they issued new shares, so you've got the owners putting money into the club."

Dropping into the National League meant Tranmere took a hit financially. It was something Palios had to deal with quickly, and he has already touched on how being in the fifth tier led to central funding cuts.

The amount of TV revenue they received decreased. The sum paid by BT Sport for National League games was, as you would expect, considerably lower than Sky pay for the Football League.

Furthermore, once Rovers had spent two years in the division, they lost their parachute payments from the Football League and the fee they received for running an academy. It was a huge blow, and led to Palios deciding to strip back on the club's youth system. They had been ploughing plenty of cash into finding the next Aaron Cresswell,

Jason Koumas or Clint Hill, but given the restrictions of the Elite Player Performance Plan, the rewards were minimal.

This was one of several cost cutting measures, as Maguire explains: "I think the first thing Mark Palios did was to identify and cut waste. You look at everything with a magnifying glass and ask 'why are we paying so many people to work behind the bar, and getting them from 12pm when the fans don't arrive until 2pm?' He was making simple decisions.

"There was an issue with making sure that if they were using external suppliers, they sourced them appropriately and ensured it was not just a case of using the same people as the year before. They may well use the same person, but they've got to be competitive, so it was a standard business approach to first of all cutting unnecessary costs and then secondly the issue of trying to identify alternative sources of income, because for most clubs, it is match day, broadcast and commercial.

"In terms of match day, people will only come to watch a winning side, so that's outside the control of the owners. You can give the manager a budget, but whether he spends that budget well or not is a footballing issue and it can take one injury or a loss of form to change it.

"I was working with Andy Holt, the Accrington owner, and I think it's well documented that their centre forward Billy Kee has had a number of personal problems, limiting the amount of time he's been available, but he's a good footballer.

"Footballers are human beings. I think this is one of the things which fans forget. They just see them as a product. They just see the shirt, not the human being below that. Match day income therefore is, to a large extent, outside of the control of the owners.

"Broadcasting income is also outside of their control because it's arranged centrally by the Premier League with what trickles down. The Premier League have just changed the rules too, meaning less trickles down into League One and League Two, because millionaires deserve more money, or that seems to be the argument put forward by the elite.

"But your third source of income is commercial, and this is where Tranmere have really pushed, and it's noticeably increased as a source of income."

The third source is what Palios has worked on tirelessly, and it has led to Tranmere increasing their turnover significantly. When Rovers were in League One in 2013/14, accounts show they made £3.5m. By the time they returned to the Football League four years later, it had increased to £4.5m.

"Comparing it to 2013/14, which is a League One season, shows turnover is up significantly," continues Maguire. "It was £3m in 2014, £2.8m in 2015 and in 2016 it had dropped to £2.5m. It was not looking great. That becomes a vicious circle. What they have managed to do is reverse it on the basis of getting promoted back into the EFL pyramid.

"That's on the back of the third wheel, the commercial streams. This is where the club is trying to generate the growth, with a view of asking what's achievable and more importantly what's sustainable.

"Palios has been focused on recruiting people for the non footballing side of the club, as well as the footballing side. He realises that these are the people who can go out and start to get the new sponsors and they pay for themselves.

"They feel very comfortable in League One, and I think they feel on the back of that they could get promoted to the Championship. I think that's it, then. For them to be in the Championship would be a hell of an achievement on the basis of these income streams."

As well as creating new businesses, such as the International Soccer Academy, Centre of Development and what is happening in China, Palios has been keen to utilise the assets he already has.

Prenton Park has, for years, been a drain on Tranmere's finances. The roof of the old Main Stand often requires repairing after bad weather, and caused one game, against Rochdale on Boxing Day in 2011, to be postponed because a chunk blew off in high winds.

On top of that, the stadium was not being used for anything other than hosting matches. That meant it lay dormant for around 340 days of the year, despite, as Palios saw, having the potential to be used for hosting parties, functions and meetings.

"I came with a blueprint that was about creating the breathing space," he explains, "which I did by extracting the organic potential. I've shown what that means, and that was in front of me with Prenton Park.

"I used to walk in every day and think 'fucking hell, we've just got this massive overhead'. I used to have a dialogue with the supporters; 'do you want to live in Prenton Park? It'll cost you a million quid. Do you want a team with a top end budget? That's another million and a half. So there's £2.5m. How much do you get from your gates, plus you've got the overheads of your managers and all that kind of stuff? That's another million.

"So where's the rest of it coming from? How much do you get from the Football League? Well we were getting nothing in the National League. But you're still talking those type of figures. You've got to build something out."

One of Palios's first tasks was giving the suites in the Main Stand a slick re-design, making them a better fit for the purpose of matchday and non-matchday functions. He also launched numerous community events in the Recreation Centre that helped bring people into the club, perhaps for the first time, as well as ensuring the facility behind the Kop is a constant money maker.

"Mark and Nicola have been pretty smart," says Maguire. "Football is a dumb industry. Your biggest asset is your stadium, but 340 days of the year, it's not doing anything. It's just standing there and the grass is growing. You're not generating any income.

"Even on match days, if you think about it, people turn up at 2pm, they leave at 5pm, and for 90 minutes during the intervening three hours, they're watching the match. There's very little opportunity to make money from the actual football, as such."

"What's unique about Tranmere is they've gone 'well we've got the facilities, can we use them for other purposes?' I think Mark describes this as the private sector provision of public sector services.

"We all know that there are wealthy and less wealthy areas of Merseyside and there are schools which struggle to get kids to come to school in the first place. If you say 'well we can connect your education to football', all of a sudden, because football is a social gathering and a community item, you can use it for a greater good.

"So they've linked the two, be it through education programmes, health programmes or welfare programmes, which can't always be done particularly well by local or national government services because they're a bit tainted to a certain extent.

"If you say to a kid, 'we're going to get our sport science people from Tranmere Rovers to teach you about better diet or the importance of education in your life, oh, and by the way, one of the players might walk in,' all of a sudden, we're changing the mindset. So Tranmere have taken that approach.

"It's involved further investment, but it's starting to pay off, because we've just seen with the recent Indonesian investment that it makes the club more attractive to overseas investors and also to domestic investors.

"Those investors have realised that, all of a sudden, the club and stadium is going to be open more the 25 days a year for three or four hours at a time. Mark Palios has sold the club to potential commercial sponsors and partners, whereas previously that attitude might have been 'we're Tranmere, nobody is interested in us'."

The result of all this is that Tranmere have been a success on and off the pitch. The football has improved, with Rovers climbing back up the divisions, meaning more people are coming through the gates. They have a bigger commercial footprint, and not just across the North West of England, and the finances have improved.

By 2018, accounts show they made £4.5m. The debt had dropped by around £5m. The club are very much on the up, and that led to the investment that Palios touched upon when, in September 2019, Indonesian firm The Santini Group purchased a minority stake in the club.

The chairman says: "People said I was smoking dope when I came here and when I said 'this is valued at £10m in the investor narrative'. The recent investment from Indonesia puts the club at a value of about £16.7m.

"They're not mugs, the Indonesians! If I'd said to you 'I will try and get an investment from a successful Indonesian conglomerate who are on the other side of the world and they'll invest with a minority stake', you'd have said 'wouldn't bother'.

"If I'd said to you 'would you try to take a fifth tier football club into the hottest football market on the planet, which is China, because President Xi has targeted the World Cup by 2050', the answer to that would have been 'no, don't bother' and you'd move onto the next question. But the reality is we've done both of those things."

It has taken a significant amount of work and effort to get to this stage though. And it all comes back to that business plan the chairman was working on, just hours after Tranmere were relegated from the Football League.

Maguire concludes: "There are good owners and there are bad owners. I've done a lot of work recently with issues to deal with Bury and Bolton and the criticism gets levelled at the fans, but actually it comes down to the quality of ownership and the quality of management.

"Looking at it from an academic point of view, if you look at any successful business, it's all down to the quality of management. What do you associate with Apple? Steve Jobs. Why was Microsoft so successful? Because of Bill Gates. Why was Ford so successful? It was Henry Ford. If you think of Virgin, the first words you think of are Richard Branson.

"I think to a large extent, the reason why Tranmere have not ended up in a Bolton or Bury situation is because of Mark and Nicola Palios. They have a vision for the club as part of the community and they're not in it to asset strip, unlike what we've seen with other clubs in the North West - and I could mention quite a few here!

"This is part of their history. Clearly with Mark, there is an association both as a player and an owner, which is fairly unique. They are using their business skills to turn the club around."

Chapter Seventeen
The Dressing Room

As important as sorting Tranmere's financial issues was, Mark Palios was aware of just how crucial it was to address what was happening on the field. The club were failing. They were tumbling down the leagues. Managers and players were coming and going and there was little connection between those wearing the jersey on the pitch and those wearing them in the stands.

It was a recipe for decline and became a vicious circle. Supporters stopped coming through gates, because they were less than thrilled with the football served up, and as a result, there was less money for the manager to spend on getting better players.

Iain Hume could barely believe the situation when he returned to Prenton Park in 2015. He had always been keen to come back to Tranmere, but found the place to be a shell of what it was when he departed a decade earlier.

He says: "When I was here for my first spell, we called the main pitch at the Raby training ground 'Wembley', and that was because the groundsman, George, had it in such a good condition.

"Obviously he had a bit more budget behind him then, but it was perfect and you could only touch it on a Friday. You weren't even allowed to walk on it! He had it coned off and you had to walk around it!

"When I came back when Micky Adams was here, it was just a bog. I know they put drainage in years and years ago, I don't know whether that had changed, but you were running around and your feet were sinking in. I don't know why it's gone like that, but for some reason it was a lot different and way below the standard. It used to be kept immaculately.

"As far as the quality of the squad goes, I think any football fan will look at it and it's more evident to me. When I was coming through as a kid, football was a men's game. Every player that played was in their late 20s, or so it seemed.

"You had some young kids, like Andy Parkinson, Clint Hill and Ryan Taylor, but look at the team when I came through: I was playing with people like Steve Yates, Micky Mellon, Wayne Allison, Dave Kelly and Andy Thompson.

"Now, not specifically with Tranmere but football as a whole, you get much younger teams, 18 to 21 year olds, and then a few who are over 26. That's the hardest thing for me, because I'm at the other end of the spectrum now.

"Football on a whole is all about image and how good do I look on the field. If you watch teams through the Football League and Premier League, how many players just 'do' a Roy Keane, as in going to win the ball and then passing it on. How many do what Javier Mascherano did; running, smashing somebody, taking the ball and playing it?

"Everyone now has to do a trick. It's even worse the lower you go down, because a lot of them are players from Premier League academies and they're on loan or have been released. As technically gifted as they are, the winning mentality has gone.

"It used to be winning at all costs. I came through with Clint Hill in my team. If you ever wanted somebody to go to war with, it was Clint. The same goes for Steve Yates, Gareth Roberts and Dave Challinor. That was our back four and you had to draw blood to get past them. That was the way I was brought up.

"In training I was getting smashed everywhere. Clint didn't care who you were. He'd clean you out in training and then apologise afterwards. Now, it's a lot more centred on your tricks, flair and technical abilities.

"I'm not saying it's worse, but it's a lot different to what I've grown up with. It's entertaining to watch, but you've got a lot of teams who go and play sexy football, but when it comes to a battle, they lose."

Hume barely had time to get to know his new teammates in 2015. Players would come and go, while he himself was cast aside from the main squad. But he noticed differences to the Tranmere he used to know and love.

"When I was here for my first spell," he continues, "the attitude was win at all costs. It was that way under John Aldridge, Dave Watson, Ray Mathias and Brian Little. It was always the same.

"We had so many bad games in 2004/05, when we reached the play-offs. I remember one away at Hartlepool. I think we beat them 2-0 thanks to Chris Dagnall, but I had a shocker, an absolute nightmare. I came off and Chris scored two. We were woeful. We got battered. They were just relentless. But we beat them 2-0, got on the bus, happy days, let's go.

"In the dressing room when I was here second time around, there was disappointment after losing a game, but you didn't see it during the week. You'd go into training and everyone was the same whether you won or lost. It never changed.

"Go back to the squads under Aldo or whoever, and you didn't accept being second best. If you'd lost a game, you'd have players in training who were raging until the Thursday. When it was Friday, they'd get ready for the next game.

"Now, people are too busy. They jump in their car and drive two hours to go home. They'd shower as quickly as they could after training and go.

"We used to have head tennis set up under The Kop. Les Parry had a big set there, and a little one by the dressing rooms. The only reason we were in that corridor is because we smashed loads of tiles playing it in the gym! We were banned from playing up there!

"We had queues of players waiting to play after training. Everybody wanted to. Our young lads at the time, people like Paul Linwood, Danny Harrison and Ryan Taylor, we didn't want to leave after training. We wanted to do more.

"Now, people just seem in a hurry to go home. You've been training for an hour and a half, two hours. You'll still be home by 2pm if you do a bit extra, such as working on something yourself, asking the coach for help or going to the gym.

"It's very seldom that you see that now because it's just a matter of 'I'm done'. That's probably the biggest difference between the last 15 years of football.

"Also, when I was here the first time, we had a couple of players who lived away, but the majority lived in Liverpool or on the Wirral. It was our club. That's how we felt as players. It wasn't 'I'm playing for Tranmere', it was 'I'm playing for the club that I live next to and with all the guys who I go for a drink with at the weekend'.

"I'm not condoning going on a night out and drinking, but it's life, you do it. How many of current squads, outside of the Premier League, where obviously you've got the money to relocate at the drop of a hat, go out and have a night out or a meal together? Very few, because where they live is so different. That's just the way of the times."

All of this meant Tranmere's fans had no connection with the players. Once Ian Goodison had departed in 2014, who could they look to as somebody who had the potential to become a club legend?

It was an issue Palios was keen to address. At first, he worked on bringing in local players who knew what it meant to play for Tranmere Rovers. Not all of the signings were successful, such as Gary Taylor-Fletcher and Michael Higdon, but at the other end of the spectrum, the likes of Steve McNulty and Jay Harris gave their all for the club every time they were picked. They got it.

"I think team spirit has been a massive feature in four of the last five years," says Palios. "It's something I'm pretty keen on. Scott Davies has signed a new long term contract, which is nailing some of the planks of stability in the place. Micky signed last February for another two and a half years.

"The difficulty of having moved up the divisions so quickly is that we've shaken some of those foundations, because we had to. We had more players come in that normally would have.

"I work on eight, eight and eight, which is eight under contract, eight re-signing and eight new signings. It has been a bit different with the promotions, but Tranmere never used to do that. It would be all about one year contracts late in the day.

"One of the things that I'm keen to do is getting people to understand what it means to represent Tranmere Rovers. I knew it was easy with Micky Mellon, and then Mike Jackson was an ex-player as well.

"We began to build this team of people who all knew what the club was about. Therefore they could make a better connection with the fans. That then started to build."

Having local players, such as McNulty and Harris, is a good way of building that connection with the fans. Most supporters have held that dream of donning the club shirt. When they see somebody from just around the corner stepping onto the hallowed turf, it is as if they are living that lifelong ambition through somebody else.

The best way of channeling that is through a homegrown youngster coming through the club's academy. Tranmere have done better than most out of their youth system in the past, creating stars such as Jason Koumas, Aaron Cresswell and Ian Nolan, who all went on to win international honours.

But with the constant chopping and changing of managers, the conveyor belt dried up. Bosses were under pressure, and they simply were not willing to blood a youngster when the stakes were so high.

Shaun Garnett held various roles in Tranmere's academy for roughly a decade. He ended up as the man in charge, and was tasked with firstly developing the youngsters before recommending that they be taken on as professionals.

Of course, the changing nature of youth football means it is tougher than ever to find that hidden gem. The Premier League big-boys can now hoover up talent at a minimal price, without being restricted by rules such as the player having to live within a 90 minute drive of the club's training base.

The Elite Player Performance Plan has, in short, relaxed all the restrictions which were in place to protect those at the bottom of the pyramid. As such, Tranmere's academy has not produced as many regular first team footballers over the last decade.

But in the opinion of Garnett, that is not solely down to the regulations. First team affairs have had an effect too. "It was a thankless task in a way," he admits. "As we moved on from 2004/05 towards 2010, it was hard because we replaced our managers fairly regularly.

"I asked one about giving a professional contract to a young player and his words were 'no, he won't keep me in a job'. I understand, because it would have come off his budget, but it was hard.

"Will Vaulks is a great example. He's one young player I recommended that we take on, which we did, and to be fair to him, he's a great kid and I'm made up with where he is now. He went to Scotland with Falkirk, moved back to England with Rotherham and then got a big move to Cardiff.

"But he signed professionally having played as a centre-half and centre-midfielder, and then in pre-season he was put at left-back. That was never going to develop him. He moved on to fulfil his potential.

"Aaron Cresswell was another one. The manager said to me he couldn't see him playing in the first team because he was too small. It would have to come off his budget but I pleaded with the manager to give him six months. In the end he gave him a year and the rest is history, but he needed that time.

"We'd had these great years under Warwick Rimmer producing players who played in the first team. We could sell them after that. During my first few years, it was hard achieving the goal, which for any young player coming to Tranmere Rovers, was to play in our first team. It was getting harder and harder because there was so much at stake.

"It's a massive risk playing a young player. I didn't really realise that until the first time I stepped up, to help Les Parry when he replaced John Barnes. I realised the gulf between youth team football and first team football.

"Okay, we have a bridge with the reserve team, but nowadays, you don't get many pros playing in that, it's mostly the young ones. It was definitely an eye opener. I was pushing somebody like Aaron Cresswell, but he probably wasn't ready at the time because the gulf between youth and first team football is massive.

"The Elite Player Performance Plan has changed the face of youth football massively, and the money being ploughed into the Premier League has changed their outlook on it. It's allowed them to trawl so many players, which has a massive impact on the smaller clubs. It's hard now. You're all looking to produce a gem.

"Are there as many kids playing football? I'm not sure. I put that down as one reason. But the EPPP, from the smaller club's point of view, has made it very hard for us to churn out another Jason Koumas, Alan Rogers, Ryan Taylor, Aaron Cresswell or Max Power. I think it would be extremely hard to have those days again. With the EPPP, compensation for younger players is suited towards the Premier League clubs rather than us."

Tranmere stripped back their academy towards the end of the 2017/18 campaign. Promotion back to the Football League has helped, as it resulted in increased funding from the EFL, and also meant clubs could not come along and sign their best young prospects for free.

They are still waiting for the next big talent to burst onto the scene. Eddie Clarke showed plenty of ability before leaving for Fleetwood when his contract expired in 2018, whilst Evan Gumbs, although blighted by injuries, has impressed when involved.

The policy now is to try and find the players who have been cast off by other professional clubs. Football is all about having a manager who will take a chance. While one boss might not rate a youngster, another may. As such, they focus on those who have been released in the hope of turning them into first team players.

"I think the only way you can identify a player now is by looking at bringing in a player aged 18-21," continues Garnett. "If they've been unable to get a pro contract at another club, we then look at them and develop them and get them in our first team.

"That's another avenue you can go down in terms of bringing a fee in for a player. Under 16, it's very hard, because we'd lose our better players cheaply. Clubs only have to pay £3,000 per year for a player.

"Going back, the financial restorations are always a big issue. Even if we give a young pro the basic wage, it's possibly still going to be £5,000-£7,000 out of the manager's budget.

"That was another thing that made me realise where the club was at in terms of the financial state of it; we were debating whether to give a young player a contract. That money, say £7,500, when you come to sell Aaron Cresswell or Max Power is not a lot of money.

"We have a system now with under-23s, filling the void between 18 and 23. If I look back now at the position the club was in, I do feel there are some players who would have benefitted from that.

"Thinking of it, there were two or three players who if we'd given a little bit of time to, they'd have gone on and played for us. Luke Denson is definitely one. He was a Bebington lad who I'd have taken a chance on.

"A couple of first year professionals didn't get the opportunity either. Will Vaulks is another good example and so is Ryan Fraughan. I just wanted to give them a year to see what they could do."

Chapter Eighteen
Micky Mellon

Traditionally, Tranmere has been a place where managers stay for a significant period of time. They might not have always been successful, but at least they were given the opportunity to develop their plans rather than get an unceremonious sacking if early results disappointed.

The same could be said for most football clubs, but as the game has changed, owners and fans have became more impatient. The pressure for immediate success has grown and as a result, managers are given less time and opportunity to turn things around if they go sour.

When Rovers were relegated to League One in 2001, they turned to Dave Watson as the person to try and guide them back to The Championship. He was the first of seven bosses to have a go at returning the club to the second tier, one of whom enjoyed a couple of spells in charge.

Few of those managers lasted all that long in the job. Watson was sacked after a couple of heavy defeats in pre-season friendlies, just a year after being handed the role. Ray Mathias replaced him, but again, he was only in the hot seat for just over twelve months before chairman Lorraine Rogers decided to swing the axe.

Brian Little followed, and he came the closest to promotion as Rovers failed in the play-offs in 2005, dumped out at the semi-final stage after a penalty shoot out defeat to Hartlepool.

A year later, budget cuts had taken their toll on the squad, with the likes of Ryan Taylor and Iain Hume sold to Wigan and Leicester, whilst Eugene Dadi and Paul Hall, both amongst the top scorers in the previous campaign, had been let go.

Tranmere would only save their League One status by beating MK Dons in the penultimate game of the season. Little left by mutual consent, making way for club legend Ronnie Moore to take over.

The former Rotherham boss remained at Prenton Park for three years before being sacked after that Scunthorpe game in 2009. Following his dismissal, Rovers became a revolving door for managers, with John Barnes, Les Parry, Moore again, Rob Edwards, Micky Adams and Gary Brabin installed and dismissed over a seven year period.

The club tried all different kinds of manager. There were returning fan favourites, such as Moore and Mathias, and up and coming newbies like Watson and Edwards. Little, meanwhile, had all the experience, and at a much higher level, having guided Aston Villa to a League Cup success in 1996.

None of them managed to get Tranmere promoted though. All that happened was the club drifted further and further away from challenging at the top end of the table.

In September 2016, Mark Palios decided he needed to make another change. Gary Brabin, who had been in charge during Tranmere's first season in the National League, had a terrific start to the season, winning six of his first seven games, but then results started going the wrong way. A defeat at Sutton was the final straw.

"I had to make a decision in the summer as to whether Brabin was the guy," Palios explains, "because we'd failed miserably against Wrexham at the end of the 2015/16 season. But next year, we won the first five games.

"I wasn't necessarily convinced about the performances though, and for me they matter just as much as the results, if not more than the results. If you're getting reasonable performances, then over a period of time, it will come.

"The fans never really took to Gary Brabin either. That wasn't the reason he went, though. I just didn't think the performances were where I wanted them to be."

Mark Bartley is another who did not like what he was seeing out on the pitch. "Even when I think of the games we won under Gary Brabin, they were poor," he says. "We scraped wins. People weren't convinced he was the best man for the job.

"I went to the Sutton game and people didn't want another season of Non League obscurity. We wanted to get out of it. I think when we made the change, it was the right move. I liked him, I really did. He brought in some good players, but we needed to make a change.

"His relationship with the fans was very poor. He did come to one Q&A very early on in his tenure. But one of the disputes I've had with Mark Palios is that TROSC were doing another Q&A session and Brabin was meant to come along. A few days before it, with us having advertised it, we got told he wasn't coming.

"That was what Brabin was like. He didn't want to liaise with the fans to that level. There wasn't the same relationship there. When results started to go badly and people thought we were going to have another season of Non League football, they were very unhappy.

"At that Sutton game, you could walk all the way around the ground. There's no segregation. So some people walked all the way around and were shouting at him. He got sacked the next day."

This was a pivotal moment in Tranmere's history. They had already fallen off their perch. Now there was the threat of being a Non League team for the third year running. Once that happens, you are no longer a sleeping giant. You are just part of the furniture.

Mark Palios had to get Brabin's replacement right. And he did. The manager who became available was somebody with a great track record, having won two promotions with Fleetwood and one at Shrewsbury.

Crucially, he also had a bit of history at Prenton Park, having enjoyed two spells with Rovers as a player, captaining them in the second with Brian Little as his manager. His name? Micky Mellon.

***

On October 7th 2016, the Scot was confirmed as Tranmere's new manager. He brought another former player, Mike Jackson, with him as his assistant. Three years and two promotions later, he was the tenth longest serving manager in the Football League, and Rovers' longest since John Aldridge's departure in 2001.

But what makes him so special? Scott Davies knows the manager more than most. Not only has he become his club captain, but he was also part of the Fleetwood team that Mellon guided from the National League North to League Two.

"I've got two or three different relationships with the manager," he says. "I'm very close to him. He's done more for me than anybody else has in football. He's been there for me in times of my life when I needed a father figure.

"When it comes to work, it's always manager and player. I know what he expects and how he expects people to act. I know what he wants on the training field and he knows what I'll always give on the training field and on a day to day basis.

"Do we talk? Yes, but not as much as people think. He'll say something to me if he feels something needs to be said and if he wants a message getting to the group. The same went for Steve McNulty. Nine times out of 10, he trusts that we're big enough influencers in the dressing room and that we won't accept shite or any bad behaviour.

"We won't accept people not pulling their weight or not policing the building well. We have a standard to adhere to and I think with those standards, and when those standards are met, football takes care of itself.

"I've been with the manager for over half my career. I know what he expects and he doesn't really need to speak to me to expect that to happen. It's just a given. It's down to trust.

"That's probably one of the best things with the manager: he's trusting of the people around him. If you spoke to him, he'd tell you he signs good people. He doesn't just sign anybody. He signs people he knows he can trust and who will buy into what he's about.

"I think another big thing about the manager is you need to know the people you're dealing with, and he does. He recognises that and he recognises when people need help away from work.

"We all do. We all encounter problems and the gaffer has been there on the pitch and off the pitch for me. I'm a big believer in him and he's given me crazy success in my career. I'm thankful to him on many levels."

Davies is not alone in the dressing room. All of the team have a deep trust in the manager and a belief in what he wants them to do.

"He's a brilliant manager to play under," adds Connor Jennings. "I wouldn't say he speaks to me or certain players very much. I know what he expects and what he wants from me. I feel like he can lead me into it. There's a lot of trust together and a lot of respect for each other.

"He's helped me out quite a few times and I'm thankful for that. Hopefully it will continue. He's improved me as a player too, technically and with experience. I've noticed a big difference with myself over the last three and a bit years. It's been a good journey so far."

Developmentally, the manager is superb too. Jamie Vardy is an established Premier League striker who played for England. He blossomed under Mellon at Fleetwood. James Norwood went on to bigger and better things after working under the Scot at Tranmere.

"He's intense and doesn't let you have a bad day in training basically," explains Liam Ridehalgh. "If you come in with the mentality that you're just going to stroll around, he won't let that happen. I'd like to mention Mike Jackson too. He's the exact same.

"They've improved and changed my mentality. They keep banging on about how important mentality is, and the older I get, the more I realise that. It's not always about how good you are on the ball. If you're going through a hard spell in a game, you've got to get your mentality right and that will see you through."

Danny Holmes had a brief loan spell at Fleetwood shortly after he came back to Tranmere. He was struggling to break into the Rovers first team at the time, and Micky Mellon made the call to Les Parry asking if he could take the right-back to Highbury. He only played three games, but that was enough for the Scot to make a lasting impression.

"Micky Mellon is exactly what you get on the tin," he says. "Every interview you watch of him, that's what he's like in the changing room. He's got this strong Scottish accent, and when raises his voice, it isn't pretty!

"Fleetwood were challenging for the league when I went there and we won the three games that I played. He dropped me because his first choice right-back was back from injury. I was completely fine with that because he's got to gain promotion for his team. I just trained and carried on with it.

"Micky Mellon is the only manager, other than Les Parry, that I've played under who truly gave me an answer as to why I wasn't starting. He would always tell you exactly what he wanted from you in a game.

"Even when I wasn't involved in the Fleetwood team, because his first choice player was available again, he'd pull me to one side and tell me what he feels he wants from a full-back.

"Even though he had his first choice right-back, I still knew what he wanted if that lad got injured again. The training was brilliant. The month I spent under him was brilliant.

"Getting away from Tranmere was key at that time in my career. I needed to prove myself. It was good for me to go away, work under someone different and be somewhere fresh. In the short space of time I worked with Micky Mellon, he was a top, top man. I haven't got anything bad to say about him."

***

Mellon embarked on his managerial career shortly after hanging up his boots. He played his final matches for Lancaster City in the 2005/06 season, before a brief stint as the club's assistant boss.

He also worked as a youth team coach before taking charge at Fleetwood in 2008. He was sacked there in 2012, but only after gaining two promotions and was not out of work for long as he received a call from David Flitcroft to be his right hand man at Barnsley.

It was after leaving Oakwell that he was handed the reins at Shrewsbury before making his return to Tranmere. During his playing days at Prenton Park, he gave an early indication of how his future in the managerial game might pan out.

"He was my captain during my first stint," says Iain Hume. "Michael Jackson was my captain as well. These are two guys who've led the team out. They know what it means to be inside a successful squad. They were when they were here last time.

"With Micky as captain, when Ray Mathias was in charge in 2002/03, we had the highest points tally to not make the play-offs. We finished on 80 points! Cardiff got 81. We were hell-bent on getting into the play-offs. Cardiff had the same mentality and set up as us. 'Listen, we're not losing'. We won six of our last seven games.

We were unbeaten in 15. But they got one more point than us.

"It's come a full circle now. You had the near misses with Les Parry at the helm, Ronnie came in, the shit hit the fan a little bit with Micky Adams, Gary Brabin brought in some good players and now there's Micky Mellon.

"He's come in and he's steadied the ship and he's got a belief. I know what he was like as a player, so I'm imagining he's the same as a manager. He's brought back that whole 'bloody win' attitude.

"He'll back his players to the hilt, but they need to give him everything. That's what you see every week. I went to the Burton game early in the 2019/20 season. It was a poor game. But they played for 95 minutes instead of an hour. If you get a leader who has the mentality that he wants to put across to you, then you get a winning mentality."

Parry was at Tranmere during both of Mellon's stints as a player. He reflects fondly on his relationship with the midfielder, having got to know him pretty well when he was out injured.

"I got on really with Micky," he says. "I still meet up with him. He didn't like losing when he was a player. He had an opinion. Him and Alan Morgan, I don't know how many fights they had on the training ground with one kicking the other.

"There was a game away at Plymouth and we got turned over 6-0. John McMahon was in temporary charge. After the game, Tyrone Loran had said something. We'd watched some clips, all of us, and everybody walked out except for Tyrone who was still in there with the coaches. He blamed Micky.

"There was a bit of shouting and Eugene Dadi said 'just leave it, we'll sort it when we get back' and I said 'leave it, you don't even talk to each other? You talk behind each other's backs, like Tyrone blaming Micky after watching the DVD. Instead of saying it to his face, he waited for you to all go out.'

"Micky turns around and says 'you what?' The two of them went out on the pitch and had a fight at Plymouth. That's typical of Micky.

"The other thing he is is a real student of the game. He loves football. He'll watch other coaches. He really believes in what he's doing. I thought he was a great appointment as manager at Tranmere. I obviously like him, though, so that helps!"

Parry now works at Manchester United, where he is in charge of the club's loan players, assessing where they should go on a temporary deal and how they are doing whilst away from Old Trafford.

Rovers took Cameron Borthwick-Jackson on a season long deal from United at the start of the 2019/20 campaign. The left-back made his Premier League debut under Louis van Gaal, but his career had hit the buffers. Parry was happy for Tranmere to take him to Prenton Park.

"I feel very comfortable sending players to Tranmere now Micky's in charge," he admits. "His desire in life is to make players better. The by-product of that for his players is that they play better and they win games. I think if he wasn't a manager, he'd be a development coach. Because of that, it's a fantastic environment."

Mellon is a genius when it comes to finding that little bit more in a player. He not only thrives upon developing one of his squad into somebody who can perform at a higher level. He also prides himself on it. On top of that, he is a born winner.

"He's an awful loser," laughs Scott Davies. "But I also think his group are awful losers now. We've had players sign for our club who have found it hard to adjust to how we respond to defeat, because it's the end of the world.

"If you came into training on a Monday morning after a defeat, it's like a morgue. Nobody speaks. That transcends down from the manager to his coaching staff, to his captain and his players. 'This is how you behave when you get beat'. You go back to square one and put everything right.

"There was a time, and we've all had it in our careers, when you play for clubs and it's seen as acceptable to get beat, as long as you come back in and start working again. The gaffer never accepts that.

"Whether you're competing with Tottenham and Manchester City or Boreham Wood and Dover, you should never be able to accept a defeat because we're paid to win games of football. He's definitely a bad loser.

"This club has now learnt to be bad losers through the manager. The group and staff have learnt that. We all know how to act. The players who come in now have to quickly get used to how we are as a football club and a group, because it's not acceptable to be beaten at any time.

"There was another key thing that happened when he came to the club: the ambition of the group changed. The Micky Mellon I know, whatever job he's going to do and whatever club he's going to lead, the kind of person he is, he'll only ever want it to go that way because he's a winner.

"At that time (when Gary Brabin was in charge), I think us as a group of players, and maybe staff, as much as you could say we wanted to go up, I don't think we showed it. That to me shows we lacked ambition. There wasn't enough fight for it.

"When the gaffer came in, there was a huge change in mentality. I was approaching 30 and there were players similar to me, like Steve Jennings, Jay Harris, Steve McNulty, Andy Mangan. We'd probably reached that point where we thought that was it in our careers.

"When Micky came in, he probably relit the fire in us all. We could all see we had a good few years left and more success. Obviously it was disappointing not to go up when we lost in the play-off final to Forest Green, but that didn't change the mentality.

"The core of the group stayed together and we knew we'd do it the year after. Obviously we didn't start as well as we hoped but we got there in the end and that was relief. It was a justification of the journey we all took."

Mark Palios sees a little bit of himself in Mellon. "He's the same as me," he laughs. "I'm a bad loser too. He's a proud man and he's proud in his ability, so every defeat hurts him.

"There's no point in me going to him if we lose, because it's not a question of passion and I know it's not a question of not working hard or technical ability with Micky.

"Yes, you look at losing a dressing room, but I never want to contribute to him losing a dressing room. Whatever goes on between him and me will therefore be between him and me.

"It's quite simple. If I see it as he sees it, I don't even have to have a debate with him. If I don't see it as he sees it, then I will.

"What makes him so successful? He works hard, that's the first thing. Secondly, he thinks a lot about the game tactically, from a coaches perspective. Therefore, he can change games because he sees what's going on in the game and knows what he needs to do to change it. Not all coaches can do that.

"Thirdly, the players know their jobs when they go out there. There's nobody who goes out there and doesn't know what he has to do. He drills them and works on the training pitch with them.

"That's what you want him to do. It doesn't really matter what players he gets; you know he will get the best out of them.

"If he's ever under pressure, I don't really say anything to counter people saying on social media 'he's got to go'. I don't come out and give him a vote of confidence. What I do do, is when I have the opportunity to talk about the guy, I will say what I think. I think he's a great coach. I think he's one of the best coaches, certainly in the leagues we've been in."

Mellon's relationship with the chairman is a key one. They have had their quarrels, but work as a robust team. That means if they do fall out, it all gets settled pretty quickly, because for both men, everything is done for the good of the club.

"My relationship with him is as tight as a drum," Mellon confesses. "We've had loads and loads of crossed words and argued loads, but we always finish the argument and move on, because it's always for Tranmere.

"It's a brilliant relationship. He's very, very honest to me and very loyal as well. He tells me that he knows I work really hard and he tells me that he believes that I know what I'm doing.

"I'm quite calculated in what I'm doing. I have a plan in my head, so I'm crystal clear in where I'm at. If I'm right, time will tell, but I believe I'm on the right track with things, and I'll tell that to him.

"The chairman is an unbelievably intelligent man and the lady chairman is an unbelievably intelligent woman. What they've done with this football club is incredible. Sometimes I just think 'wow' at how he does stuff. It creates something and then we get investment and I just think 'you clever bastard' because he's good at it.

"I have a really good relationship with all the family. I'm very respectful of them and I enjoy working for them. He always says to me 'Micky I want you to go to the top' and if that opportunity ever comes, he says he'd more or less take me there. We have that kind of relationship. I get on really well with him.

"We both want the same thing; Tranmere winning games, playing well and all the rest of it. We both enjoy working for Tranmere, the same with the lady chairman.

"I get on well with everybody here; Dawn Tolcher and Michael Kinsella and everybody, because we all want the same thing. Whenever they ask me to do something, I realise they've got a job to do.

"Christine Roberts will ask me to get the players down to an event and I'll say 'yes, it'll be good', because I want the fans to see the players. We all work really well together, which is good, because we all want the same thing."

There is another relationship which is key to Tranmere's success, and it is the one Mellon has with his assistant manager Mike Jackson.

The pair worked together at Shrewsbury, with the latter coming to Prenton Park just a week after Mellon had been confirmed as the club's new boss. But they go back a lot further than that, having played together, albeit briefly, for Rovers under Ray Mathias, as well as crossing paths years before.

"He is everything that I'm not," Mellon explains of his assistant. "He's a football fanatic, like me. He's passionate about improvement, personally and making the players better. He's meticulous in his preparation, to the inch. He writes everything down. He has to have everything right. The training sessions are always meaningful and towards what we need to do as principles.

"He listens to me and I listen to him. We've never fallen out. People will say that's not healthy, but we've never fallen out. We have a good, healthy view on how things should be.

"Shaun Garnett is the same, and all the backroom staff, Michael Vernon, our analyst, Andy Hodgen, our strength and conditioning coach. We're task focused. We all try our bollocks off.

"The same goes for Ian Liversedge and John Stokes, down to Andy Parkinson and Alan Morgan in the academy and people like Tony Coombes who work on the off field kind of things.

"What I'm saying is we don't really piss each other off. We all know we've got a role to play and don't overplay our role. It's a great environment that we have as staff. If you go into the office, they'll be laughing their heads off. Other times, it'll be silent because we're all grafting.

"Jacko and I watch about three or four games a day on our laptops. We speak about football all the time. 'Did you see this' or 'did you see that'. Our relationship is very good.

"I can take a step back and view it from a different angle, but Jacko has to be in the middle of it all and he's 100mph. Sometimes it needs that. We really all get on really well.

"We don't over play our parts. I'm not sitting here like Caesar. I'm really not precious about me. I want them to go and express themselves and improve. I'm not sitting here thinking I know everything. I wouldn't even bother telling everybody that, that I don't know everything.

"But what I am quite good at is saying 'how do you think we can do that better'. I can be quite humble in that way. I don't have all the answers, but I'll work my bollocks off to find out maybe what the answer is.

"So we all get on well. It's a good place to be, but a very driven place. I think if you weren't like us, you wouldn't like it, because it can be aggressively ambitious at times. It can look fiery and feisty. Some people don't like that, because it's so driven.

"Some players couldn't accept being like this. This morning, me and Jacko must have been into five or six of them: 'What the fuck was that? You can do that better. No, I'm not accepting it.' Better. Better. Better. All the time. Get into them.

"The players understand that we just want them to be good. You'd need to ask them, probably, what they felt about us. But I would hope that they would say 'yes, he's tough on us, but we accept it because he just wants me to the best that I can be. He will not stop until he thinks he's got the most out of me. And then unfortunately, when he thinks he's got the most out of me, he will think about Tranmere, or the club that's he's managing, and they will take precedence and he will try and get someone else in, but that's just football. He won't mind doing that and he will do that, because Tranmere have to come first.'"

Chapter Nineteen
The Future

Mark Palios reaches past several stacks of paper on top of his overcrowded desk for a notebook. He finds the first available blank page and starts drawing a diagram of the Wirral peninsula in pencil. A few inches to the right, he depicts the Liverpool coastline, with the River Mersey in the middle.

He is about to outline how he sees Tranmere's continued existence. He has already developed the club into one that is almost unrecognisable to the one he bought in 2014. They are thriving in areas which had previously been left to decay. So what is his next move? How does he make them sustainable for years to come?

On the North East corner of the Wirral, he draws a small circle, filling it in with the heavy grey of his pencil. This is to mark The Campus, Rovers' large training ground since 2016.

It is the ideal base for any team. There are multiple grass pitches, used by Tranmere's senior and youth squads, as well as Liverpool Women FC. Housed inside the main building are, amongst other things, numerous classrooms, a canteen, changing rooms and a home for the medical staff.

Palios slides his hand slightly down the coastline from Leasowe. He next draws a rectangle, roughly where Bidston Moss is. This is where he hopes, one day, to build a new ground.

Leaving Prenton Park is a subject that the chairman has been wary to breach. He knows all too well that a football ground has a romantic hold over every supporter. They cherish the seat they have sat upon for season upon season, perhaps witnessing some of their most treasured memories.

Yet Tranmere have spent in excess of a century at their current home. It was fully renovated in 1995, at which point it perhaps lost some of the decaying charm of the old terraced Cowshed stand and sloping Kop.

There have been a handful of alterations since, such as new disabled sections and the removal of the iconic red and yellow seats in the top two corners of the Main Stand. It is still very much a modern venue, and the envy of many teams Tranmere have played host to over the last five years.

But Prenton Park is not without its faults. It is too big for Rovers based on their current attendances. Spare a few sell-out cup matches, it has rarely been packed to the rafters over the last two decades.

The geography of the ground is not great, either. It effectively lies in a valley, at the foot of two steep hills and that means whenever the Wirral is subject to heavy rain, the pitch becomes saturated and, increasingly in recent seasons, has led to matches being postponed.

On top of all of this, the stadium comes with huge overhead costs. The Main Stand is decrepit and has been draining the club of money for years. These are just some of the reasons why Palios thinks leaving CH42 is a necessity if Tranmere are going to kick on.

He has done the sums. If Rovers are to become a self sustainable Championship club, as opposed to the model that Peter Johnson funded to reach the second tier, then they simply must move with the times.

Yet there is much more that he can do, as opposed to simply building a shiny new stadium. With The Campus, he already has the ideal location to start developing and showcasing the Tranmere brand. For now, that takes priority.

The chairman is keen to piggy-back on the footballing success of the world famous city that sits on the other side of the water. Across the

Mersey, he sees huge financial benefits that could propel the club to the next level.

Football tourism is becoming increasingly popular in the current day and age. Every time Liverpool are at home, hundreds, if not thousands, of supporters will fly into John Lennon Airport. Many come from Scandinavia, where the Reds have traditionally held a large fanbase for years, whilst others come from more far flung corners of the earth.

Tranmere are already reaping the rewards. If their matches at Prenton Park coincide with weekends when Liverpool are at home, then some of the football tourists will make an effort to watch a Rovers game as well.

If they enjoy the experience, they will come back. When they return, they might buy some merchandise in the club shop, such as a shirt or scarf, and they may start encouraging some of their friends to take the same trip. Palios reckons Tranmere can capitalise on the trend.

"We've got our campus in Leasowe," he says, pointing his pen at the dot on the North East corner of his diagram. "It's right on the tip. I'll put a budget sport hotel on there.

"I don't have to do the maths, I will, when I need to, but I'll get the council and Liverpool City Region to fund the feasibility study. I'm starting those conversations now.

"I've built the relationship with the Liverpool City Region, the Council and so forth, they probably will eventually fund it. When you've got that, you attract people in to be partners in it.

"If I put a hotel on there, a 3G pitch and a purpose built school on there too and then we own The Campus, we're pulling everything into there.

"So potentially you could have all of it for ours as the International Business, to bring them in here. Here, I'm saying put the school in, put a hotel on it and we'll take it and deal with it. I'm ten minutes from the centre of Liverpool."

Football tourism is already coming into the Wirral. People are coming to watch Tranmere play, so why not give them somewhere to stay and increase your income stream?

It is a clever plan, and Palios already has an idea of how much the club could benefit from such an idea, as he has seen first hand how much money visitors will spend.

For the last few years, Rovers have had a connection with Inner Mongolia and China. They have been providing coaching to school children out there and in return, coaches have come to the Wirral to learn how to best develop a young prospect into a professional footballer.

"The international business was a bit of innovative thinking," Palios continues. "It started a little bit with my background as chief executive of the FA.

"Martin Best, who's one of our directors, happened to meet the representatives from the IMG who were over on an exchange visit in Liverpool. At the same time, coincidentally, we were going out to Hohot in China because a local lad, who was a teacher out there, had tried to tie us up with a Chinese educationalist, who wanted us to send teachers out there.

"They'd send kids over here for football holidays. Then the Chinese coaches came over as well. We know that when they do, they spend between £2,000 and £3,000 per person.

"Inner Mongolia was the pilot province for the development of football in China. When the Inner Mongolian government found out I was going out there, they hi-jacked the visit and asked me to help them develop what they were doing.

"I thought I'd give it it a go and then I got the concept of selling the

North West of England, which I consider to be a unique piece of footballing geography. There's a graphic which shows the majority of the England players in the last World Cup all came from the North West of England. There's a few who are from just over the border in Yorkshire, but the Chinese can't tell because it's not that far away!

"So I sell the potential of the North West of England, firstly to develop a playing programme, which they can't get in China but I can do it here, and secondly, we can sell the whole of the North West.

"On top of that, we've moved from Inner Mongolia, because that was a three year MOU, and we've moved into the Chinese private market. I might be getting a small investment from China and then they want us to joint venture.

"I want to get into the Chinese private sector and also The United States. We've invested in The States in the last year, and that'll start to come in. They're coming into the home of football in the old country and stuff like that. All of this comes in.

"So it ranges from elite to sport tourism and so forth. I've just focused on that. We've had over £3.5m from the international business in just less than three years."

This is all about future proofing the club. An extra income stream from a hotel will help provide much needed money that can be used to boost the first team's playing budget.

The ultimate goal is to get Tranmere into the Championship, but with the current finances, Palios estimates that it would be tough to keep them in the second tier.

At the 2019 Annual General Meeting, he provided a brief overview of what kind of budgets teams in the Championship had been operating with for the 2017/18 campaign.

Burton had the least money of all, with about £10m spent on the playing side of things. Staggeringly, Aston Villa at the top end of the scale pumped in over £70m. These are the kind of figures Rovers would be looking to compete with.

Should they get promoted to the second tier any time soon, Palios estimates an increase of £8m would mean they sat at the top end of the lower third of budgets in the division. A further £10m on top of that would put them around mid-table.

Naturally, their central funding would increase should they go up, but only by just under £6m. There is therefore still a funding gap to bridge, and that is where moving stadium comes into the equation.

Should Rovers reach the second tier, attendances would go up, but not enough to increase the budget significantly. The average match day ticket costs £10. If 14,000 came through the turnstiles every week, it would only add £2m in revenue.

The issue is something the chairman has been looking at for some time. He has scoured the Wirral for the best possible site, settling on Bidston Moss, as depicted on his diagram.

"If you then put a stadium at Bidston Moss," he explains, moving his pencil up and down the coastline, "you've got Wallasey Docks nearby and then over the water there's Liverpool.

"We've got the infrastructure, because we've got the M53 coming all the way in. It's the last turn off before the tunnel. You go off at junction one for Solar Campus. If you come through the tunnel, the first turn off is to the docks. I haven't got to put an infrastructure in. You've got a station and you've got the roads.

"On top of that, it lifts up all the residential values in the surrounding areas. It primes a regeneration of the dock area which has been sitting there for years. It's the biggest project in Europe and it's never been done.

"This is a catalyst to the whole area. You will have cafes and buildings around it. Regeneration experts can do that. I don't need to know. I just know intuitively that that will work. The council are very keen on regeneration. We have spoken to them about it on a number of occasions."

It looks like a plan with legs. The chairman is convinced it is the next natural step for the club if they are to be able to compete with some of the big hitters in the Championship. So what does he envisage a new ground would look like?

"The Campus would have a budget hotel," he continues, "The stadium would have a conference centre. Rotherham's ground is a great example. It's a 12,000 seater stadium, but it looked full with 8,000. I'd go for 15,000 at least to start with.

"I'd do a proper feasibility project and then you step it up. One end has all the conferencing facilities and if you want to build up or increase it, you can. It'll be double grass fronting and you're looking at Liverpool.

"I want The Campus done first, and then move on to the stadium. If I have to pass that over to somebody, there's a pathway for the club to get to becoming a real Championship club.

"But if go out and say that, people will scoff. There's a lot of things to do. But show me the maths; do you want to be a League One club or do you want to be a Championship club. If you want to be a Championship club I can show you that this can be done. I haven't got all the answers but it feels like something that could be done.

"I'm after more equity coming in. The Indonesian investors have the option to make a further investment over the next two years. It's an investment that moves us on. Would they want to partner up and build a hotel on the campus? Maybe?

"We've got Essar. They've got 16% of the oil coming into the UK. The relationship with Essar has been growing.

"There's a lot of stuff that you can do. Has the club turned around? Well it's not finished. I've got to make us stable League One club and then I've finished my job. It will be a stable League One club with an opportunity to become a Championship club.

"I've got to start working on that now. I have been working on the stadium for two years. Some weeks I won't do anything on it, because it's all about priorities.

"It's on my whiteboard, at the bottom with a dotted line around it. So is The Campus. They're the medium term things that I need to every so often check and ask if I need to keep moving them in the right direction."

Part Three
Bridging The Divide

Chapter Twenty
A Disjointed Fanbase

Football fans can be a fickle bunch. When things are not going well, they will let the powers that be know. Sometimes that anger will be directed at the owners, on other occasions the manager. Even players will bear the brunt of it.

The point at which you really start to worry is when people simply stop caring. Supporter apathy is, without a doubt, the most dangerous threat to a professional outfit. You tend to find a struggling club is riddled with it.

Tranmere supporters became apathetic during the difficult years, post the play-offs near miss of 2009, when the club's ambitions did not seem to extend beyond survival.

The Wirral public became apathetic. People lost interest in a club who spent thirteen years in the same division and by the end of that time were simply treading water, failing to provide any real possibility of mounting a promotion challenge.

Fans want to be excited. They want to watch players who will get them off their seats. They want hope. If you are not getting any of those things, then, understandably, their interest will wane.

There is little chance of encouraging new supporters through the gates, either. People make that journey through the turnstiles for the first time because they are intrigued by what is happening on the pitch.

They have seen the impressive results and heard the stories. Perhaps entertaining football is being played or there is a particular individual getting his name in the headlines and they want to see him. Are they glory hunters? Maybe. But you have got to start somewhere.

Tranmere were not giving anybody any of those reasons to come and watch. Their matches did not produce many goals and those fans who came were not relaying positive reviews. It had all become stale.

"I've supported Tranmere since I was about 10 years old," says Mark Bartley. "I used to live right by the ground and my dad finally took me to a live game after years of persuasion.

"We played Port Vale and it was Johnny Morrissey's debut. He had just signed for £8,000 from Wolves. Frank Worthington was in charge and we got beat 2-1. Morrissey scored.

"My dad felt a bit sorry for me though, so a few nights later he took me to a game against Mansfield and we lost that 2-1 as well. My next game wasn't until about Boxing Day and we beat Burnley 2-1.

"So obviously I was into football from a young age. Because Tranmere were just up the road, it was quite cheap to get there. You couldn't really get to Liverpool or Everton games and it was a hassle to get tickets.

"I started going along to Tranmere and soon I went with my friends. So I've been going fairly regularly since I was a teenager.

"Now I take my kids. They actually live with their mum in Nottingham, but it's been enforced from a very early age that they're not supporting Forest! They're supporting Tranmere! And they do. They're big fans, they wear their kits to all their training sessions and although my wife comes to the odd game, it's mainly me and my children who go."

Convincing a child to support the club is not an easy thing to do. There will be many lifelong Rovers fans on the Wirral who have struggled to get their kids along to Prenton Park. They are dazzled by the bright lights of the Premier League, which can be so accessible on television.

Following Liverpool or Everton, or even Manchester United and Manchester City is the 'cool' thing to do. Mo Salah, Jordan Pickford, Paul Pogba, Raheem Sterling - all bigger names than those they can watch at Prenton Park.

When you consider that for a time, Tranmere as a team were losing their identity, failing to produce any exciting or winning football, then a problem was building.

"My kids are 13 and 10," Bartley continues. "The first season they can probably remember is when Ronnie Moore was in charge. They went towards the end of the 2011/12 season and it was difficult to try and persuade them to support Tranmere.

"But for my eldest, he did see a lot of the season when we were playing really well and I was lucky with that. If it had been twelve months earlier, it would have been a struggle! They'd have been sat on their phones or iPads because the football just wasn't entertaining."

Tranmere spent over a decade haemorrhaging fans. Their first season in League One in 2001/02 saw an average crowd of 8,577 attend Prenton Park. That dropped over the next couple of years until 2004/05, when supporters could see the club was showing some ambition.

A team including the likes of Ryan Taylor, Iain Hume, Theo Whitmore, Paul Hall and Eugene Dadi, as well as former Liverpool man Jason McAteer and long term servants John Achterberg and Gareth Roberts gave people a reason to come to the matches. A certain Ian Goodison was just started out on The Wirral too.

Brian Little guided his star-studded side to third place in the division that year. They lost in the play-off semi-finals, beaten on penalties by Hartlepool. But word of mouth got around and home matches were watched by an average crowd of 9,044 that season.

After that, attendances dropped alarmingly. 1,800 had been shaved off the gate the by the end of the following season, slipping to a staggering 5,130 for 2011/12. There was a little lift to 6,196 for the next year when Ronnie Moore was back in charge, but come 2014/15, Tranmere's final campaign in the Football League before relegation, it had dropped again to just 5,192.

"It was fairly depressing being a Tranmere fan at that time," adds Bartley. "I can understand why there was such apathy from the Wirral public. You'd be paying to go and watch a team draw 1-1 or lose 1-0. It wasn't an entertaining way to spend a Saturday, certainly not for a new person. It wasn't entertaining at all, it was just depressing."

He starts browsing through the fixture list from the 2011/12 season. Football fans often have terrific memories. They can look at games and recall moments, despite how irrelevant that instance might have been on the outcome.

"I remember a defeat at Preston when Jose Baxter scored," he says. "I went to Sheffield Wednesday as well when Ian Goodison scored near the end. I remember the defeat at Brentford too.

"But there were also quite a few games that I might have gone to on different days, but I just couldn't be bothered. I'm looking at the fixture list right now and I can't remember half of them. I did lose motivation to go at times."

Even those fans who had stayed loyal through thick and thin were losing interest. They are the lifeblood of the club. The ones relied upon to turn up week in, week out, spending their valuable money at the ground.

Even when they got to Prenton Park, the match day experience was poor. The ground was disheveled, the bars were empty, the atmosphere was a negative one and the football was getting worse.

Yet nobody was reaching out to those supporters to try and involve them. It was almost like they were taken for granted.

"Attendances were dropping alarmingly," says Shaun Garnett. "That was possibly due to the style of football, but my gripe with the club at the time is that we didn't interact with people. For example, we did not reach out to the local grassroots clubs. Because we were Tranmere, we never seemed to build bridges with them. We just took their players.

"We just used the community without giving much back, and we paid the consequences for it, because the community just said 'get on with it, you've made your bed, lie in it'."

Former physio and manager Les Parry admits "style of football" was a major reason as to why attendances dropped away at Tranmere.

He added: "You can either set up to win a game or you can set up not to be beaten. I'll be the first to hold my hand up; when I was manager we set up, in the first instance, not to be beaten, and then try to sneak a win.

"The fans know that. They know how we used to play. I don't think there was a harder working team in the division. Were we the best team in the division footballing wise? No, we were probably one of the worst. But the aim was to stay in the division, which we did."

Chapter Twenty One
Give Us Hope

Football fans thrive on belief. If their club appears to have no chance of being promoted or winning a cup competition, then what is the point? Why bother going to watch a team when the ambition is simply to tread water?

Unfortunately for Tranmere, the latter is exactly what they became. From a club who in 2005 had a shot at the Championship after a four year absence, they became one for whom staying in League One was an achievement.

Outwardly, of course, a club will always state that they are hoping to challenge at the right end of the division. They need to provide some form of optimism to try and convince people to come and watch. But fans are not stupid.

"This is the thing with football," explains Les Parry. "There are two agendas. There's one that goes to the fans, and there's an agenda of reality.

"Unfortunately, directors will never let the fans know what the reality one is, because you go into every season and they want the manager to talk about aiming for the play-offs.

"I was actually on a bonus to keep us in League One. That says everything about expectations. That was the aim, to stay up. We had to maintain our League One status."

"Between 2009 and 2015, I never thought promotion was a possibility," adds Shaun Garnett. "I just didn't think the squad was good enough. We always had one or two players who were okay.

"I'd talk to managers, because I'm always interested in how they do it and what their beliefs are, and the biggest feedback was 'you get what you pay for'.

"You can pick up the odd gem. You can get a James Norwood, have him for two or three years and then sell him on, or an Ian Muir who was about to be released by Brighton, but the majority of the time, you get what you pay for. We paid a lot of money for John Aldridge and we got goals. That's football, more so now than ever."

The fans were noticing the lack of interest in going up, too. It is no coincidence that attendances dropped off so significantly. They wanted to watch a team attempting to get promoted, not one who were scrapping for every point possible to stay in the division.

"I don't think there was any ambition," says Mark Bartley. "We were on a downward spiral and there wasn't a great deal that was done, I don't think, to stop it.

"There was that one season, under Ronnie Moore, when I thought things looked up, but it wasn't necessarily through investment. It was just that the stars aligned for six months and we were putting in brilliant performances. We then got hit by loads of injuries or players returning to their parent clubs and we were back to where we were before.

"You never looked at the team before the start of the season and thought we were going to challenge for something. When Les Parry was in charge, the aim was just to try and stay in League One, and that's all we just about achieved.

"I think he was probably a little bit a victim of circumstance. I don't know what his team talks were like, or much about his player recruitment, but it just felt like the whole club was on a downward slope.

"Les unfortunately came in the middle of that. I don't know whether you can blame him or not. He was just part of the unfortunate process.

"I think Tranmere just wanted to stay in League One. That was the aim of every season. Don't get relegated. There was never any drive towards promotion.

"At the end of the day, we probably couldn't afford it. The money had stopped flowing in. We had to make ends meet. We didn't have a particularly good business model at that time either, certainly not when you consider what's going on now. The budget was cut accordingly and we probably were living above our means. We probably were a League Two team."

***

Mark Palios understood that lack of ambition when he bought Tranmere. He saw a club who had suffered from years of underinvestment, and as a consequence, fans were making their feelings known.

Plenty were still turning up on a match day, around 5,000, but they were just going through the motions. They would arrive at 2.45pm and leave as soon as the match finished. They were not engaging with the club because the club was not engaging with them.

"For me, ambition is the lifeblood of the game," he says. "I used to shut my door on a frosty November morning and I'd go out to play in the Sunday league when I was 50 odd. I still had ambition to win that game.

"I used to live in houses that were right next to the fields. I don't know why that was, it was a coincidence, but I always remember that ambition is the lifeblood. You can't not have it.

"It's one of the big issues with the football pyramid. Why is it so successful? Because ambition never ends. If you get into a league like the Scottish Premier League or our Premier League though...

"I remember going to West Ham at the start of the season and they were playing Chelsea. Their fans were saying to me 'our seasons starts after today. Let's get it out of the way because we're going to lose it'. In my day, West Ham would have fancied their chances against any First Division club on their manner. It was a lack of ambition because of the killing of competition.

"Where we are with this is if you're getting to the position where we're trying to sell the club and there's a lack of investment, that will drip down on to a lack of ambition.

"The fans are the club. The fans have ambition. That's why when I talk about the move from Prenton Park, I say 'tell me when I'm wrong with the figures, I'm happy to have the debate, but absent of structural change within the football industry that fixes the gaps, you are condemning yourself. You're at the height of your ambition being a good cup run and staying in League One.'

"That becomes a problem, potentially. I think the club clearly has to have ambition. We have ambition to be at least a League One club. At least. The difficulty is that there's a tension between credibility and leading people, not in terms of leading people up the garden path, but keeping their heads up.

"I came in and said 'I want to get us to the position whereby in five years time, we can be a League One club that's capable of going up and not coming straight back down'.

"Since that time, the gap has increased, but that was where I wanted us to be. We still had the ambition to potentially be a Championship club and not come straight back down.

"If we were a League One club at that stage, in five years time, which we are, we're not quite at the top end of the table but the gap's increased with the likes of Sunderland and Ipswich and they've got the money dripping down from the Premier League.

"The ambition is back. I wouldn't say it's changed and massively increased because I think you've got to have ambition without arrogance or entitlement. You're not entitled to be a Championship club or a Football League club. Ambition is the lifeblood and you've got to respect it."

There are a number of people who think the Championship is Tranmere's natural level. The fact is, though, they have only ever spent eleven seasons in the second tier in their entire history.

One of those was in 1938/39, but Rovers were relegated with just 17 points and a goal difference of minus 60. Manager Jim Knowles left his position in January, less than a year after getting the club promoted to the second tier, replaced by Bill Riding.

It was not until 1991 that Tranmere returned to Division Two. John King, managing his team of club legends such as Ian Muir, Johnny Morrissey, Jim Harvey, Dave Higgins and Eric Nixon, led his side to a play-off final win over Bolton at Wembley, Chris Malkin scoring the only goal in extra time.

They would spend the next decade at that level, three times knocking on the door of the Premier League by qualifying for the play-offs. They fell at the semi-final hurdle on each occasion, in 1992/93, 93/94 and 94/95.

At this point, Rovers were bank-rolled by Peter Johnson. It was his money that allowed King to bring in the likes of John Aldridge, Pat Nevin and Liam O'Brien, all of them fully fledged international players.

When the owner crossed the River Mersey to buy Everton in the 1990s, that money dried up and so did Tranmere's chances of getting into the Premier League. By the end of the decade, they were struggling to make ends meet.

In 2001, Aldridge's Rovers side were relegated back to the third tier. They finished bottom of the First Division, as it was titled then, accumulating only 38 points from their 46 league games, a stark contrast to their form in the cup competitions as in the same season, they defeated Premier League opposition in the form of Leeds United, Everton and Southampton.

Come to Prenton Park now, and you still see the remains of a Championship club. The ground is huge, far bigger than Tranmere need given their current attendances. Mark and Nicola Palios have brought a professional touch to the facilities around the stadium, something that was more than needed after years of deterioration, and the training facility far excels what they had before.

"On my whiteboard," the chairman continues, "in between on pitch performance and fan experience you've got the institution. It isn't about me or the manager or any individual. It's the institution; the club itself.

"It is the club's ambition. Not an individual's, because they may not match. A manager may want to go. That's all well and good if you've done your job. But it's all about the ambition of the club and it's got to be realistic, otherwise you'll have heartache.

"I don't think the ambition has changed. I see my job as stabilising, future-proofing and trying to show them, the fans, the ambition.

"If I went out today and said 'we're going to be a Championship club', well I'm not saying that. It's the ability to be a Championship club. There's certain things you've got to do to make that happen.

"I'm plotting a pathway to the Championship. Whether I'm here or not, it doesn't really matter. It's not the individual. It's not me. It's about where the club can go if it keeps on course. It's a relay race where you just have to hand over the baton and be further up the track. I think we're further up the track than when I got the baton. But I still think we can get further up the track."

That ambition has been exceptionally well received by the fans, who are turning up in their numbers. Of course winning football helps, but those supporters want to see the kind of pathway that Palios talks about.

The average attendance for the 2018/19 season, Tranmere's first back in the Football League after a three year absence, was 6,541, their highest since 2006/07 when Ronnie Moore's side were watched by a regular gate of just under 7,000.

Towards the end of the campaign, the public really started to respond. Over 8,000 were at each of the club's final five home matches, something that had not been achieved in nearly 15 years, whilst the Prenton Park turnstiles clicked round over 150,000 over the course of the season.

"I think re-engaging the club with the fanbase and the community has been one of the biggest achievements during my time here," Palios continues. "It fuels so much in terms of what we do. It makes things so much easier.

"It's a real virtuous circle. Fans come up to me and say 'I'm proud of my club again'. They can go into school or work on a Monday morning, and I know that it isn't just the results on the pitch. It's much more holistic than that.

"It's the fact that we can collect toys for kids who don't have toys and give them a Christmas that they didn't otherwise have. I was in care and I know what that's like. To know that you've affected that many people is really good, and the fans do it.

"The club used to give stuff to Radio City's Cash For Kids. I said 'no, we'll do our own,' and we set up 'Super White Christmas'. The schools have weighed into that. Calday Grange have been brilliant. From what's a relatively affluent part of the Wirral, they're bringing stuff over to kids on the less affluent side and giving them a Christmas, which is just fantastic."

Chapter Twenty Two
Fortress Prenton Park

Your home ground should be your fortress. Teams should fear coming to visit, because they know to expect a red hot atmosphere, with no inch given by either the home fans or players.

Under Johnny King, Prenton Park was like that. Tranmere were almost unbeatable on home soil and the bond created between those on the pitch and those in the stands bubbled through the game. The team could always count on the supporters.

But Rovers lost that. Fans had become more than weary; they were angry. Their club was going nowhere for years and then suddenly, after treading water, the papering of the cracks stopped working and the negative momentum kicked in.

As such, Prenton Park flipped. It was still a tough place to play, but for the home team instead of the opposition. Not how it should be.

"When I took over," explains Micky Mellon, "I asked a few questions of people I trusted. They told me what the situation was. I'm an experienced manager, so that's the kind of thing you do.

"I asked 'what's happened' and they'd say 'the fans hate the players and the players hate the fans. There's a real dislocation between all of it. The fans are pissed off. They're still turning up in their numbers but they're pissed off and the players weren't gelling.'

"So I just came in, spoke to the chairman, and it obviously helps that I've come here with an amount of success. A lot of people possibly looked at me and thought what I'd done before, I could do it again, because there was a desperation to get out of non-league. I had also played for Tranmere before and that helped.

"I came in and I said, straight from the start, 'you're eating yourself from within. If we're going to be successful, then we've got to do this together. We must. We mustn't keep punching ourself in the face'.

"I told the players some stories and told them how managers were coming here, keeping things tight for 20 minutes and then the Tranmere fans would turn on the players and the players would go under. I told them that they were using you as a tactic. They couldn't believe it."

The squad were well aware of what it could be like to play at Prenton Park and some of them found it hard to deal with.

"The atmosphere was quite nasty at times," admits Liam Ridehalgh. "It was tough. We were losing every week and the fans expected more. After 20 minutes of a game, they were on your back."

Mark Palios returned to Prenton Park when the atmosphere around the place was at its very worst. Prenton Park was only a third full on a match day, so any cries of anguish or bellows of fury were easily audible as they echoed around the empty stands.

As the 2014/15 campaign wore on, the fans became more and more hostile. Manager Micky Adams bore the brunt of it as those supporters grew tired of what was happening to their football club.

"I wasn't really expecting it to be a fantastic scenario," admits the chairman about how he found the atmosphere when he returned. "I knew it would destroy people, if they felt people were out there and they weren't doing their best for the club.

"There was a spot-fixing allegation against a couple of the players. That would just be an anathema to anybody who knew Tranmere Rovers. And then you had the situation with Ronnie Moore.

"On the pitch, we'd been top of League One at Christmas in 2012, but before that, there were constant relegation battles. So I expected the atmosphere to be as it was and I knew it was going to need rebuilding."

Unfortunately, things did not get much better once Tranmere were in the National League. Expectations were high and in the first season the team sometimes did not deliver.

Traditionally, Rovers have always been superbly supported on the road. Their fans get behind them and travel in numbers to every corner of England. But Palios recalls one infamous trip to Barrow in January 2016 when events at Holker Street looked somewhat different.

The team had gone through a sticky patch under manager Gary Brabin, losing to Macclesfield on New Year's Day and winning just three times in 13 games. It was not the form expected of a side who were supposed to be challenging at the top end of the table.

They went to Barrow hoping for a first victory of the calendar year, but found themselves 3-1 down with just three minutes left. Future Tranmere striker Andy Cook was amongst the goalscorers for the hosts.

Things turned toxic in the away end. Brabin was on the end of a significant amount of abuse as some of the supporters pushed as close to the dug-out as the stewards would allow.

What happened next on the pitch was incredible. Rovers performed the mother of all comebacks, scoring three times, with Jake Kirby netting a deflected winner deep into injury time after Jeff Hughes and Lois Maynard had also been on target.

"The fans were giving dog's abuse to the manager," Palios recalls. "I remember saying at a supporter meeting 'that's what going the 90 minutes means'. On the Thursday before, I'd said 'going the 90 minutes means supporting the team right until the end and you can make a difference'.

"That was one of the things I wanted to get across to the fans. I look at it and think 'what's stress?' Well it's when you can't influence what's going on. So if you're a fan and you're sitting there and watching it and it's crap, you can influence it. You can make the players run a bit harder and go the extra mile.

"Building that oneness was one of the things that was massive. That Barrow game was an example of where the lads went all the way. I came back afterwards and said 'that's going the 90 minutes'.

"Just before that, we'd had a player come on as a substitute at Halifax, Ben Tomlinson, and he stood on the touchline and the fans were booing him.

"I remember saying on that Thursday night 'you can come and stand in the car park and boo me and Nicky when we get out of the car, but we're not going to work any harder for it'.

"It was one of those subjects that's a difficult one to tread, but I knew that there was more that the fans could do and they would enjoy it more. They'd get that oneness together.

"It's something I've worked on quite hard because as a player I know what a difference it makes to you, and what a difference it makes to the opposition as well. When they come, the game plan is the same as it always was.

"It was even worse in non-league because the opposition just shut up shop, frustrated the fans, who then got on the back of our players because the expectation is there and that made it all worse."

Chapter Twenty Three
Detached From The Community

As well as improving the match day atmosphere at Prenton Park, Tranmere were desperate to attract new fans to their home matches. Crack that nut and they really could start motoring forward.

They faced a real problem though. The Wirral was almost embarrassed about its local football team. The community was completely detached from what their only professional sport club was doing, either on or off the pitch.

"I'm not sure we did enough to embrace the Wirral," says Shaun Garnett. "Losing the sponsorship (from the local council) and not having Wirral on our chest was massive.

"It was iconic. It gave everyone a little bit of identity. It was where we are and who we are. When it went, we lost a little bit with the Wirral. All of a sudden, it ended, and I know all things come to an end, but as a Tranmere fan and employee, I feel it knocked us.

"From the John Barnes era onwards, it was hard. A lot of people got bored of Tranmere. They got fed up and consequently, it filtered down and the first team suffered."

Wirral Borough Council's logo was first emblazoned across the front of a Rovers kit for the 1989/90 season. It remained for 24 years, the longest running shirt sponsorship deal in English football and third longest in Europe.

It was synonymous with the club and it was a source of pride amongst fans, although the amount of money paid was fairly small compared to what other teams across the division would have been taking in.

A freedom of information request by the Liverpool Echo in 2013 discovered that Wirral Borough Council paid a little over £1.3m between 2000 and 2013 to be on the front of Tranmere's kit. The cost of sponsorship for the 2012/13 campaign was £125,844.

That money was not spent solely on player wages or transfer fees, though. It went far beyond that. Tranmere's Football In The Community arm has always been long reaching.

Players, to this day, go on school visits every week. Soccer camps and soccer schools are run across the region and the Rec Centre behind the Kop offers a multitude of programmes to disadvantaged children and adults. The club also ran a 'Return To Work' scheme as well as carrying out health and education initiatives.

Such stories do not write headlines, though. At a time when the council, like many others across the country, was having to cut costs, the sponsorship became highly controversial. It was even the source of a telephone debate on the Jeremy Vine show on BBC Radio 2, allowing ill-informed callers who had no idea how that money was spent to get in touch and lambast the deal.

"A council has renewed a £125,000 sponsorship deal with a professional football club while closing care homes for the elderly" reads a typically inflammatory subheading from an article in the Telegraph, dated 16th April 2012. It was the kind of piece that people across the country, not just the Wirral, would read and it cast the club in a negative light.

The 2012/13 season was the final one in which the council sponsored Tranmere's shirt. They were replaced by Home Bargain, perhaps a metaphor for where the club were shopping for their players during that era. With the company's name on their kit, Rovers were relegated twice.

In the intervening years, Mark Palios has worked tirelessly on improving the club's relationship with the council. Indeed, he sees it as key to what direction they go in the future.

"When I was at the FA," he explains, "I could see that clubs seemed to be constantly fighting with their local council when in fact their local council is the context within which they live. Therefore it was something that I felt was very strange and should and could be fixed.

"I was pretty keen for us to align the club and the community, education and international (tourism) work that it was doing with what the council wanted to do. We've worked very hard at trying to get into a position whereby the council isn't just giving us money to go on the shirts. They're acting as a true partner with us in lots of the things we're going to do.

"Lots of the things I've been talking about, and what I want to do in the future, relates to a good relationship with your local council with us delivering stuff in the community. It was all part and parcel of the same thing. It was an important piece in the way I tried to structure the club, to have a working relationship with the council that meant something on the ground for both parties."

***

Tranmere were also in dispute with some local residents over the sale of their Ingleborough training ground, which the club had owned since 1995 but had become surplus to requirements.

It had been used by the Centre of Excellence, with hundreds, if not thousands, of kids spending many happy hours kicking a ball around and trying to convince youth coaches that they could make it as a professional.

Rovers, however, also leased a site not far from Clatterbridge Hospital called Raby Vale. It had a creaking shed for changing rooms and boggy pitches that were often out of use in the winter months.

In truth, it had become barely fit for purpose. But it was still used by the first team for training and the under-18s for matches.

With that facility, and what they had at Prenton Park, Ingleborough was no longer needed. The old pavilion had become a little rundown and the land was used far less frequently. Given its position, just a five minute walk from the ground, it was also perfect for any housing developers. As such, it was valued at around £5m.

Tranmere hoped to get planning permission for nearly 90 homes to be built on the land. They would then sell the land to developers and use some of the money to pay off a chunk of the club's debt. Another sizeable amount would help purchase a new state of the art training base that could house both the first team squad and the youth team.

It all sounds ideal, but there was a catch. Such planning permission had been sought for some time, but it was opposed by a handful of residents due to the historic use of the land.

Ingleborough was previously owned by the Birkenhead Institute and served as a memorial to 88 pupils who lost their lives during World War I. One of those students was the renowned poet Wilfred Owen. As such, there was a covenant on the land which stated it had to be used as a facility for sport and leisure.

Dean Johnson from the Wilfred Owen Story was the lead campaigner. He accused the club of wanting to "desecrate a war memorial" in one article in the Wirral Globe.

In another interview with the paper, he said Rovers' actions were "morally bankrupt" and that "the shame they have brought on the town will reap a whirlwind of bad publicity for Wirral".

These were all seriously unhelpful headlines. At a time when Rovers needed to embrace the community and get as many of them through the gates as possible, the local public were reading stories that damaged the reputation of the team. The Wirral was turning its back on Tranmere.

Johnson approached Tranmere for comment on several occasions, but they refused to do so. Instead, the Trust offered him an olive branch, keen to find some middle ground.

Mark Bartley explains: "I think the club had initially talked to him, but then decided to distance themselves and resorted to a "no comment" type basis with regards to his demands.

"Myself and Ben Harrison decided to take on the role as "peace moderators" and arranged to meet him and his partner at Ben's coffee shop. We had a pleasant evening where we discussed how the plans could benefit the community and we suggested it would be possible to build a permanent memorial on the site which would be accessible all year round.

"He seemed to be interested in all of these pragmatic ideas but then the next day decided to completely go against what he said during the meeting and continued with his opposition to the plans."

Rovers were always acutely aware that any changes made to Ingleborough had to be respectful ones, given its history. There would be 88 trees planted around the new development, one for every pupil who lost their life in the Great War. They would also ensure there was a landscaped memorial area on the site that had public access.

That was a stark contrast to the on-going situation, where the old pavilion, used as changing rooms, and the playing fields lay behind locked, rusting blue gates that were only open when training sessions or matches were being held.

"It's strange," Bartley continues, "Because the fields had been open every Remembrance Sunday for years due to them being used as football pitches, but there were never any visitors then. As soon as it got closed they were outside doing a PR stunt.

"Johnson managed to get himself in the Wirral Globe fairly regularly and it was obvious he liked the self-promotion. He made some terrible posters which had poppies growing amongst gravestones and superimposed them on the Ingleborough field."

Tranmere's plans went hand in hand with wanting to build a new training base, which was originally mooted to be in Woodchurch. If they were successful in getting the covenant lifted, they legally had to ensure those new facilities were built.

But facing such strong opposition, the club withdrew the original blueprints in early 2012, taking time to reconsider what they wanted to do. Later in the year, they were resubmitted and they were given the green light, firstly by the council in 2013, and then the Department for Communities and Local Government, who were called upon to check everything was above board. Eventually, the Secretary of State Eric Pickles decided not to halt the project.

This was merely a case of the covenant being lifted, though. Only after Mark Palios bought the club was everything ratified, and with a more than slight tweak to the original plans as well. Instead of moving the first and youth team training base to Woodchurch, Rovers would take control of some of the facilities at Solar Campus, a pupil referral secondary school based on Leasowe Road, Wallasey.

This all came into fruition in early 2016, with Gary Brabin the first Tranmere manager to be able to use the large site, which houses multiple pitches, a gym, cafeteria, classrooms and offices.

Things have moved on at Ingleborough, too. Glance across to where the playing fields used to be from the top of the Main Stand now, and you can see the houses poking up where grass fields used to be.

"I think the sale of Ingleborough has been vital in the resurgence of the club," Bartley adds. "Without that we would not have had the ability to develop Solar Campus and the new facilities there. It also paved the way for Peter Johnson to sell his stake and bring Mark and

Nicola Palios into the picture."

* * *

Those headlines are now long forgotten. Tranmere are as embedded in the local community as ever, and that is down to the hard work not only of Mark and Nicola Palios, but also the Tranmere Rovers Supporters Trust and TROSC.

They have each engaged themselves in a number of activities across the Wirral peninsula, working to break down any boundaries built up by issues from the past.

Fundraising initiatives have helped pay for valuable repairs to the Recreation Centre roof, where a number of classes and courses are held for disadvantaged and disabled members of the public.

The homeless have also been welcomed to Prenton Park for Boxing Day home matches, 24 hours after their Christmas Dinner has been served. The SWA2 campaign donates tickets to those who would not otherwise be able to afford to come to matches and Nicola Palios is one of several employees who has taken part in 'Kip On The Kop', spending a night sleeping under the stars to raise money for those who have no bed of their own.

This is just the tip of the iceberg. Tranmere have not just started reaching out to the Wirral public. They have become its heartbeat.

"When I came here," Mark Palios continues, "I did say it was a working class club, Jeremy Corbyn picked up on that, and I said it was a community club, one that needs to be rooted in its community.

"I knew that we could leverage the brand. I knew that the club could do things that other organisations on the Wirral couldn't do and I set about doing that. That split into the community business and the education business. We built an education business, mainly with

Michael Kinsella who came along and Dawn Tolcher.

"There's so much more that you can do, and that's the organic potential of the club. I think that connection with the fans is really good. Nicky plays a large part in that because of her social media presence.

"I don't like social media to be honest. I look at Twitter and will Tweet a few times now. I never used to Tweet at the start. It's difficult because it's an unrelenting master and it can turn on you. You should be cognisant to what's going on on Twitter and social media, but not a slave to it.

"Nicky gets the balance right on that. She talks to the fanbase and gives them a good connection with the board and the heart of the club. That's one of the ways we compete with Liverpool and Everton. Size militates against access, but here, we can give access that none of the other clubs can.

"For example, when we gave back the play-off trophy, the first one, we had to bend the lid to fit the cup because it had been so battered! It had been everywhere! People asked for it to go to places. We went to a tennis club with it. That just gives access to a club that you can't get.

"The boardroom used to be panelled, hidden and shut. It had no windows. Everybody went into this mysterious room. It's now opened. Some people say I've gone too far, but I'm fairly casual about it. Businesses have access to the boardroom and the people who come to the boardroom. It's one of those things that a club should be.

"We've always been good as a club, well before I came here, in terms of players going into the community and doing stuff, but I think that the stuff we're doing on the community business side, the alternative provision with Alzheimer's, health, inclusion and all that kind of stuff, it contributes to utilisation of the premises.

"Financially it works, but the reality is it also massively works in terms of extending the brand. I've often said to Dawn Tolcher our managing director, if we break even on community, it's still the best marketing we can do."

All the pieces of the jigsaw are now beginning to fall into place. You have the ambition. The community is working on your side, as opposed to actively campaigning against you. Attendances on a match day are going the right way. All that is left to do is put them all together and make them work in your favour.

Chapter Twenty Four
Putting It All Together

The Tranmere Rovers Supporters Trust first came to prominence with the fundraising initiatives they ran when Les Parry was in charge, such as Les Aid. Their work has been terrific, not only in providing some much needed money for the club, but also raising awareness of the good work they do throughout the Wirral peninsula.

Yet a Supporters Trust should equally challenge at board level. If a question needs answering or a major decision has had a negative impact on a large scale, they are the organisation who are expected to make some noise.

The same cannot be said for a supporters club. It is a nuanced difference in wording, but a key one. And it is a department in which Tranmere were lacking.

"Mark and Nicola Palios told the Trust that they wanted an official supporters club," explains Mark Bartley. "And that's how I became involved with the Tranmere Rovers Official Supporters Club. I was the vice chairman of the Trust at the time and I was concerned about what would happen to the supporters club if it was run in conflict with the Trust.

"You hear of some clubs where there are four or five different supporters clubs who all hate each other and are trying to undermine each other. We didn't want that. Because I was running the coaches and doing quite a lot of stuff that a supporters club would normally do, it was suggested that I went along to meetings about initially setting it up.

"The definition of a supporters trust and club are somewhat

blurred. In my opinion, a Trust is the group that wants to own and advise at boardroom level, whereas a supporters club focuses on the fans, which is what I was doing.

"So I went along to a meeting at the club that was hosted by Christine Roberts. A good few other people turned up, but it was a bit haphazard. I didn't really know who was doing what.

"Another meeting was arranged, and only three people turned up to it. I therefore fell into the role. I said I'd take over and I'm still doing it today! But it came along from three of us around this table to what it is now. It's moved on so much."

From that meeting, TROSC has become a vital arm in the club. They put on coaches taking fans to every single away game and run Aldo's on a match day, now a bustling hub for supporters to visit, instead of a deserted, rundown function suite.

"We've grown from just being a simple membership to a group that turned over £120,000 last year," Bartley continues. "When we first started, it was about £7,000 of membership and nothing else.

"We run coaches to every single away game, no matter what. Even if it was a Tuesday night away game at Lancaster City in the FA Cup, we'll always do something. That turns over a lot of money. It doesn't bring in a great deal of profit margin though, because we do it for the fans.

"With Aldo's, people used to walk in at half-time, see a small bar and it would be busy, so they'd walk out again. We set up a bottles bar. We pay rent to the club for that.

"The supporters' club made a £15,000 profit last season and all of it will go back into the club. That's not taking into account the money we pay in rent or donations. We were instrumental in setting up the SWA2 campaign. We did that in the first season and it won an award. It's now been taken over by the club because it's seen as such a positive thing, and they've got more capability.

"I had a little look online to see what other supporters clubs do. Peterborough only turned over about £5,000. We're doing so much more than others. We are a fully functioning supporters club.

"There are about 10 or 12 of us who do it and it's a full time job! I feel knackered with it! But the club recognise us in a positive light. Mark Palios sent me an email after our AGM in 2019 thanking us for everything we've done; our contribution towards the club, our contribution towards the atmosphere, we appreciate it. Having something like that is a world apart from in previous eras."

Bartley has not always been in Mark Palios' good books though. He laughs as he recalls the match at Sutton at the start of the 2016/17 campaign.

"A group of us congregated near the away bench at the end of the game," he says. "It was a terrible performance. Some fans started to sing 'we want Brabin out' and I filmed a bit of it on my phone and uploaded it to the internet.

"Mark Palios wasn't very happy with it. He asked 'why is the chairman of the supporters club singing about the manager getting sacked?' Technically I wasn't singing it! I felt it, but I wasn't singing it!

"He said 'I can see you on TV! You shouldn't be doing that. You should be supporting the club.' My response was that I have an opinion as well. I wasn't singing with them, but I agree with them."

**

Membership of the Supporters Club has grown significantly since its formation. For the start of the 2019/20 campaign, well over 1,000 fans were signed up, each paying their yearly fee of up to £10.

But it has not been without its criticisms. One of the benefits of joining is that you get earlier access to tickets for away matches. So for games when allocations have been particularly tight, such as trips to Wrexham and Chester in the National League, members had a window, sometimes no more than a couple of days long, when they could purchase their seat before anybody else.

In reality, this only ever led to a portion of tickets being claimed ahead of general sale. There were still plenty of others left up for grabs for everybody else. But some supporters argued that this was the only reason for anybody to join TROSC. That is a claim Bartley vehemently denies.

"We have about 1200 members now," he adds. "When we started off, it was included in people's season tickets, so they obviously just thought 'I'll tick that'.

"We had a situation with away tickets in the National League though. People used to say 'people only join the supporters club for away tickets' but that's not the case at all. You can get away tickets easily now, but we've got a higher membership now than ever. People see the value it gives.

"We've put banners up outside the ground on lamp posts. We've done things with the Trust for ground improvements. These are those little things that the club might not necessarily do because they're focused on so many other different avenues. Having a mural painted or something, it's not on their list or priorities. But as a fan, it is that kind of thing that makes a difference.

"We're working on getting stuff put up all the way down the Johnny King Stand at the moment. Just things on the history of the stand, because there's some quite interesting stuff. Little things like that, fans can do it. Clubs can to an extent, but it's better when it comes from the fans."

***

One of the main tasks Mark Palios set for TROSC was to improve the match day experience at Prenton Park. That included, but was not limited to, making sure the atmosphere created by the fans was something that helped the home team, not hindered it.

"That's exactly what we wanted to get to," Palios explains. "It was the same when I played. 'Keep it tight in the first 20 minutes, their fans will become your friends. They'll get on your backs.'

"They had it in spades in the National League because teams put a block on and destroyed the pattern of the game, which played right into that scenario.

"When I was a player at Crewe, they always used to say teams would come through the tunnel and say 'have you packed your shinpads, you're going to Tranmere'. So I want people to think that way again. Prenton Park is a fortress and the fans can make it that."

So how could that happen? Firstly, the fans had to be embraced as a force for good, and that had not always been the case. Those who wanted to chant and sing had previously been discouraged from doing so in the Lower Kop, for fear of elder fans complaining about the noise.

As such, the more boisterous supporters had spread throughout the ground. Some sat in the Johnny King Stand, towards where the away fans were situated, until they were moved because that particular section of the stadium was closed.

They then found themselves in the expanses of the Main Stand, whilst others were towards the top of the Kop. Making a noise up there is pointless if there are only a handful of you, it simply escapes into the atmosphere.

"Years ago," says Bartley, "I used to play the drums. When we went to face Leicester at Wembley, I was doing it then! But at Prenton Park we were parked right at the back of the Kop, miles away from anywhere."

Mark Palios did not want anything of the sort. He wanted them as close to the action as possible, creating a heated atmosphere that Tranmere could thrive off and that had the potential to make the visitors wilt before your eyes.

"We were told 'we want the supporters club to help improve the atmosphere'," Bartley continues. "It's very difficult to force an atmosphere on people, but what you can do is give them the means to do it.

"So we got the banners up, bought some drums and got some people who could play the drums, rather than just hit it!"

TROSC was formed in 2015. It took them some time to really change the atmosphere at Prenton Park on a match day, but then these things cannot happen overnight.

The inspiration for the ideas they put in a place came from a trip to Lincoln in December 2016. Tranmere actually lost the match 2-1, Micky Mellon's first defeat as Rovers boss, but it was what the Imps fans did that impressed Bartley so much.

"They were pretty noisy," he says. "They had a section with loads of banners and flags and they had the air raid sirens too. We were looking on with a bit of jealousy. They've only got a small ground but they had a section in the corner for making a racket. It picks up the team and they got promoted, so we were thinking that we could do something similar.

"We were jealous of the atmosphere that they had. Mark Palios asked us if we could start getting something together like that. If the club had suggested putting a band in the tent and trying to create something, it would fall flat, just like Aldo's or the Marquee did.

"But if you give these things to the fan groups, like the Trust taking the Marquee, decking it out and making it a trendier place to go, it'll pick up very fast. Obviously it was helped by the on pitch performances.

"We started getting the band together and we put some banners across the middle of the Kop - just a couple of the ideas that Lincoln had used. They weren't ultras, that's an overused term, but it's a section where people could go if they wanted to shout, stand or sing. Nowadays, if the opposition are taking a corner in front of the Lower Kop, there's a good atmosphere down there."

Later that season, things started to click into place. There are now numerous examples of matches when the fans had a real impact on the result because of their support late on. Interestingly, Bartley and Palios both pick the same starting point.

"The night that it all clicked was Dover at home," says the chairman. "They just got it and I was sitting there thinking 'wow'. It makes me emotional thinking about it now.

"Nobody knew we'd been working on that one thing. The waves came out of the Kop that night. It's quite good that that it happened, because there is no love lost between Dover, the Dover chairman and us! From that time on, the fans got it.

"I think it was the season that you started to hear managers actually say 'it's a tough place to come, the fans keep going'. A visiting captain said that too. That's quite a nice thing.

"All through this, there's just been that extra special piece of the away fans at this club. They're fantastic. I'm really proud of them. There's the odd idiot, but by and large, clubs tell us our fans are fantastic. Fans from other clubs say it. That's the reason I got all those texts after the Plymouth game. The club was well liked.

"Those fans have a great sense of humour too. How can a hot-dog run onto the pitch and then try and jump back into the crowd without being seen? He's dressed as a hot-dog! That was the start of the journey where we kicked on."

Bartley agrees, adding: "The Dover match was an evening game and we won 1-0. That was the game when the band kicked in and people started to say they could sense the atmosphere. We'd had the decline. We'd got ourselves in the National League and stabilised the ship.

"For that game, the atmosphere was amazing. I remember when I was walking out, people were giving each other high-fives. The bars were busy. We were really looking up. It seemed to take off from there.

"I think the whole match day experience we have now is infinitely better. If you compare 2012 or whatever to now, people used to just come for the game and then go home.

"Now, they arrive early and they've got a choice of places to go in the ground. They know that if they come and spend their money in the ground, it stays within the club and supports the club, so Aldo's is busy and so is the Marquee.

"The game itself has a much better atmosphere. If you're in the Kop, people are singing and there are new songs. Players have got songs again, which they didn't have for years. The facilities are better. The catering is better. The bars work better.

"After the game, the facilities like Aldo's and the Marquee are still open. We put bands on after the game and people come and watch that. People stick around. Sometimes they arrive at midday and go at 8pm.

"They spend all day there. It used to be coming for the 90 minutes and getting away as quickly as possible. It's infinitely better. Everything.

"There's another match that sticks out recently. We beat MK Dons 2-1 and Connor Jennings scored. It was a busy afternoon and everybody was enjoying it. It was so much better than what it had been.

"I enjoy going to the game more, although I don't see as much of it now, partly because of my role in Aldo's. We have the live feed on in there so I can watch it while I'm working but I spend quite a bit of time watching the TV!"

**

Just a few years ago, Tranmere's players, fans and the local community were three different entities. All had their own frustrations and anger, and when displayed, it worked to the detriment of the club.

It is absolutely no coincidence that since the atmosphere at Prenton Park on a match day has improved, the club have started picking up results. But it should also be pointed out that it is equally no coincidence that the improved atmosphere has happened at a time when the team are picking up results. The two go hand in hand.

The efforts of the supporters have not gone unnoticed. Prenton Park is once again a tough place to come for visiting teams, whilst the hosts thrive in what can become a bubbling cauldron.

"The chairman was brilliant through it," says Micky Mellon. "He's a very clever man. He started to hook up with the supporters club to get an atmosphere going, and we gave them work to do.

"We told them to support us because we needed them. We gave them the 12th man role. Never mind all that shit with flags and that. We said 'be the twelfth man. Go on. Be it. Less of the bullshit. Let's drive ourselves out of this together, which means be a supporter. Back it up, carry it. Be what the word support means'. And it changed with the click of a finger, I'm told.

"I've only had one guy shout something negative at the team at Prenton Park. It was during the 2018/19 season. He shouted something at the team and I turned around and said 'are we going to start that? Why don't you just support the team? They need you.'

"And do you know what? The whole stand stood up and went

252

'you're fucking right. Yeah.' So they stood up, and that impacts the Kop, which impacts the Johnny King, and they all stood up and away we went again.

"They applauded the sentiment. They knew the statement was right. They wanted to get back on track again.

"Now we have this phenomenon, which I haven't seen anywhere else, where with 15 or 20 minutes to go, there's a rise. They know. They take a bit of pride in it. They like it. They go 'when we do this, we get results'. Recently, they've done that and we've got results. There's that connection.

"Plus we've celebrated a lot together, so there's the winning thing, and we know each other. They'll come and say 'Hi Micky, how are you doing?' and we'll talk to each other.

"I try and be really straight with them all the time. When I'm talking to the camera and the media, I'm talking to the fans. When I'm asked 'so Micky, what about this?' I look at that as the fans asking me a question. I'll then answer back to the fans, to the best of my knowledge and opinion, with what I think is happening.

"I will acknowledge if the fans are pretty pissed off with anything. I think that they quite like that. They might not always like my answers, but I'm giving them the straight truth. It's what I think is happening and I say what I'm going to do next. It's the best way I know how to do it and we all go again."

"Just look at the attendances now compared to a few years ago," adds Shaun Garnett. "We're all in it together now. If you talk to people around the Wirral, they're asking about Tranmere. They're very much interested.

"We're taking over 1,000 to away games. There's a buzz back within the club, and I think that's very much because it's gone back to being a family club.

"The fans really have had a massive impact. If we have an open day now, you're looking at thousands of people turning up. Five years ago, you'd be lucky to get 200 or 300 people, and it would be the same ones who always turn up. They were very loyal through the hard times. But there's a buzz now.

"If we bring out a new shirt, it gets record sales. We'll take phenomenal support wherever we go. That's a credit to the owners and the manager."

The gap between the club and the local community has well and truly been bridged. Whereas once there was an apathy from both sides, there is now an understanding. Each group reaches out to the other. They depend on each other. No longer do fans turn on the players sharply. Instead, they back them until the death, knowing a result is still possible.

The Tranmere Rovers Official Supporters Club should take some credit. So should Mark Palios, and those who turn up to the games determined to play their part from the terraces. It really has been a complete team effort. Scott Davies also thinks somebody else should take credit.

"I put it down to the manager personally," he says. "I think the fans recognise that they've got somebody in charge who knows what it is to be Tranmere. They recognise that the lad in goal knows what it's like to be Tranmere. They know the core of the group knows what it's like to be Tranmere.

"Any fan who comes to watch Tranmere would rather watch eleven guys who know what it means to be Tranmere, fighting, scrapping and doing whatever is necessary, bleeding for the shirt, rather than ten who can, on any given day, put the ball in the top corner after six step overs. I think that's what we became.

"I think the fans recognise that. I think they fell in love with that. If you go back to the song young Jordan Edwards did, that said everything to me. It showed where we were as a team and as a club.

'This is how it feels to be Tranmere'."

Liam Ridehalgh has been through the whole journey. He was on the wrong end of that fanbase on several occasions as Tranmere tumbled down the leagues. Now, he gets to step out at Prenton Park every other Saturday safe in the knowledge that those same supporters will give the players the extra lift they need to get them through the 90 minutes.

"The way they've changed helps you massively," he reveals. "We had a recent Tuesday night game against Peterborough and it's the perfect example. I thought we were brilliant in the first half and then we lost two goals really quickly. They still cheered us on and kept us going. We came back and got a 2-2 draw.

"There was a game in the National League against Sutton and that's when it all changed in my opinion. If I remember rightly, I made a mistake for their second goal, but then Michael Ihiekwe scored in the last minute and we won 3-2.

"That was one of the first games when they brought the drums and the trumpet and the atmosphere was just incredible. It was really late on when they scored the equaliser and they just carried on. They got us through. Every credit to them."

Connor Jennings was playing that night too, although he had been substituted with fifteen minutes left as Micky Mellon threw Adam Mekki on in an attempt to get a vital three points in the title race with Lincoln. That was his first season as a Tranmere player. Now in his fourth campaign with the club, he can reflect on how very different things are around Prenton Park from when he joined in 2016.

"I think the biggest thing that's changed is the fans," he says. "I look at it now and they're such a community club. That's down to everybody who is involved; starting at the top with Mark and Nicola Palios. They've done a fantastic job.

"Then you're filtering down to all the people in the stadium, the manager, the players and all the unsung heroes. There are loads of them. It's transformed. The difference is incredible.

"These days, I don't expect anything less from the fans. Home or away, they're there in their thousands. They've been brilliant, they really have. You couldn't ask for anything more from them.

"At home, you have all the drums and the flags, which helps everybody else with the atmosphere. It gets everybody going ... and winning games obviously helps too!"

Part Four

Two In A Row

Chapter Twenty Five
Building For League Two

On May 12th 2018, Tranmere were promoted back to the Football League after a three year absence. James Norwood's late header secured a 2-1 victory over Boreham Wood in the National League play-off final and sparked scenes of jubilation at Wembley.

"Mellon's Mission Accomplished" roared commentator Adam Summerton on the BT Sport coverage. Except it was not, far from it. The manager still felt that his job at Prenton Park was nowhere near complete. He wanted to return Rovers to League One, at the very least.

He knew it would be a tough ask. It had been 27 years since Rovers were last promoted. They had no recent experience of going up, let alone back-to-back successes. Mellon, though, had won promotions before, getting a couple in three years at Fleetwood, so he was aware just how big a step up they were making.

"When you do transition from league to league, it's always really difficult," he said. "I'm glad I'd had the experience of doing it before with Fleetwood. I knew that there was a step up in tempo and quality from the National League to League Two.

"Then you have to adjust and adapt to players leaving because their contracts are up, and that's their right to do that. You have to try and find the right type of quality with the finances you have, which is always important, to try and replace some very good players. We recruited to try and replace.

"We tried to keep the nucleus of the squad because we thought, quite rightly, that it deserved another go. We weren't going to get emotional about it, but there was a lot of quality still left in the group that we felt would be able to compete in the league."

Returning to League Two was not enough to convince some of the club's most influential players to stay at Prenton Park. Andy Cook, out of contract once his two year deal expired, joined Walsall on a free transfer, whilst Oli Norburn was sold to Shrewsbury for an undisclosed fee. A third major loss saw Jeff Hughes return to Northern Ireland as he penned a lengthy deal with boyhood club Larne.

It meant Mellon had something of a rebuilding job on his hands. He still had the core of a more-than-capable League Two side but it needed strengthening. And he did not have a lot of money to play with.

"The way it happens here," he explained, "is we don't really have the ability to recruit until probably nearer the end of the summer. Certainly since I've been here, the summers I have done recruitment in, I've not really had the finances to go and do things at an early stage.

"That's just the way it is. Tranmere are bigger than me, so I'm not going to complain about it. I know what happens. I have to be patient and try and do the best we can when we're able to do the recruitment."

The manager was nevertheless able to bring in some quality players. Paul Mullin, a target twelve months earlier, joined from Swindon on a two-year deal, whilst Jake Caprice signed after his contract expired at Leyton Orient.

Zoumana Bakayogo was another arrival, coming back to Tranmere five years after departing for Leicester City, then in the Championship. The defence was further bolstered by Mark Ellis, an experienced centre-back, coming from Carlisle.

A couple of familiar faces also returned to Prenton Park. Manny Monthe and Ollie Banks had both been on loan with the club during their final campaign in the National League, with the former playing a huge role in the win over Boreham Wood.

These were two players who had already shown the Super White Army what they were capable of and Mellon is a manager who likes to sign players he can trust.

He continued: "When you get the opportunity to bring real quality with potential and ambition into your group, like Monthe and Banks, it wasn't really a tough decision. They've both gone on to prove that they had qualities we believed were good enough to keep moving the club forward.

"When we see a player is a good player, we go into his character and find out what type of guy he is. If he's still full of ambition to kick on, then he's easy to work with. Those two certainly wanted to kick on with their careers.

"We looked into their character as much as you can do, asking people what kind of characters they were. Eric Nixon knew Ollie Banks well, so we knew they were the right types to add to the group to try and keep moving the group forward."

The loss of Cook also led Tranmere to change their style of play. The striker had been superb in his two year stint at Prenton Park, netting in excess of 50 goals, including 27 in the 2017/18 campaign.

He had also formed a lethal partnership with James Norwood. Both had finished that promotion season with over 20 strikes to their name, and both had scored at Wembley in the play-off final.

Mellon brought in Cole Stockton, returning to Prenton Park just 12 months after he had departed for Hearts in Scotland. The striker was supposed to partner Norwood in attack, but he struggled to settle back on the Wirral, scoring just once in 16 league appearances.

Eventually, the manager decided to play with a lone front man. Connor Jennings, if not out wide, would be used in a slightly withdrawn role as a number ten and Rovers would set up with a five man midfield.

"When we lost Cook," Mellon continued, "I knew that Norwood was going to be a better striker up front on his own. I had the feeling that he was a lone striker anyway.

"I always felt that when they played as a pair, because of the way Norwood plays, they got in each other's way. When one came short, the other one never really read the other one.

"As I got to know Norwood better, I kind of thought two centre-backs playing against him, with the amount of runs he makes, if we can create overloads and try and find his runs, we'll be a real force. I knew I had Connor Jennings as a ten to play off and around him. So I was quite comfortable knowing that I had those two.

"I always had to try and bolster the squad, because I need 20 odd players. You've gone up a level, so the intensity is going to go up, so you also don't know how players are going to handle that intensity jump, injury wise. Everything goes up a gear. Everything is quicker, so there's more toll on the body. You have to be robust. So you don't know."

***

As crucial as it was for the club to be back in the Football League after a three year absence, it created a challenge for individuals within the team. Several of those who had played a significant part in getting Tranmere out of non-league football were returning to a level at which they had not played for many years.

Norwood, for example, had made his debut in League One with Exeter in 2010, but then spent nearly a decade in the fifth tier. The same can be said for Jay Harris, who had last played in League Two for Chester in 2009, whilst Steve McNulty had dropped into the National League when he moved to Tranmere from Luton in 2015.

Scott Davies is another who had fought to get back to a level at which he believed he belonged. Released by Fleetwood in 2015, he was considering walking away from football before Tranmere manager Gary Brabin came calling.

"It was massive for me to get back into the Football League," Davies said. "When I left Fleetwood, I'd had a bad loan spell at Accrington where things just hadn't gone well for me.

"I wasn't enjoying my football and I was probably in a place where if it had ended that year, no joke, if my career had stopped that summer, I had said to my wife 'I'm happy to finish'. That is with no disrespect to Accrington, but I struggled with the unprofessionalism.

"Anybody who knows me in football will know I've always been a very good professional. When I'm out there working, I give 100%. I'm a big believer that what you're doing Monday to Friday. If you do 1000 repetitions of one thing, on Saturday you do 1001.

"When I went to Accrington, I struggled with the unprofessionalism. Listen, you've got to credit John Coleman and his people. They've done unbelievably well with the resources they have. But I was used to a certain standard of training and professionalism and when I went there, there was no goalkeeping coach.

"We'd be training on astroturf one day, then training in the gym the next day and then on a 4G pitch and then a park field. I struggled. Mentally I wasn't in it. I wasn't training well and my performances were poor.

"It was just an accumulation of things and I wasn't in a good place personally. I'd fallen out with Fleetwood. I'd had a good loan spell at Morecambe prior to Christmas. I went there, I knew the goalkeeper coach and manager and had a good relationship with the fans because of what I'd done previously. It went well.

"Financially I was on really good money at the time, but Morecambe couldn't match what Fleetwood wanted, so I had to go back and I had even more of a fall out because I wanted to go back to Morecambe. Then on the last day of the transfer window, I got a phone call at 10pm telling me to go to Accrington. I was like 'pfff, might as well,' and in hindsight I shouldn't have gone there.

"But that's football. You make decisions and you live or die by them. It wasn't a good time and probably at the end of that loan I would have been happy to walk away from football."

That phone call from Brabin therefore saved Davies' career. He joined Tranmere on a one year contract as their first choice goalkeeper, replacing the departing Owain fon Williams. And he has not looked back since.

"Tranmere came knocking," he continued, "This old, big club, and I thought 'I'll have a go at that' because I saw ambition in it. I decided to have another go and I said I wanted to get back to League One.

"In my mind, I thought it would be a quick transition. Then the first season turned out how it did and it was difficult, mentally more than anything, because I don't think everybody was pulling in the same direction.

"I think there was a disconnect between us as players and the fans and the management staff and the fans. The group of players we had, we should have got out of the league, or at least got into the play-offs, but we were miles off it. I know it doesn't look like we were miles off it if you look at the table, but as a group I feel like we were.

"When we did finally get back into the Football League, I felt relief more than anything and justification of the route I took. Those lows that you experience in football, without them, you don't experience the highs. If you look at me after the promotions, you can see the emotion in me, and that all stems from moments and spells when I was written off."

***

The last time Tranmere were in League Two, they had finished bottom of the table. The 2014/15 season had started in a spirit of hope and expectation, with many supporters believing they could mount some kind of challenge for a place in the top seven. But it did not materialise.

This year was different though. Supporters held many different opinions on how they thought Rovers would do. Some believed just finishing above the relegation zone would mean the campaign had been a success, whereas others had loftier ambitions.

Micky Mellon insists his hopes were slim, saying: "I wouldn't for one minute say that we believed we were going to get promoted. We didn't have any thoughts. You've just got to get going with it, see where it's going and go game to game, because you just don't know.

"There were so many players coming into the Football League for the first time, so you don't know how they're going to do, because it is a step up and you've got to give them the opportunity to make that step up, whilst making them aware of that step up in quality."

Mark Palios, on the other hand, was always confident of a successful season. "I honestly believed that we could achieve the play-offs," he says. "Then of course when you're saying that, you're saying promotion is feasible. I honestly believed that. I wasn't smoking dope!

"If you'd asked me what the chance of going up was, I'd have probably said slightly less than half. But did I think we were going to struggle? No. Did I think we'd be in the top half of the table? Yes."

Chapter Twenty Six
A Steady Start

Tranmere's first game back in the Football League saw them travel to Stevenage, and a brace from James Norwood ensured the visitors came from 2-0 down to grab a point. It was a promising start to the season.

Over 1,000 fans made the journey to Broadhall Way, and they were slightly surprised to see Scott Davies named in the starting line up, given the goalkeeper had missed a large proportion of pre-season.

"I wasn't fit," he admits. "I got injured in Scotland in week one of pre-season and tried to play against Liverpool a few days later but I had to come off. I'd torn all of my glutes and I had an impingement in my hip.

"I went for a scan and was told I'd be out for three months, so we signed Shamal George. I ended up getting an injection along the way and me being me, I didn't just want to sit it out and have an operation on it. You're a long time dead, aren't you? You can do that later on in the day.

"So I ended up training the week before the Stevenage game but didn't fully train with the lads until the Thursday. Eric Nixon and the manager said if I was fit, I would play, so I did."

Davies was testing that injury after just 20 minutes as he picked the ball out of the back of the net; Jimmy Ball giving Stevenage the lead, before Joel Byrom doubled the advantage a few moments later.

It was a bitterly disappointing way to get the campaign underway, but Norwood soon pulled one back and in the second half, Tranmere looked far more at home. Davies admits it took a stern talking to from Micky Mellon to get them going.

"We were 2-0 down early on without really laying a glove on them," he says. "It was a boiling hot day, as the first day of the season often is, and it felt like a pre-season friendly.

"Nors scored to give us a lift, but when we got in at half-time, the gaffer gave us a little bit. He told us to up our ambition. 'We've not come into this league not to compete. What's your ambition? Just to fucking survive or to go and lay a glove on them?'

"Second half, we did lay a glove on them. We should have won the game and we showed what we're about. To start the season, you'd have taken a point, going to Stevenage, but after the game, we were disappointed not to win."

Mellon's reasoning for the half-time team talk is slightly different. "It wasn't really ambition as such," he insists. "It was a wee bit of belief. When you start the season, it's a bit like the monster in the wardrobe.

"You know there's a monster in the wardrobe. You know the Football League is a big ask, but it isn't until you actually open it and you confront it that you can say 'well actually, it's not as big and as scary as what I thought it was going to be'.

"It got to half-time and I was asking 'why have you got the handbrake on? What are you waiting for?' It was a bit like they were expecting more.

"By half-time, it certainly hadn't come. We found ourselves a couple of goals down, but they took the handbrake off and then I started to see it. I think Stevenage quite fancied themselves to do well and it was a good early indicator of where we were as a group, because nobody knew where we were.

"When we got on to the front foot, they performed really well and it was a really pleasing start. We should have won the game. We had numerous chances to win it. But it certainly showed me enough to suggest that we were going to be alright."

A week later, Tranmere got their first Football League win for over three years as Norwood was again on target, scoring a screamer from outside the box in a 1-0 victory over Cheltenham. They had lift off.

"It's a terrific result for us because it's the first time we've won a Football League game for many years," Mellon said afterwards. "To get that off our back is really important. That's obviously on the players' minds as well.

"I just have a special thing for the crowd too. It's amazing. They were magnificent and the atmosphere was electric. Again, they were a very educated crowd. They knew we needed them at the end and to a man, woman and child, they got behind us. It's a great bond that we've got now. There's great togetherness. They know when we need them and you can see them rise. It gave the players that extra lift.

"I'm so pleased that I was the manager to walk out for the football club in their first home game back in the Football League. A club like this has to be in it. It was fantastic. They showed what a terrific football club they are."

***

It was a strong enough start to the season; four points from the opening two games. In the final ten games before relegation in 2015, Rovers accumulated only five.

So it looked like they were going to be just fine. They had got their season underway. Most supporters would have bitten your hand off for such a tally from those first couple of matches.

But as well as the club adapting to life back in the Football League, some of the players were trying to get to grips with a division they had not played in for some time.

Connor Jennings had started his career with Stalybridge Celtic before being signed by Scunthorpe at the age of 21. He managed only a handful of appearances for the club though, leaving two years later after loan spells with Macclesfield, Grimsby and Stockport.

"I found that League Two was a lot more technical than the National League," he says. "You probably get a bit more time on the ball. The players are a lot better at pressing. It was a bit different from the National League, but I wouldn't say loads.

"It suited me, because I'm a technical player, but then you've got to have the end product with it. It's alright having the time, but you've got to do things with it and back it up.

"In League Two, we were still a big club, but we were a club who had just been promoted. In the National League, we needed to win games, so a lot of teams were camping in and making it difficult. In League Two, they were attacking and we were good on the counter attack."

***

Tranmere's first defeat of the league season came in their next game. They had raced into a 2-0 lead down at Swindon, but Jay Harris was sent off after just 18 minutes and after that things turned sour very quickly.

They eventually lost 3-2, and a fuming Mellon said afterwards: "We were cruising up to that point. It's a big moment in the game and changes pretty much everything.

"We defended poorly for all the goals. We will not look for excuses. For the last two goals we have our whole team in the 18-yard box and they get two side-footers to score.

"I have no question about the sending off. If you go in reckless like that, you run the risk of leaving us with 10 men for a long, long time. We paid the penalty for that. Up to that point, we were knocking it around for fun. We looked like we were going to get more.

"They were dead. They were gone. The crowd was turning on them. They had run out of ideas and we kept catching them, continuously. I don't know what's going to happen after the sending off point, but up to that point we were very much the better team."

It would take Harris sometime to get back into the team after that. A three match ban followed, as did the arrival of Luke McCullough, a former Manchester United youngster who joined on loan from Doncaster.

The Swindon result did not derail things too much, though. Rovers somehow escaped with a 0-0 draw against Mansfield, much fancied for promotion, before beating Port Vale 1-0 thanks to a late goal from Norwood.

A couple of 1-1 draws followed, against Northampton and Colchester. Things were ticking along nicely. Tranmere had settled into the division and, even at this early stage, had positioned themselves at the right end of the table.

The only thing that was missing was an away win, something that would be rectified in the next game as they travelled to Brunton Park to face another team tipped for promotion, Carlisle.

It could have been very different though, as Richie Bennett hit the bar with a header before the hosts were presented with a golden chance to take the lead when Scott Davies was adjudged to have fouled Gary Liddle in the box.

Jamie Devitt stepped up to take the spot kick, firing a fierce shot to Davies' right, but the 'keeper stuck out a strong left palm and beat the ball away to safety.

"It was a big moment for me personally," Davies admits. "It was game over when I saved the penalty, but it was never a penalty anyway. The guy has tried to shoot, I've tried to block it, the ball has gone past the post and the referee has given a penalty. I couldn't believe it, because if I don't dive at his feet, he scores.

"I don't think goalkeepers get the credit for moments like that in games a lot of the time, unless it is a penalty, because there are times in games where you make saves at 0-0 or 1-0 to keep yourself in the game and then the team comes back to do their job at the other end of the field.

"I think personally, as well, I'd made a mistake against Colchester the week before. I punched one and the lad volleyed it in from the edge of the box. I put my hands up to it in the dressing room and the week after I remember the gaffer saying 'that just shows you that we have a different hero every week, even if you do make a mistake'.

"I've gone on to play over 200 games and I think that's a great example that if you play 200 games, more or less back to back, at any club, you have to have a mentality that you're not going to be perfect every week.

"One week you'll be a 5 or 6 out of 10, but if you're able to come back and hit your 7 or 8s and live at that level, that shows a strong character. On a personal level, that's proof of it."

After Davies' penalty save, Carlisle's heads dropped. Tranmere took the lead five minutes later when Tom Parkes turned Jake Caprice's low ball into his own net. Then Paul Mullin secured a 2-0 victory by curling a trademark right footed shot across goal and in at the far post.

"It felt like we belonged at that level after that," Davies continues. "It felt like the fans believed we belonged at the level. Even though Carlisle had the penalty, we were by far the better team and we showed we were a good team that day. We were comfortable too.

"I didn't realise it was our first away win! We weren't losing many games though, home or away. We'd only been beaten by Swindon on the road."

The win at Carlisle gave everyone associated with the club a real belief that a second successive promotion was achievable. It left Rovers on the cusp of the play-off places, behind Bury only on goal difference with 13 points from the first eight games.

Davies adds: "I said after the game 'we know in there what we're fighting for, but we're not going to say it as as group'. In the summer, we knew we had a good group, but we knew we'd have to look at the first five or ten games to see where we were at.

"Once we had seen those first five or ten matches, if I'm totally honest, I thought 'easy, we'll be in the top seven without a doubt'. We knew we'd be fighting for the play-offs. We wanted to get promoted."

Micky Mellon is always fairly pragmatic with his approach to management. Outwardly, at least, he rarely makes bold predictions or piles pressure on his team by setting targets. He simply takes things one game at a time. But he felt he knew he had a good squad on his hands.

"The games are what I call exams," he explains. "That's how they measure you. When we went up to Carlisle, they stuck to the plan and were a constant threat, keeping the shape and doing everything that we'd worked on, such as the principles we'd established in pre-season. They just seemed to get them.

"When a team starts to believe in their principles and starts getting results, it's great for the momentum of everything, because then they start building that trust in each other. That's what you start to see evolving.

"I was always wary though. I was never really carried away. I just thought it was a good start, but that's all it is. There was still a lot of football to be played. A lot of people would get to know us when they didn't at the start of the season. Then they started to respect us.

"I go one game to the next game. It's always the way I've been. I'd be too worried about thinking long term in football, because things can change very, very fast. But I was certainly pleased with where we were at, and I had a benchmark then. When you've got a benchmark as a manager, you can relate back to it and say 'no, we've fallen below that'. But I don't get carried away.

"Scott makes that penalty save though and it shows moments can change games or seasons. That's the reality of football, although perhaps not the beauty of it! Moments can change the course of a hell of a lot of stuff. That was certainly a massive three points."

Chapter Twenty Seven
A Dip In Form

Prenton Park had become a bit of fortress for Tranmere during the National League era. Although teams came to the Wirral and set out to frustrate the hosts by putting 11 men behind the ball and defending for the lives, they were not successful that often.

The game plan from the opposition was slightly more expansive in League Two. At least there was more emphasis on attacking football and less of an interest in time wasting from the first whistle.

Newport were the first side to inflict an away win at Prenton Park, Fraser Franks scoring in the fifth minute in a 1-0 win. Ironically, they were one of those teams for whom gamesmanship was a clear plan, although it only kicked in after half-time.

Rovers took plenty of joy in beating Lincoln 1-0 in their next home game. It was a tactical masterclass from Micky Mellon, who saw his side completely outplayed in the opening 45 minutes and somehow get in level at the break.

At that point he decided to switch things around, throwing an extra man into the midfield by bringing on Harvey Gilmour, a summer loan signing from Sheffield United, as a replacement for Cole Stockton.

It worked a treat. Tranmere were impressive in the second half, with the fifth midfielder helping them both defensively and in an attacking sense. They won 1-0, James Norwood getting the only goal before being sent off in injury time.

"I thought Lincoln were a better side than the one we played in the National League," says Scott Davies. "I was expecting crash, bang, wallop, but in the first half they footballed us to death. They were very good.

"I made a save off a header down low to my right of early doors and there was one cleared off the line as well. I think we survived the first half. I think it showed that they'd kicked on, where were we at?

"Second half, Nors scored a good goal. That was when you started to see that if I played well at one end and we kept the ball out, Nors could always nick one. We were starting to nick games.

"We'd done it the year before, but we were keeping that winning mentality. They were games that in my first year we'd probably lose. There were a lot of games last year that were on the edge, but they'd be defined by moments, such as a save by me or a block on the line by someone, then Nors would score.

"Those things always went in our favour, but not through luck. It was down to hard work. Beating Lincoln was a big moment. After the Carlisle game, we knew what we were fighting for and we had full belief that we had faced, especially in MK Dons, where we drew 1-1, Lincoln and even Carlisle, teams who were supposedly the better teams in the league and were paying the biggest money.

"We'd gone toe-to-toe with some of them and beaten them. We showed where we were as a group and the ability we had. Over the course of the season, it proved correct."

There were further home wins against the likes of Macclesfield, a Friday night special with Gilmour getting the winner, Crawley, who were battered 5-1 and Exeter.

James Norwood scored doubles against both Crawley and Exeter, taking his tally for the season to 12 goals by the start of November. He would add another six by the end of the calendar year.

It was a quite remarkable return. Every time the striker ran through on goal, you felt confident he would score. That had perhaps not been the case in his early years at Prenton Park, when he was often left cursing one on ones.

He was getting better and better, to the point where he was one of the most prolific players in the Football League. Scott Davies saw comparisons with an England international with whom he had played earlier in his career.

"I remember speaking to Nors in his first year and I compared him to Jamie Vardy," he says. "I played with him at Fleetwood and I was also at Blackpool when they had Brett Ormerod. He was a player who just used to run and chase after lost causes and earn something for himself.

"Nors reminded me of that. I always said to him that one day everything would start going for him if he just kept believing, and it did. Last season, against better players, he enabled us to be good defensively because we knew we could leave him up there on his own and he could do something.

"I can't credit him enough. I think he's brilliant. He's a great footballer and a great lad who was a huge part of the group and the team spirit we had here. I miss him loads but I wish him well.

"He deserves every little bit of success he goes and gets because he earned it here. I think he epitomised everything we were trying to do. Having been here for the time I've been here, I think a Tranmere fan recognises effort, desire and willingness to run through a brick wall for the shirt over anybody who can do ten step overs and put it in the top corner. He epitomised that. I hope he goes on to have an even better career, because I think he deserves it.

"When he was here, we always knew that if we stayed in the game, we'd score. That was part of our game plan. Anybody will say the same. We spoke about fighting for the nil, because if we stayed in the game, we had a goal scorer."

***

Whilst Tranmere were proving tough to beat on home soil, away from Prenton Park things were not quite as good. Davies talks of fighting for the nil, but they started to ship goals left, right and centre.

Rovers got away with conceding three at Morecambe and still won, sneaking a 4-3 victory thanks to a last gasp strike from Gilmour as they came from 3-2 down. But that win, in early October, would prove to be the final time they picked up three points on the road until mid-January.

They lost 3-1 to Forest Green, 3-2 to Crewe and 5-2 to Grimsby, a game in which they actually took the lead before crumbling after the half hour mark. Another three goals were conceded in a 3-2 defeat to relegation threatened Notts County before a 2-1 loss at Bury.

Five away league defeats in a row. It was not the form of a team fighting for a second successive promotion and it was having a serious impact on the team spirit.

"It was a very tough period," Davies continues. "I think the group started to fracture slightly. The gaffer started to make changes and it took a lot to keep us all together.

"I'm not going to blow smoke up my own arse too much, but I think it was big that we kept the group together. I remember taking the lads on a night out and keeping the spirit as high as we possibly could.

"When the FA Cup replay with Southport came around, it was put back a week due to TV, which meant we lost our Christmas party, so we had no team bonding prior to Christmas, which for me makes a big impact. It was very hard.

"I think we got into a bit of a losing mentality. But what the gaffer always does, and Mike Jackson, is detail. If you get the small details correct, over the course of the rest of the season, it'll take care of itself. We went back to basics to be honest. We went back to fighting for the zero."

Micky Mellon, though, is adamant that Tranmere did not deserve a Christmas party. He says they had not earned one because of their poor form and the only way to turn things around was by winning games. He also knew where things were going wrong.

"We stopped running," he says honestly. "Our intensity dropped. I remember the midweek game at Grimsby. It was an appalling performance, because we just came right off the plan. People weren't shifting across the pitch.

"We never went there wanting to run. We just tried to play the way that we fancied playing, rather than attacking the game. It was a big learning curve for us really, that we weren't going to get it all our own way, and the reason why we were doing well was because we were working bloody hard.

"We didn't work hard enough on the night. It was a windy night. We allowed the game to drift away from us. We scored first and then just came off all the things that were making us a decent team and all the things that I worry about all of the time.

"But we made sure that they knew about it after the game and before the next game. We told them that we're not good enough to go places and not work hard. It was a disappointing performance.

"As far as the Christmas party is concerned, we weren't doing well enough to have one. The priority was football. Team bonding is fine. They went out for a meal the other evening and that's fine. But the best teams that I've ever had, the successful ones, are the teams that were winning, and they had a great team spirit. You have that because you're winning games of football and you're achieving in your career.

"It's nothing to do with going paintballing. There's certainly a place for that, but never have I seen a better team bonding than a team winning, or a team coming home on a winning bus or celebrating after a game in the dressing room.

"That's the best way for team bonding. A team digging in for each other in the last ten minutes and getting a 1-0 win, that's team bonding. People often get it mixed up with other stuff or look for reasons. You'll find that the teams who are winning have the best team spirit.

"Did I notice that it was bending? It's nothing that I haven't been surprised about. Things will always dip a little bit when you go through a wee bit of a bad spell. Players will look at each other and they're very young in terms of maturity.

"What you don't know back then, you certainly know now: you've got to look at yourself first. But back then, you would be looking at everybody else because you don't know how to blame yourself and you don't want to.

"So you would have people saying it was them, this or that and then the people who aren't playing want to play because the team's not winning or performing the way it is. It's just a natural thing that happens in a football club.

"I know that I've just got to get them back to basics. I know that we've got to score the first goal and keep a clean sheet. Get them on that mentality or get their mentality on scoring the next goal. That'll eventually turn it all around."

At around this point, Liam Ridehalgh was introduced back into the team. He had suffered a lengthy injury absence, an unexpected one after seeing red in the National League play-off final, forcing Mellon to bring in Zoumana Bakayogo as left-back.

His first league appearance came as a substitute in that Grimsby game, and he admits getting back into the side was a bit of a struggle.

"It was a difficult start to the season for me," he says. "I did my knee in the tackle that got me sent off and it was a double blow for me really. It was tough to take, especially coming back into the Football League.

"I thought Zoum was doing brilliantly, as well. He started the season really well. He was up and down the wing, like he always is, and I was wondering how I was going to get back into the team.

"But I've never changed my approach to anything. I always just work hard and go home, because I know how quickly things can change in football.

"When I came into the side in November, I didn't really think about promotion. The gaffer goes on to us all the time about concentrating on the next game, and then the next game, and that's really what we do here."

Unfortunately for Ridehalgh, it did take some time before Tranmere found their second wind. Even the home form took a dip, with draws against Oldham and Yeovil, but defeats at Prenton Park were few and far between as they also registered victories over Morecambe and Cambridge.

They were, however, slipping behind the chasing pack in the promotion race. Something needed to happen if they were going to catch back up and reignite that push for a place in League One.

***

Away from their efforts in the league, Tranmere were also in the midst of their finest FA Cup run for four years, reaching the third round for the first time since 2015, when they lost 6-2 to Premier League side Swansea.

They did not make life easy for themselves, despite being handed what was, on paper at least, a straight forward draw. Firstly, they welcomed National League South side Oxford City to Prenton Park, where a late James Norwood equaliser spared their blushes in a 3-3 stalemate. That took the tie to a replay, which Rovers thankfully won 2-0, Norwood again on target alongside strike partner Paul Mullin.

That game was also notable for Liam Ridehalgh making his long awaited comeback from injury. As luck would have it, the man in charge of the replay was Craig Hicks, the same referee who showed him that red card for lunging in on Ricky Shakes.

"We didn't say anything to each other about that at the time," he laughs. "But I've seen a photograph and he's got a very cheesy grin on his face, so I think he liked that one more than me! I got a lot of stick from the lads about it."

The victory over Oxford earned Tranmere a local derby with Southport in the second round. Again, this was a fixture they should have won comfortably given the two division gap between the teams, but the initial tie at Prenton Park ended 1-1.

The replay, shown live on BT Sport, saw Rovers put things right as Connor Jennings struck twice, including one magnificent volley from long range, in a 2-0 win. And that teed up a quite magnificent third round clash: Tottenham Hotspur at home.

This was the kind of occasion Tranmere had yearned after for years. It had been some time since they had welcomed such a big club to Prenton Park. At the turn of the century, such games were fairly regular, with the likes of Leeds, Southampton, West Ham and Sunderland all sent packing.

But the club's decline in league status had also seen them become significantly less successful in the cup competitions. So it was no surprise that the visit of Mauricio Pochettino's side, who would reach the Champions League final in June, drew plenty of interest.

Prenton Park was a sell out for the occasion, although hundreds of Spurs fans purchased their tickets without any intention of making the journey to the Wirral. They just wanted the loyalty points for later on in the competition. The match was also chosen for live TV coverage on a Friday night, all valuable revenue in the club coffers.

Not everything went to plan, though. Tranmere started superbly, pressing the visitors, who included Dele Alli, Lucas Moura, Heung-Min Son and Davinson Sanchez in their starting line up.

Yet despite all their good work, Serge Aurier struck just before the break and it completely deflated the hosts. They went on to lose 7-0, with Fernando Llorente netting a hat-trick and second half substitute Harry Kane getting on the scoresheet.

"The game for me as the manager was a nightmare," admits Mellon. "I've got this thing at the minute about football and sport. When you play Tottenham and you're Tranmere, it's difficult to see the sport in it, because the players that they have are so far ahead that if it was a boxing match, you wouldn't let a heavyweight fight a flyweight. It wouldn't be allowed. In golf, you'd have a handicap.

"To go toe-to-toe with Tottenham at that stage of the season always worries you, because you think if you get a heavy defeat, how will it affect the group? Yes, people will say you never expected to win anyway, but I always had one eye on the fact that I might have to pick things back up again.

"If we get tanked, yes, it's great for the finances and everything, but I've got to try and pick a group up. It will affect them, trust me. And it did. But we quickly sort of got over it because we'd done it before when we were at Shrewsbury.

"We had tough games against Premier League teams there, such as Manchester United. We had to get ready as quickly as possible because we had bigger fish to fry for Tranmere."

The players, meanwhile, were left somewhat red faced by the result. Yes, Spurs had a strong team, worth hundreds of millions of pounds, but 7-0 is a deflating scoreline regardless of the opposition.

"It hit us pretty hard," admits Jennings. "Losing 7-0 hurt me. I was a bit embarrassed. It took a good few games to get that out of our system. We had done well up until the 40th minute when they took the lead. After that, the game totally changed.

"The only positive out of it was that the manager was able to bring in a few players in January who I thought were the perfect match. They were brilliant. They fitted right in. We had one game when we all started, against Northampton on a Tuesday night, and we played some good football but we didn't really get the result."

Chapter Twenty Eight
January Transfer Window

You would not normally associate Tranmere with being particularly busy in the January transfer window. Indeed, aside from Micky Adams making significant changes in 2015, rarely in recent years have Rovers added that much to their squad during the winter months.

It would also be fair to say that those who came in had generally not been too successful. Rob Taylor and Adam Dugdale were a couple of the arrivals under Adams, whilst Stephen Arthurworrey, David Amoo and Ryan Brunt are just a handful of the other players to have joined in January in years gone by.

Some, though, made an impact, including Tony Warner and Andy Robinson. But you perhaps have to go back to 2008 for the most impressive transfer of all; when Ian Thomas-Moore made his return to Prenton Park, rejecting a move to Oldham in favour of playing under his dad Ronnie.

Over the next two and a half seasons, the striker would be a vital cog in Tranmere's wheel. He scored on his debut in a 2-0 win away at former club Leeds, and in total netted 38 times in 141 appearances.

When Tranmere were outside the Football League, there was no need for them to get too involved in the January transfer window, because the regulations did not apply to National League clubs. Likewise, before they went down, they were still permitted to sign players on emergency loans, even once the deadline had passed.

FIFA, however, recently tightened those rules. The emergency loan window is no more for clubs in the Football League and therefore when Micky Mellon wanted to patch up some problems in his squad, January was his only option.

Tranmere had been faltering. They badly needed some additions. But Mellon insists this was not a defining moment for the campaign if they were going to re-energise a promotion push that was slipping away.

"I don't think the January window was make or break," he says. "I just think Tranmere are a continual thing. Even now, we just try to keep making it better. There's never a plan to get promoted. The plan is just to get better.

"Read about Toyota. They're the best company on the planet for continual progress and finding ways of fixing things and continually moving forward. Keep trying to improve it every day. As you move through, look for things to make better.

"That's all we do, whether that be with the playing staff, the way we train or the facilities. All the time, we're continually making things better, even now. Did I bring those players in to get promoted? No, I brought them in to continue the development of the football club.

"It's just a continual improvement. That's where I mentally am at the minute. I believe if I keep improving it, the results will take care of themselves."

With some adjustment to the squad required, Mellon was, in theory, assisted by that run in the FA Cup. They had three games televised, each bringing in some much needed funds from BT Sport, as well as collecting the gate receipts from the Spurs fixture.

Mellon, though, saw little of it added to his transfer budget. "It was a big game because it was what the club needed," he says. "It needed a big game to keep the momentum of the club moving forward, because don't forget we were recovering. So it was big in terms of media interest and the spotlight coming back on Tranmere. For a long time, we hadn't had that.

"In terms of the finances, it didn't make that much difference to my budget. We didn't start to suddenly lash money around. We brought players in, but we also moved some on, like Cole Stockton and Ritchie Sutton.

"When they went, I got their wages for some of those who came in. You can see the chunks of money leaving the club and I'd get those chunks back. Maybe because of the Tottenham game, the chairman would add a certain amount on top of that, and that's the way it's always been here.

"I wouldn't even expect the money that Tranmere made from that though. It went towards helping to secure the club's long term existence. The chairman is very clever, and it's been a real learning curve to me, how he does it. He creates sustainable business around about the club in order to feed the football side.

"He won't blow that money into the atmosphere and not allow us to see the long term benefits of it. That money went into fixing things like the Rec Centre roof and repairing a lot of the financial damage that was done for years because we didn't have that kind of funding.

"So there would have been a little bit that came to me, but nothing that would make you say 'wow, that's significant'. The chairman runs the club very, very well and that's why it's in the position that it's in, because we're not stupid with it."

It proved to be a busy month. Harvey Gilmour made his switch from Sheffield United a permanent one, whilst Ishmael Miller arrived on a free transfer from Oldham and Chris Dagnall came from Bury. A trio of players also arrived on loan, with Sid Nelson, Ben Pringle and Kieron Morris joining from Millwall, Grimsby and Walsall respectively. Nobody, though, had the same kind of impact as David Perkins.

The midfielder, 36-years old and with bleached blonde hair, made the switch from Rochdale. In the previous season, he had been promoted to the Championship with Wigan and he brought bags of experience with him to Prenton Park.

Mellon knew him well, too. He was Barnsley's assistant manager whilst Perkins was plying his trade at Oakwell. And although some people were mystified by his signing, the boss knew exactly what he was getting.

"I loved that people scoffed at him signing," he admits. "I love being able to sit here now and say that none of the scoffers, or certainly not many, having come back and said 'Mellon wasn't stupid'.

"An awful, awful lot of them couldn't believe that I was bringing in a lad of that age and at that stage in the season. But I was probably just waiting for the impact. I knew it was going to happen. I knew how good he was and how good a professional he was. I knew if I could keep him fit what a massive player he'd be for us.

"On and off the pitch, he lifted everything the moment he walked in the door. He started to do pull-ups and all of these players, who had been non-league players the season before, were looking at him and going 'oh that's why you're 36 and you're still playing!'

"He'd be doing 100 pull-ups every day throughout the day. He wouldn't leave the building until he'd done it. All of a sudden, I had a pull-up group! He had an influence on all of them.

"I didn't say too much about what he was like on the pitch. I just allowed it to happen. The first moment that I saw him doing something, I listened and the crowd went 'what's happening here?' I knew I was bringing in a lad of great influence who would drive us on again with his standards and his quality and that's what he did.

"I was so pleased that I got it exactly right with that one, because if I didn't, the scoffers would have been all over me like a ton of bricks. I probably gained a lot of trust from a lot of people with that one."

In terms of impact, Perkins is arguably one of Tranmere's most successful signings in years. It took him a couple of games to settle, but once he did, he was outstanding. His influence was felt throughout the club, both on and off the field, and Scott Davies reckons he dragged the performance level of his teammates up.

"David Perkins is a great lad," he says. "I was with him when I signed professionally at Morecambe at 17 or 18. He was four or five years ahead of me, so we both went the same route. I've known him well for years. He's a character!

"I think the biggest thing when he came in was that the gaffer was trying to change the mentality. It wasn't a non-league mentality, but I think it was almost settling for being a League Two team instead of pushing on.

"Look at Perkins. He was 36-years old when he came in, he'd played in the Championship for a chunk of his career, earned good money, played for good clubs and won promotions. He had the right to sit there with a cigar in his mouth and then come to Tranmere for a final pay day.

"But after the goalkeepers, he was the first person out on the training pitch every day. He was at the front of every running session, he was the loudest in every training session and he worked the hardest.

"I think I'm doing people a disservice if I say he embarrassed them into working hard, because we had a group of players who did work hard, people like Jay Harris. But you get ones who are floating in every squad. They're coasting through the rest of the season.

"He embarrassed them into working at a higher level, because they looked at him and thought 'fucking hell, if a 36-year old who has been there, seen it and done it can do it every day, why can't I?' So the level of training came up and then you go into the games and it became a bit of a joke, the amount of running that he did. He was here, there and everywhere.

"So I think Ollie Banks would then look at him and think 'I want to play at the level that he played at'. Jay Harris probably looked at him and, knowing Jay, wanted to be better than him and be even more competitive, so his level came up again.

"With where he'd been and what he'd done already, to still be doing it and ahead of everyone else, I think it raised everyone's game. They wanted to compete with him and they wanted to live with him. He set a standard, it's a simple as that."

All the January arrivals made an impact. Even if he only made one and a half appearances, Ishmael Miller had his say on the season, scoring on his debut away at Cheltenham. Sid Nelson would come into his own at the tail end of the season after Mark Ellis injured his knee ligaments, whilst Kieron Morris and Ben Pringle had sprinklings of success from out wide.

Each of the six signings brought something different to the side, be it their defensive capabilities, leadership qualities or ability to make something happen in the final third. Mellon explained why he targeted each particular player.

"If you look at all their backgrounds, each signing was a Football League player," he continues. "I work really hard on trying to improve my knowledge by going around, finding things and trying to bring it back to Tranmere.

"One of the things that I read about was The All Blacks and that they try and make sure they have plenty of caps on the table. So if they're going into a game, they look at the amount of caps, the amount of experience that they have. Basically, I just tried to put some caps on the table.

"They had to be good players, but because we were going through that bit of a wobble, I wanted to make sure that I added more caps to the group. More appearances, more experiences, good professionals.

"I wanted to move it forward. I wanted to teach the players the proper mentality of a Football League player. In order to be able to do that, I had to bring in good professionals. Ishmael Miller is a good pro, David Perkins is a great pro. So are all of the rest of them. They're experienced and they had experience of success. It was calculated, what we did. The chairman was involved. It worked for us."

***

There was another key contract signed during the January transfer window. Micky Mellon put pen to paper on a new two and a half year deal, meaning he would be staying at Prenton Park until the end of the 2020/21 campaign.

This was a huge bit of business for the club. Tranmere had a manager who had already led them to one promotion. He was targeting a second. His success had not gone unnoticed.

At the time, Mark Palios described Mellon's signature as the club's best bit of business during the window, whilst Mellon himself added: "When you're at a football club and you have such a personal relationship with it, it makes it that little bit more special when you're winning games.

"The fans will be able to see I'm a no bluffer type of guy. I wear my heart on my sleeve. When I get involved in anything that's good about Tranmere, I celebrate it like a fan.

"Of course we're very professional, but we also have that wee added bit, when a club means so much to you, to achieve things with it. That's a really nice place to be for a manager."

Reflecting now, Palios stands by his statement. "One of the things I think about professional footballers is they are a little bit fickle," he says. "Once they think the manager is going, they'll think they outlast him and he becomes less effective as a consequence. Lame duck management, I call it.

"Look at Manchester United when Alex Ferguson said he was going at the end of the season, first time around. He had a really difficult time with the players, because they knew their contracts were going beyond him. It wasn't them they were worried about. They'd outlasted him.

"So one of the things you've got to be fairly careful about is not to undermine the manager in that scenario, because he becomes less effective and it becomes a vicious, downward spiral. As a result, he's not getting the results he should get.

"Another thing that was important was not turning a disappointment into a crisis. We had a disappointing December. I was disappointed with early January, including the Tottenham result. I don't think a Tranmere team should fold in the way it did. I didn't need to say anything to Micky, because he's well motivated anyway.

"At the moment, he's the tenth longest serving manager in the Football League, which is an inditement on the game really. So there is an element of stability, and then you're always building on that."

Mellon is able to reflect on that key word, stability, too. He thinks signing a new contract helped settle everybody down, from the players to the fans, as it put to bed any speculation about being prized away by another club.

"If there's a manager doing well, then things are going to get said," he says. "The football world is a small one. If anybody thinks that they need a manager and then they look and they see who the managers doing well are, that manager can become a target. Nobody is daft enough not to think that.

"I sat down with the chairman and I was on a rolling contract. I said 'I want to know where I'm going to be for the next two and a half to three years. Let's sit down and make it so that you know I'm here, I know I'm here, then get on with the job'.

"It settles everyone down, including the players, because they know who they're working with. I'm going to be here for the next two and a half years, unless the chairman comes to me and says 'Micky, that's a great opportunity for you to go and manage X'. That's the relationship that me and him have.

"The players know the manager is going to be here though, so it settles them down, and it settles the fans down too. We felt that it was just the right time to do that and I was comfortable doing that."

Chapter Twenty Nine
Mansfield Away

Tranmere's promotion charge looked like it could be drifting away after they visited Mansfield on January 26th. A 2-1 defeat at home to Swindon a week earlier meant they had registered just three victories in eleven league games, a run that saw Micky Mellon's side slip out of the play-off places.

The Stags, with one of the biggest budgets in the division, were one of Rovers' main promotion rivals. They had a team packed full of experience, thanks to the likes of Neal Bishop, Krystian Pearce and Jacob Mellis, whilst Tyler Walker and Jorge Grant provided youthful exuberance.

The latter was a thorn in Tranmere's side all afternoon, rolling around whenever a defender came near him, but also proving a tricky customer to handle thanks to his quick feet. Indeed, he netted the opener after just 22-minutes, brilliantly firing a free-kick into the top corner.

Rovers tried to rally, but their afternoon went from bad to worse before half time as Ollie Banks was shown a second yellow card for hacking down Malvind Benning right in front of the dugouts. They created a few chances after the break, but the damage had already been done and they eventually succumbed to a 3-0 defeat, Grant adding another and Nicky Ajose also finding the back of the net.

It rounded off a miserable afternoon for Tranmere, but some felt the result was a little harsh. "We were alright up until we got a man sent off," says Micky Mellon. "I was looking at the game and we were well in it against one of the fancied teams in the division. It was good. I was just thinking: let's stay in it."

"I look at a game, watching how we're defending and making sure it's how we should defend and nobody is coming off that, including the midfield or the frontmen, and then I'm looking at how we're attacking. We were sticking to that. We were fine. We were cruising and we were well in the game. They obviously have some talented players and it was two different systems, plus things were breaking here and there for them and you have to accept that. But it was fine.

"Then Ollie stupidly gets sent off. It was a stupid, crazy tackle and it put us down to 10 men. From that point, you know you've got it all to do and we just couldn't get going.

"But the weird thing was, we put on Ben Pringle and David Perkins was making his second appearance, and even with 10 men, the game suddenly turned. We started to knock it around and really became a threat.

"Of course we lost 3-0, which isn't what you want to do against the teams you're challenging with. But it wasn't about coming away from that and changing everything. It was about getting them right and back to the way we play and getting people like Ollie disciplined and telling him that he let us down because he put us down to 10 men in a big game.

"So we say what we have to say after the game, come in on Monday, do the DVD work and get back on the grass to get them back on track. We had a little bark at them to tell them that we weren't accepting it because they'd let the project or the team down, so get your arses back in gear and let's get going again, which they did."

Scott Davies was put up for post match media duties. Two of the goals Rovers conceded had seen the 'keeper stop fierce shots from distance, but the ball had bounced off him and with no defenders following in, the rebound had been tucked home. It was a tough afternoon, but despite the result, he was in no mood to give up on a second successive promotion.

"Correct me if I'm wrong," he retorted, "But is it not the first time all season we've lost two on the bounce? We're in this league. We're fighting in this league. We're fighting for the play-offs. I don't know where your question is going, to be honest.

"There's no dent in the confidence. We're a group who fight hard every week and go out there and put everything on the line. We'll continue to do so. We'll fight for each other. If you look at the season as a whole, it's a lot more positive than negative."

The result left Rovers five points off the play-off places, but rewind just over twelve months and they were sitting in sixteenth place in the National League after 1-1 draw at Hartlepool. They eventually finished the season in second place, and Davies insisted a repeat charge could happen.

"There's 17 games to go," he continued. "At the start of the season, you'd look at these games and maybe these are the ones you'd think you might not get points from. The ones you can get, you take. It's one scratched off.

"We've got a lot of home games to go. We know how many games we need to win. Bring it on. We're a confident group. We've got good players. We'll be fighting until the end.

"We're new to the league. We weren't expected to go and do what we've done. It's football. It's going to happen. It'll happen to better teams than us."

Davies was fuming. Tranmere, as a club, had been on the up because everybody had been fighting for the same thing. But here he was, facing questions over whether their season was over before the end of January.

"I think people lost belief in us," he reflects. "I go back to that game all the time. I'll never forget it because I was shocked. There were 90 mile an hour winds, it was pissing down with rain and we went and got beat, but by a team who probably had one of the top three budgets in the division and who were expected to piss the league. Plus we had 10 men for more than half the game!

"If you'd said prior to the season starting that we'd get beat at Mansfield in the middle of January with 10 men, I would have probably agreed.

"I wasn't shocked by the fans, because I think we got to a place where they believed that much in us, that any time we didn't win, they'd get disgruntled, but that was down to our success and how good we'd been. They just thought 'fucking hell, we shouldn't be getting beat there', which I can take.

"Some of the reporters after the game though - they should be on our side and not against us. I've said it on numerous occasions, when everyone pulls together, we're a more successful team and football club, from top to bottom.

"I faced a few difficult questions after the game and I came out fighting, firstly because I believed in the group, secondly because I thought what they were saying was nonsense, and thirdly, because it was January! It wasn't April or May. We should be judged over a season. We still knew what we were fighting for. We had a couple of new players. Was it a bad defeat? Yes. Was that the end of that team? No. I was a bit disappointed with it.

"After the game, our secretary Tim Roberts sent a text to me, because I'd made my own way home from the game, and it was about my interview. I said to him: 'I want to give it to someone'. I was absolutely fuming. He calmed me down and said 'you'll get your day'. Every couple of weeks I'd still be wanting to give it to them. But he kept saying it, 'no, you'll get your day'.

"There are certain folk, and fans as well, I don't know what it is, but they like to see you fail. That hurt me at the time because of what we were doing as a football club and where we'd got it back to. The feel good factor that 99.9% of people had was surrounding us. The 0.1% of people were happy to bring us down.

"I can only believe that when the club fell from where it fell from, that was probably relevant more than ever. To be able to stick two fingers up at them come May, I was delighted."

It was a somewhat out of character interview from Davies. He is always one to fight his own corner, especially when he feels there has been an injustice, but he will often do so in a much more reserved way. Not that day though, and he thinks it was because he was beginning to share skipper duties with Steve McNulty.

"Big Mac was still captain but he was coming out of the team," he continued. "Maybe it was a bit of a penny dropping moment for me, too, where I had to take on the responsibility, but I believed in the group.

"Anybody who knows me knows that I speak my mind. I don't hold back. If I see something, I'll say it how I see it, no airs and graces. That was just what I thought at the time. They were my emotions. It was exactly what I felt. I was speaking for the group and if they saw that and took belief from it and took some sort of comfort from it, then great. I'm just the kind of character who stands up for what I believe in."

The players did see the interview. They often watch what their teammates have said pre or post match, and take a particular interest in what Micky Mellon's got to say as well, something the manager has mentioned in the past. They hate it when he forgets to mention one of them when recounting his injury list.

One of those who did watch what Davies had to say was Liam Ridehalgh and he says they all took heart from the fighting spirit the goalkeeper had shown. "I can remember feeling very upset that we'd lost the game," he says. "Ollie Banks got sent off and we got battered really.

"After that, it just picked up. I think Scott Davies' interview after the game really helped. All of us look at the interviews because we care and it helped us. It gave us self belief."

There were still 17 games to go and 51 points left to play for in the season. Tranmere's form would soon pick up once the new signings bedded in, although two of them, Sid Nelson and Kieron Morris, were yet to arrive. And with over a third of the campaign still to go, Davies knew there was still plenty left to play for.

"Without doubt, knowing what we'd been through the year before, coming from behind, gave us the belief we could do it again" he continued. "Honestly, the reaction after the Mansfield game, I couldn't believe it. Even if we were 10 points off the play-offs, there were still about 50 to play for.

"I've been in football long enough to know it's not the team who are 1st to 7th in January who win anything. It's the team who does it in the second half of the season. The team who have legs to carry on. It's a 46 game season.

"We've all seen teams start well when the weather's nice and then come January, they start to plateau and their legs have gone. We are as fit as anything. We worked hard and kept going as the season wore on. Our fitness coaches were unbelievable.

"We work on detail I reckon more than any team in the league. We've got an analyst who goes through everything. Every goal gets combed over. The goalkeeping coaches were unbelievable with me, the same with Michael Jackson with the back four. Over the course of a season, you end up where you deserve to be and we knew that come May, we'd be where we deserved to be. We knew we had a group that should be there."

Tranmere would lose their next game, beaten 2-1 by Northampton at Prenton Park. Nelson and Morris both made their debuts, whilst Pringle and Perkins were also involved.

After that, though, their form picked up dramatically. Davies' interview had the impact intended of it. The season was nowhere near over.

Chapter Thirty
Seven Wins In A Row

Tranmere's home defeat to Northampton was their third in a row and left them in tenth place in the table, eight points off the play-offs with 16 games to go.

It was an irritating evening for the hosts, who had their chances, but could not add to James Norwood's strike midway through the first half. Two goals from Sam Hoskins proved decisive.

"We're very frustrated," said Micky Mellon afterwards. "You'd have to say that we've lost goals at the worst possible times. That's has a massive factor in the way the game was played.

"We kept trying to pass it. There are loads of things that I could say that we could've been better at but giving away an early goal changes the mentality and everyone wants to force it.

"It would've taken that wee bit of quality in vital areas or a wee bit of magic and imagination to try and open up a whole body of defensive players on their 18-yard box.

"We lose the goal when we do, just before halftime which obviously is the worst possible time to lose it, if you're getting back into it again. I think that was pretty much the story of the game."

The belief that Tranmere could make the top seven remained unwavering within the dressing room, though. This was the first time a number of the January arrivals had all played together, with Ben Pringle, Sid Nelson, David Perkins and Kieron Morris all in the starting line up.

Four days later, Rovers finally got that allusive win as they beat

Stevenage 2-0. Morris got the ball rolling, nodding home Connor Jennings' brilliant clipped cross at the back post on the stroke of half-time. Norwood doubled the lead after the break and everybody at Prenton Park breathed a sigh of relief when the final whistle came.

"We must give the lads great credit for the performance," ordered Mellon at full-time. "We have, quite rightly for a team who's so proud of their team, taken a lot of criticism because we haven't won games.

"We knew we had to man up today and try and get that first goal and keep a clean sheet. All credit to the boys and staff for doing that. They put in a great performance, but we've got to keep them going. The mentality was the big thing today, from the first minute to the last."

The visitors even ended that game with nine men. Ben Nugent was the first to be dismissed, chopping down Jennings and picking up a second yellow card, before Elijah Adebayo was issued a straight red late on for a clear elbow on Mark Ellis.

That led to a furious outburst from Stevenage boss Dino Maamria, who even accused Rovers of some underhand tactics. He fumed: "Tranmere probably won the game in the referee's dressing room at 1.45. They do this hand-shake with the referee and captains before the game. I sent my assistant Steve Gettings.

"Their assistant Mike Jackson complained straight away about the referee for their game on Tuesday night. I thought it was poor for him to allow him to do that. It was bizarre."

It was a bitter retort from Maamria. His team, themselves chasing a spot in the play-offs, had been beaten fair and square. Tranmere had lift off. That gap to the top seven was already down to just six points.

Seven days later, they drew an untidy game at Cambridge 0-0. The hosts probably shaded the contest, but they were kept at bay by a solid back four who, when beaten, could rely upon Scott Davies to make some fine saves and ensure a second clean sheet in a row was kept.

After that, Tranmere just got on a roll. Port Vale were beaten 2-1 courtesy of a Norwood brace, before Jennings bagged the only goal in a 1-0 victory over Notts County.

Both those teams were around the relegation zone, with the latter subsequently going down to the National League. Rovers, if they were to sustain, or re-energise, a promotion push were expected to win both fixtures.

The next test was significantly sterner; a 500 mile round trip to take on Exeter, a play-off rival who sat three points above Micky Mellon's side in the table. Win here, and that race for a spot in the top seven would really open up.

The visitors were excellent. They had a few chances early on, with Johnny Smith and David Perkins seeing shots from inside the box blocked, whilst Luke McCullough fired into the side netting.

With half an hour on the clock, they took a well deserved lead, unsurprisingly through Norwood, returning to haunt his former club. The striker latched on to a wonderful clipped pass from Ellis and converted from just inside the box, although it was a somewhat fortuitous finish, with a huge deflection wrong-footing the goalkeeper.

Once ahead, Tranmere knew how to front run. They had been good all season at closing games out. This fixture was different though. Exeter threw everything at them, and it took a quite stunning display from Davies in goal to keep them at bay.

The Rovers 'skipper made a brace of world class saves to deny Jonathan Forte and Hiram Boateng, somehow stretching out his left palm to tip a shot from the latter away from danger.

"If I'm totally honest, I think the save in the play-off semi-final against Aldershot was better," he says. "The ball was headed back across and Scott Rendell heads it back across me.

"But it epitomised where we were at the time. We had Nors at one end and me at the other, as well as bodies on the line.

"I'm a big believer in getting rewards for your work. I've worked my balls off. I work my balls off every day. Does it go for me every week? Probably not. But I work my balls off in training every day for moments like that, and it was a good moment.

"I didn't think I was overly busy in the game. It was just two saves late on, and obviously that particular save was a big one. But it wasn't just the saves. There was then the desire from Jake Caprice on the line and they were still piling men forward, but we put our bodies on the line.

"It epitomised where we were as a group. How many fans did we take too? It was superb. At one point we were looking at automatic promotion and that game summed up what we became as a team. Fight for the nil as best you can and we've got a goalscorer who can go and win us games at the other end."

One man watching on from the sidelines that day was Liam Ridehalgh. The defender missed out due to illness, with Zoumana Bakayogo taking his place at left-back. And the 90 minutes that unfolded on the pitch convinced him that Tranmere were heading for the top seven.

"We defended brilliantly," he adds. "Scotty pulled off some outrageous saves. We were trying to get in the top three at one point, but after that game, I 100% knew we'd get in the play-offs.

"Norwood's goal is heavily deflected but he's a goalscorer, and when you're a goalscorer, those kind of things happen. It happened for him that day and if I remember rightly, it was a brilliant ball by Mark Ellis.

"But Scott Davies pulled a brilliant save out of the bag, there were some blocks on the line too. We were under heavy pressure in that game and I thought we showed brilliant character."

However when Micky Mellon reflects on the game, he picks the holes in Tranmere's performance. "I have an unbelievable memory for games," he confesses, "And even now I can remember that with about 20 minutes to go, I didn't like us because I felt we went on the back foot. I didn't like that.

"I had something to work on and something to speak to them about. I watched the DVD of that and can then ask why did they go on the back foot? Why, all of a sudden, is he not getting out to press there? Why is the back four moving up and down and across? I would think that way. I'd only be thinking about trying to make it better."

The manager also refuses to entertain the idea that he knew from that moment onwards that Rovers were going to be fine in their quest for a play-off spot, adding: "I would be worried if I thought like that. I take games in isolation.

"Don't get me wrong, I'm not trying to be clever, I know when a game is a big game and when a result is a big result. But I tend to, after Exeter for example, ask what was good in that.

"Did I think there was a game when I knew we were going to make the play-offs? I don't think so. I knew that we had good results. A lot of them were big results. I remember when we beat Aldershot here in the National League and we were brilliant. We beat them 2-0 in a league game. That was a pretty complete performance. It was brilliant.

"So I know when we've been good. But I'm always wary of getting over the line until you cross the line. Of course there are games I'd like to win or ones that I know it was good that we won. I wouldn't say that I suddenly sat here and thought we were going to make the play-offs, though."

***

The win at St James' Park had propelled Tranmere into the play-off zone. They continued their fine run by beating Crewe 1-0, before hammering Grimsby 4-1, with both results coming at Prenton Park.

Victory number six came down at Colchester, another success against a side gunning for the play-offs and against a manager Micky Mellon knew pretty well, given he and John McGreal had been teammates with Rovers during the 1990s.

A week later, Ollie Banks, James Norwood and Manny Monthe were on target as Tranmere beat Carlisle 3-0, strengthening their stranglehold on a play-off spot as they stayed fourth in the table, seven points clear of eighth place.

This was also their seventh victory in a row. No Rovers team had achieved that since the great Johnny King side of 1990 won nine on the spin. From the misery of Mansfield, they had become a force to be reckoned with.

"We just felt so good," admits Connor Jennings. "We never felt like we were going to lose. Every time Norwood had a shot, it went in or we got a corner or something like that.

"The defence were obviously tight too. We were looking pretty strong and we were all so confident. Me and Nors were linking up well, but all over the pitch we were so smooth. We were working hard and getting the results.

"The Colchester win away was big, so was a 1-0 win over Crewe. It was a very scrappy game, and a big one, but Norwood scored. We were just taking things game by game. We felt pretty confident, even against the top teams."

Scott Davies had been through this kind of run before. He was in goal for Fleetwood when they went 18 unbeaten in 2011, en route to landing the National League title. That experience was a huge help.

"The belief grew with every game," he adds. "I think we went back to basics. We went back to fighting for the nil. We got beat by Mansfield and Northampton and had a meeting on the Thursday, where we just said 'fight for the 0. Somebody will score. Nors will score.'

"We started fighting for that and if you look at those results, a lot of them were by just a goal. That's how we played. Mark Ellis came in and did a good job. I had to step up with Steve McNulty out injured. I had to be more of a character because we'd lost him.

"He was our leader for two or three years. Other people had to step up as well, like Connor Jennings. You saw the spirit and the fight in the group."

It really was a staggering run of form, but Mellon, who was in charge of that Fleetwood team eight years earlier, refuses to take too much of the credit for the way things turned around in such a short space of time.

"A lot of people will give the manager some kind of credit for that, and managers will take the credit," he says. "They'll say 'I was the one who got them to win seven in a row' and then they'll lose a game and say 'the players just didn't perform today' or 'the players weren't up for it'.

"Managers should take the blame for victory and defeat. I say all the time that all I did was set the standards. I'm 'the standards man'. I make sure the agreed principles that we play to, they got back on them. They were on them mentally, physically and tactically.

"When they cross that line, if they're mentally at it and they're motivated and ready to get going, you can do all the shouting you want, but the individual is the chief executive of you. You will determine how you're going to win. It's not me telling you to move your arse or move faster. If you don't want to run, you won't run. At the end of the day, you won't give me everything.

"They just did that. We never changed anything. We just got back on track in how we believed Tranmere should play; the standards, the tempo and the intensity. If the players bring the qualities to that, away you go.

"Defensively, everybody knew what they were doing, and attacking wise, everybody knew what they were doing. Every phase in the game, we all knew what we were doing.

"We were winning games, so we liked each other. Team spirit was good, amazingly, but we never went paintballing in that spell or went to play pool! We just won games.

"We built up a head of steam and belief comes in, because you're at that stage of the season where you can look at the league table and think 'that looks quite nice'. The fans are getting excited and there's a lot of good things going on."

***

There was a stage when it looked like Tranmere could even trouble the top three, but sadly it was not to be. Their winning run came to an end with a 2-0 defeat in a rearranged game at Oldham. Although, the way over 2,000 traveling supporters reacted at full-time would have had you thinking Rovers had won.

"It was quite a flat ending," Davies admits. "I was disappointed, but I'll never forget it. The fans after we were beaten were amazing. It showed where we'd come in a short space of time.

"I would say 99.9% of them were unbelievable with us. Just imagine if that 2,500 had booed us off and called us this and that? Would we have responded the week after? I don't know. But the way that they applauded us off the pitch meant we came back and carried on."

Rovers reacted by drawing 0-0 with Newport in their next game before getting back to winning ways with a 2-1 victory over MK Dons, although that game was soured somewhat by the sight of David Perkins limping off after handing his side the lead with a superb strike from the edge of the box.

Their chances of finishing in the top three were diminishing though, particularly after an undeserved 1-0 defeat at Prenton Park to Forest Green. A trip to Sincil Bank then yielded a point in a goalless stalemate with Lincoln, enough to hand The Imps the League Two title.

That meant Tranmere had to win their final two fixtures if they wanted to sneak into the top three, but next up was the visit of Bury, who themselves only needed a draw to secure automatic promotion and, in turn, ensure Rovers would be consigned to the play-offs.

James Norwood handed the hosts the lead after just 11 minutes as Micky Mellon's outfit dominated the first half. But they failed to add to their advantage, and Bury were like a different team after the break, with Danny Mayor equalising before the hour mark.

From then on, Ryan Lowe's side played with confidence and swagger. When the final whistle went, they celebrated on the Prenton Park turf, much to the dismay of the Super White Army who had witnessed similar scenes only four years earlier. Yet the dressing room was not too dismayed that the chance of automatic promotion had gone.

"I think we knew that as much as we were fighting for automatic promotion and we'd have loved an extra four week holiday, we were realistically going to end up in the play-offs," admits Davies. "We gave ourselves a little bit too much to do, but we did unbelievably well to get to within touching distance of the top three.

"We never got disheartened. It never felt like we were disappointed after the Bury game when we drew and it put an end to our automatic hopes, whereas I think if we'd gone to the last day and then not done it, it would have been a disappointment.

"So we knew what we were fighting for. We went to the second to last game with a chance of automatic promotion in our first season back in the league, we all knew where we were at. We looked at the play-offs and I don't think there was anybody there to be scared of."

Connor Jennings agrees with his skipper, adding: "Against Bury, we played well in the first half. Second half, they came out of the traps and got the goal to draw it. That was gutting, but the best thing was it was a game before the last match of the season.

"We could digest it over a few days, but we knew we had the play-offs. If it was the last game, it might have hurt a few of the lads, but we had time to get over it, crack on and get our heads down.

"We'd had the same in the National League for the past two seasons. They're little things, but it comes to your head that you've been there before and you know how to react to it. It's all good experience."

Chapter Thirty One
Forest Green

Tranmere were formed, as Belmont FC, in 1884. It was not until 131 years later, in 2015, that they first crossed paths with Forest Green Rovers. Yet in the past four seasons, one of football's strangest rivalries has emerged.

The relationship between the two clubs started fairly innocuously, as Rovers registered a 2-0 win at The New Lawn, inspired by a wonderful debut goal from Gary Taylor-Fletcher. Later that season, Jay Harris was on target during a 1-1 stalemate at Prenton Park.

Micky Mellon was in charge by the time the two teams next met, a thrilling 2-2 draw in which Tranmere twice came from behind to grab a point against a promotion rival. They were not so lucky towards the back end of the campaign though, losing 1-0 in a crucial clash in the race for top spot in the National League, despite dominating for much of the 90 minutes.

It was in that fixture when tensions between Forest Green and Rovers first flared. Harris picked up a nasty knee injury that would rule him out for the rest of the season, whilst the Super White Army were less than impressed by some of the antics employed by Mark Cooper's side, such as time-wasting and general gamesmanship.

Such tricks would once again be on show in the play-off final at Wembley a month later. Forest Green were excellent in the opening 45 minutes, opening up a 3-1 lead after some wonderfully accurate finishing. But they then spent the entirety of the second half sucking the life out of the game with niggling fouls, rolling around on the floor and wasting time.

Cooper's side had Tranmere's number. They went up. Rovers were consigned to a third successive year in the National League, thankfully escaping 12 months later when they beat Boreham Wood 2-1.

The two teams would cross paths again in 2018/19. Rovers were battered down at the New Lawn, losing 3-1, before the reverse fixture at Prenton Park towards the end of the season was a carbon copy of the game on the Wirral in 2017.

That gamesmanship was on show again. Tranmere were by far the better side, creating chance after chance after chance, but failing to take any of them. Junior Mondal scored the only goal just after half-time and the hosts never recovered.

The rivalry continued to brew. It was not just down to what happened on the pitch, though. Cooper was often somewhat ungracious in what he said after matches, whilst owner Dale Vince said getting to League One would be "easy" after their win over Rovers at Wembley.

"I think the Forest Green relationship is just one of those little rivalries that has sort of occurred," says Mark Palios. "I don't have a problem with the chairman there or what they do. They can do what they want to with their club. I think their food is fantastic! For medical reasons I'm a vegan anyway.

"I just objected to the way in which they played football on the pitch. I told them that and I told the manager that. People call it game management but that's a euphemism, because it isn't, it's cheating, in my opinion.

"I think there are issues in the way in which they play the game and how they interpret playing the game is, for me, not the way it should be. Things like stopping the ball coming into play, for example, as opposed to keeping the ball in play but keeping it in the corner flag. The latter is legitimate because the ball is in play. If you're disrupting the pattern of the game and the play, that's not what the fans pay to see. That, I think, is the heart of what happened.

"I think on the day they beat us in the final in 2017, they were the better team. They knew how to play us with certain players and personnel. We were not up for it in the first play-off final.

"I think it's more a rivalry between the fans. I think there's a little bit of, dare I say it, arrogance from our side, saying 'we are an established league club', whereas they're newbies who are just funded to get to where they are.

"People can do what they want to do with their money. I personally prefer traditional, old clubs, as I would, but it's not for me to tell somebody how to spend their money."

Rivalries aside, it is fair to say that Forest Green were Tranmere's bogey team. That Taylor-Fletcher inspired win in 2015 was the only time Rovers had beaten the Nailsworth side in seven meetings. And then they got paired together in the League Two play-offs.

But Micky Mellon's side came into the tie well warmed up. The fixtures towards the end of the season might not have looked kind on paper, with games against so many of their promotion rivals. Yet it meant that they were already having to perform at a high level in every fixture, instead of the campaign ending with a handful of meaningless games.

"I think that definitely helped," admits Liam Ridehalgh. "Our record against the top seven sides was very good. We showed that we could do. In seasons before, we'd been criticised for not being able to get the performances and results against the top sides, but we definitely matched them in that season."

Tranmere were confident for another reason, too. Despite failing to win any of the recent meetings between the two teams, the players believed they were beginning to get the upper hand. Psychologically, going in with that kind of belief was huge.

"I knew we were a better team than Forest Green," says Scott Davies, "So I wanted them over two legs, because over two legs, the better team will win 9 times out of 10. If we'd have played them over one game, anything could happen.

"I fancied Newport over two legs, because I felt like we were a better team than them, but Mansfield over two legs would have been difficult. They had good players and it would have been a slugfest that could have gone either way.

"But, honestly, I always felt if we'd have played Newport or Forest Green over two legs we'd be in the final, and then the final is just a game of whoever bends first, loses."

Micky Mellon, meanwhile, was glad to be tackling an old rival once again. "I was really looking forward to the games," he says. "I love those type of games. It was a good managerial tactical test, so I enjoyed them.

"I knew that we had a lot of experience, a good side and we were playing well. We'd played them only a few weeks earlier and we battered them. Make no mistake of that. We had chance after chance after chance, we didn't take them and they nicked a 1-0 win. So I had that on my mind.

"When they came to Prenton Park, they never got out of their own half, in either half. We really pegged them in. I think sometimes as a manager you might think 'we maybe got away with one there' and I felt like they got away with one against us a couple of times.

"Sometimes, don't get me wrong, they blew us away. That gave us a measurement of where we were as a club and it probably helped us change some stuff at times. We thought that if we were going to be successful, we had to be able to run toe-to-toe with Forest Green because they were a good benchmark for us.

"I felt like we'd got to that stage anyway. I thought that we were overrunning them. I thought that we had good players and I knew that they had good players as well, and Mark Cooper is a good manager. So I knew it was going to be a good test."

***

Tranmere were at home in the first game. Prenton Park welcomed its biggest crowd of the season, with 9,579 fans on hand to see the visitors reduced to ten men after just 15 minutes as Gavin Gunning saw red for petulantly kicking out at Jay Harris.

Shortly afterwards, Rovers made that advantage count as Ollie Banks slammed an unstoppable shot towards goal from 30-yards. It cannoned down off the bar, but thankfully for the hosts, goal line technology, in use at Prenton Park for the first time, confirmed that the ball had crossed the line, much to the delight of most of those in attendance. 1-0.

"I totally forgot the goal line technology was being used," laughs Connor Jennings. "I'd never played with it before. So when Ollie shoots, I'm thinking it was miles in, and then I couldn't believe the referee and linesman hadn't given it! Thankfully he pointed at his watch! It was good timing to have it in the play-offs!"

James Norwood, himself perhaps lucky not to see red, had chances to extend the lead, four times failing to hit the back of the net, whilst Tranmere racked up twenty shots across the 90 minutes without extending their lead.

"Because they went down to 10 men, a lot of people thought we needed a second goal," Jennings continues. "I was just like 'we've won!' I thought winning against them was a big boost.

"It was getting one over on them. We could go there and play our game, which was usually good away from home with the counter attack."

Liam Ridehalgh believes some of the supporters were a little underwhelmed by the scoreline too. "Maybe they expected a little bit more," he says, "wrongly or rightly, because of the man being sent off.

"But at the end of the day, we still won our home game in the first leg of the play-offs. I'd have taken that result before the game, 100%, and it just proved to show when we went down there and competed with them and went through."

Forest Green meanwhile felt like they had escaped with some kind of victory. Cooper actually celebrated in front of the traveling fans at full time. He ran over to them, arms pumping, as if forgetting which Rovers had won.

"It was us against the world tonight and we came through it with flying colours," he said, somewhat bizarrely, in his post match interview. "The boys were magnificent, I'm so proud of them. I asked them to be heroes at half-time and they surpassed that. They were superheroes. Everything's to play for. I'm sure they would have been looking to put the tie to bed there but we stood firm. We were outstanding."

Micky Mellon saw the game somewhat differently. "We battered them," he reflects, "But we only scored once. I think it was a psychological blow though. They went down to ten men but we passed them to death and it was all us.

"We should have scored a few more but I was comfortable knowing that we'd landed something. I wanted to make sure everybody knew that as well, so I said that after the game, on Sky and in the press.

"I was pleased to take any kind of lead to Forest Green, because I knew we'd score at Forest Green. In fact, before the play-offs, if you'd asked me how will you be successful, I'd say we need to score at Forest Green. So the first leg made no difference to me. I was mentally prepared for having to score there. There was no real fuss after winning the first game 1-0."

Scott Davies believes Tranmere took much more out of the game than just the slender 1-0 win. Indeed, he reckons he felt a momentum shift in the relationship between the two clubs because of the result. The hoodoo had been broken.

"I think we had one of the best defensive records in the league, so I was happy with it being 1-0," he says. "I felt like I'd go there and keep a clean sheet. Obviously I didn't, but I never felt like they were ever going to score two past us, which is massive.

"I also never thought we wouldn't score. I don't know how many games we didn't score in last season, but it wasn't many. I went there knowing we were through.

"I was planning my Wembley trip, no joke. I've never been like that before, but I just had an ultra confidence and belief in the group. I think that hurt Forest Green. They felt that we knew we were better than them, and they knew we were better than them as well."

***

The away leg took place four days later. Tranmere near sold out their allocation of tickets for the trip to the New Lawn and headed south full of confidence. All they needed to do was win or draw and they would be back at Wembley for the third their year running.

"I remember being on the coach on the way down," continues Davies. "It was me, Jay Harris, Steve McNulty and Adam Buxton, that was our table. We all said 'we'll fuck these tonight'. We knew we wouldn't get beat."

Twelve minutes in, that prediction did not look so good. Joseph Mills was left unmarked from a corner and he met Mondal's corner, heading past Davies to put the hosts 1-0 up and level the tie at 1-1 on aggregate.

Mellon describes it as a "crap goal" to concede, and he is right. In that instance, Tranmere should have been better. Yet, instead of grabbing the game by the scruff of the neck, the hosts looked a little bit apprehensive of what their visitors could do to them.

"I think their manager realised that we had better players than them and they were scared of us," Davies continues. "They sat in. I was surprised. Even after scoring they didn't come at us.

"Every other time we've gone to their place, they've came at us and really put it to us, and we've buckled under it a couple of times. In that game, they were scared of us and that's where it span round. I think you could see it in the game. I think we looked a foot bigger than them, a yard faster than them and it comfortably saw us through."

There was a shaky five or so minutes straight after the goal for Tranmere. Forest Green had plenty of the ball and Rovers just had to hold strong and get over any potential onslaught. But as Davies says, it never came.

It took them only fourteen minutes to equalise on the night as Norwood got his 32nd goal of the season - against the club whom he left to move to the Wirral in 2015.

David Perkins floated the ball across from the left, and it was nodded down by Kieron Morris, who in turn picked out the striker. The finish was brutal, one brilliant swing of his right boot, connecting perfectly to angle the ball into the far corner.

The traveling fans, Premier League referee Mike Dean amongst them, went wild. Norwood celebrated by goading the home supporters, striding towards them with a sole finger pressed to his lips.

"I was just thinking 'here we go again' when they scored," admits Liam Ridehalgh. "But yet again, we picked ourselves up. Our mentality throughout the season was never say die.

"Nors scored that goal out of nothing really. It's a nothing goal. It's an unbelievable finish. We knew that meant we were only drawing on the night, but with the result staying that way, we knew we were going through. We then defended unbelievably.

"I can't speak highly enough of James. He's such a brilliant player. Having a striker like that in the team brings you a lot of confidence, because you know you can get a goal from nothing. Send a ball over the top to him and he'll score."

From that point onwards, Tranmere were just superb. Micky Mellon is a remarkably good manager tactically. He works out a way to out-think the opposition manager and out-play the opposition. And Rovers did.

They defended from the front. Norwood was a constant menace, in that he occupied the defenders for the rest of the game without actually having many chances. But whenever the ball was in the Forest Green half, Norwood was near it.

Davies made a couple of saves, from Christian Doidge and Liam Shepherd before the hosts were again reduced to ten men when Carl Winchester picked up his second yellow card for a foul on Norwood. From that moment on, there was no chance of Tranmere losing, either on the night or aggregate.

"We all know our jobs," recalls Jennings. "If we stick to them, we can beat anybody really. We were pretty confident and as a team, it was a brilliant away performance.

"I remember watching it back a few days later. It surprised me how good we were with a back four, midfield four and Norwood up top on his own. Obviously we had a bit of luck with the two sendings off, one in each leg, which is nice, but it was two good legs."

Micky Mellon meanwhile could not have been prouder of his team. "We had too much experience," he adds. "We had too much calmness and control.

"If you asked the players, they'd probably say they loved the game, which is hard to be able to do in the play-offs, because you want it done and you want to get to Wembley. But I think they enjoyed everything about it. They were comfortable in it. We got to that stage where we were enjoying that type of challenge."

It would be unfair to say Rovers held out for a 1-1 draw, because they did not. They thoroughly deserved to win the tie, and did so 2-1 on aggregate. Wembley beckoned again. After years of trying, Forest Green had been dismissed.

"If you asked any Forest Green player who played against us in the final in 2017, they thought they had our number, and I'd agree with them," says Davies. "They did. They were a good team and they seemed to know how to play against us.

"But I think the sign of any good team, and it hasn't changed that much, is that you find a way to overcome a rival, be it a boxer overcoming his rival or Manchester United or Manchester City.

"Every good team overcomes their rival at some point and becomes better than them. Over those two legs, you saw we were a mile ahead of them."

Several Tranmere fans invaded the pitch as the joy of reaching another play-off final hit them. Mike Dean was picked out by the Sky Sports cameras, fist pumping as he stood on top of a crash barrier.

Some minutes after the final whistle and once the playing surface had been cleared, the team emerged, ordered to do so by the manager, to thank the fans and join in the celebrations.

"We were in the dressing room and we were very calm, " continues Davies. "But the manager said 'you better go and see the fans'. So it was one for the supporters really.

"We knew that we hadn't done the job. But you should celebrate it. Tranmere fans might not get there again for 10 years, or even 30.

Look at clubs like West Ham, at the higher end of football, who haven't won anything for decades. Whenever you get to a final, especially a Wembley one, you should always celebrate.

"The gaffer told us to go out and see the fans, which was good. They were having their moment and they deserved it. They've been with us all season. But we knew we hadn't accomplished anything. We had a couple of beers on the bus but it was only two or three and it was a toast to working our balls off and getting to a Wembley final, so there's your reward.

"We knew we didn't want to go there and lose. Having lost there two years earlier, it lived with us until October if you look at the start of the next season. It hurt us bad."

Ridehalgh admits they needed to thank the fans for their efforts, too. Throughout the season, the Super White Army had travelled in their numbers to all the corners of England. They had had little more than a week's notice for this game, yet over 1,000 still made the journey on a Monday night.

"They were superb that night," he adds. "We had all the side stand. It might be a small stand, but it was full of Tranmere fans and they were so loud from the first whistle to the last.

"Mike Dean was circulating on social media quite a lot afterwards as well which was quite good to look at. He comes in here now and again to get a rub and have a coffee. He's a top guy."

Jennings meanwhile admits to getting a little bit blasé about the occasion, saying: "It was a bit surreal. It didn't feel like we were going to Wembley, but I think that's because in the first year we celebrated too much.

"Since then, we've kind of thought it wasn't time to celebrate fully. It was a nice feeling, and there was a long wait until the final too!"

A final word to Cooper, whose comments after the game again put a smirk on the face of every Tranmere fan as he blamed the authorities for Forest Green's failure to make it to Wembley.

"It seems like it wasn't meant to be," he mused. "It wasn't our time and I don't think they really wanted us to be in the final if I'm brutally honest. It feels really unfair and I have to be really careful what I say.

"For anyone who watched the two games, I don't think anyone can say we were given a fair crack at it. We're bitterly upset that we haven't got through. We've played half the tie with 10 men and I don't think it's fair.

"Good luck to Tranmere, they played well tonight. We were getting on top but then we were reduced to 10 men. So I think it's really unfair the way a little club has been treated. I'm sure I'll be getting another phone call from the PGMOL tomorrow saying 'we're really sorry but we've let you down again.'"

In tribute to his reaction, the Tranmere Rovers Supporters Trust brought out a limited edition drink, Mark Cooper Bitter, put on sale for £5 and with all the proceeds being put back into Tranmere Rovers In The Community.

Chapter Thirty Two
Connor Jennings and the play-offs

Connor Jennings became one of Gary Brabin's final signings as Tranmere manager when he arrived on a free transfer in 2016. He had just finished the previous season as Wrexham's top scorer, netting 14 times in 45 league appearances.

It was quite a coup, convincing the forward to leave the Racecourse, where he had also worn the captain's armband, and Rovers fans were delighted that they had managed to prize him away from their bitter rivals.

"I wouldn't say Gary Brabin sold the club to me," he says. "I already knew a bit about them. I'd obviously played there before and I'd watched my brother there. I knew a bit of their history too. Once I got the deal sorted, I was over the moon to be fair and I haven't looked back."

It did, however, take Jennings a while to settle after completing his move to Prenton Park. A change of manager always brings uncertain times for a player, especially when it comes just a handful of months after that boss has signed you.

Brabin's departure also came less than two weeks after Jennings had picked up a serious knee injury in a 1-0 home defeat to Lincoln. He would not play another competitive match until Boxing Day, by which point Micky Mellon already had his feet under the carpet and was setting his sights on promotion.

"I was out for about four months and it was tough," Jennings admits. "I went to Macclesfield on loan and it was the turning point in my Tranmere career. Since I've come back, I've played in pretty much every game, or I've been in the squad most weeks.

"There was a point when I thought I might not get back in the Tranmere team. Obviously I wasn't Micky Mellon's player, so I wasn't very positive about it. He wouldn't let me go out on loan at first. I told him I needed games.

"The team were winning at the time, so it was really hard for me to get in. But eventually, after me annoying him a lot, I persuaded him to give me four or five games at Macclesfield. Since then, he's been brilliant to me. He's put a lot of trust in me and we've been on an eventful journey together."

Jennings truly has gone from strength to strength, delivering in plenty of big moments with some sublime goals. One stunning volley against Sutton just before Christmas during the 2017/18 season helped Tranmere on their way to a crucial 3-1 win, whilst another long range effort set Rovers up for a 2-0 victory at Southport a year later, earning them that money spinning FA Cup tie with Spurs.

He is also a player who appears to be getting better with each passing year. In 2018/19, back in the Football League for the first time since leaving Scunthorpe in 2014, he netted 13 goals, a season best return in a Tranmere shirt.

And when it comes to play-off matches, something always seems to happen with Connor Jennings too. For Rovers' first trip to Wembley to take on Forest Green in 2017, he scored the equaliser, another trademark, unstoppable long range effort that rifled into the top corner past goalkeeper Sam Russell.

A year later, his involvement against Boreham Wood was in doubt due to a serious illness. Indeed, there were fears for Jennings' career as he lay in hospital on a drip only ten days before the historic match.

However, he would make a remarkable return to training and declare himself fit enough to be involved, and it is just as well he did. The forward came off the bench in the first half, and it was his cross that James Norwood headed home to give Tranmere a 2-1 win and send them back into the Football League.

As if what happened in 2018 was not traumatic enough, Jennings was hit by a family tragedy on the day of the first leg of their semi-final against Forest Green in 2019. One of his grandparents passed away.

"It was really tough," he confesses. "It wasn't the best way to start the day, especially when you've got a big game in the night.

"The worst thing was that my grandparents were down in London. All my family were down there. I felt helpless. After we got the second leg out of the way, the gaffer gave me two days off, which was a big help."

It is a measure of the kind of person that Jennings is that he did not tell anybody of the grief he was going through. He knew the importance of the Forest Green clash. They had been a bogey team for Tranmere in the past. Everyone was desperate to beat them, and to do that, it was vital they got the two-legged tie off to a good start.

"I didn't tell them before the first leg," he continues. "I'm not going to ring the manager up, am I? I just thought I'd keep it to myself. Obviously it got out, unfortunately, and I don't think the manager was particularly happy with me! I got a phone call the next day and he was brilliant. He was so supportive, just like the season before when I had been ill. We got through it."

The manager himself was only alerted to Jennings' grief through social media. Micky Mellon had absolutely no idea that one of his stars was suffering at a time when he needed him to be at his best.

"I only found out what had happened to his grandad because somebody told me something was on Twitter," he said. "He wasn't a lad who came in and suddenly he was all 'woe is me, I'm really suffering here'. He just came in and got on with things.

"I could tell there was something not right about him, but he's quite a moody sod anyway, so sometimes he can be like that. You know by the way he is and the way that he trains that there's something up with him, you get to know them quite well.

"So I knew there was something up with him, and sometimes you just go 'oh I can't be arsed with it, he'll get ahead of it', but somebody told me he'd been sent condolences for his grandad on Twitter.

"I knew he was close to his grandad and I knew his family situation. I got to know them when he was first ill the year before. It all puts football in its place.

"I hate saying it puts it into perspective, because it doesn't really do it justice. I think certain parts of life just get put into place in terms of importance when somebody gets really ill. It has to take a place, football, and it's certainly not as important as a guy's health and we'd all do well to remember that.

"I'm obsessed with football. It's my hobby. I don't know if anybody is as obsessed with it as me. I was up at 4.30am this morning because I was thinking about certain things. I got my computer and I was looking things up. What I'm able to do with my obsession with football is to still also know what's important.

"With Connor, it would have affected people who can't compartmentalise and focus, but I knew if he wanted to play or take some part in the game, it wasn't going to affect him. He would be able to do it and he would find a way. He has learnt a way of turning that into energy, which is a skill in itself. It's a real ability.

"I had no problem if he wanted to take part. It was no bother at all. It was up to him and we of course know what happened. What a terrific moment for him and his family, a perfect moment really.

"He lost his grandad and it was a real emotional time, but the emotion of football for that moment helps everybody, and that's

323

really what football does. That's the beauty of the game and that's why it is so important to us, because it makes it all worth it for moments like that."

One of Jennings' closest friends at Tranmere is Liam Ridehalgh. The pair travel into training and matches together and have got to know each other well since becoming teammates three years ago.

"We had pre-match at the ground before the Forest Green game," said the left-back, "and he walked in and I just said 'he doesn't look right'. I knew there was something up with him and it was such a sad time for him and his family.

"I travel in with him usually, but he came in on his own that day, so we did realise there was something up. He just didn't look right, but I still think he played really well.

"It must have been difficult having to hear that news hours before the game. I've been through something similar before a game quite recently. I know where he's coming from."

Sport seems to work in a different way to any other industry. If you are employed in a more normal office environment, time off when suffering a bereavement is a given. But because of the stage in the season, Jennings had no interest in stepping away from football for a few days. For that reason, it was not until after the campaign had finished that Jennings was truly able to spend the time he needed to with his family.

"It was a long three weeks," he continues. "The lads helped me through it. I didn't want to take some time away from football, but I definitely needed it. But what can you do? You've just got to get on with it.

"You've got to put a front on. You can't come in moping about. You've got to put that front on and it was pretty draining. I felt really tired doing it all the time when I just wanted to grieve.

"Playing didn't help me get through it. It's hard to describe. You are mentally tired. Especially with that first leg. My head was all over the place. My dad and my brother and cousins were saying 'just concentrate on the game, get your head right'. They knew that I wouldn't be able to. That Friday night it was just about working as hard and as much as I could."

Chapter Thirty Three
Two In A Row

And so, for the third year running, Tranmere found themselves at Wembley. They were 90 minutes, or perhaps 120, away from a second successive promotion. This was unheard of territory for the club; even the great Johnny King had not managed to go up back-to-back, instead making the jump from Division Four to Division Two in three years.

May 25th was the date. It had been a big gap between the semi-finals finishing, nearly two weeks, in fact, but that gave Rovers a chance to rest up and get properly prepared.

The fans travelled down in their numbers, with in excess of 10,000 packing out the East end of the stadium on this occasion, the opposite side of the ground to the stands they occupied for the matches against Boreham Wood and Forest Green.

"You saw all these families turning up and it's great," smiles Mark Palios. "I loved a Tweet I got from one of the fathers, because it really summed up where the club had come from to where they are.

"He said 'my lad has asked me 'dad, what time do we normally set off for Wembley?'' It was great. It summed up where the club is. That's what we want. We want the fathers and mothers to have great days with their kids."

There was one supporter missing though. Mark Bartley had given up hope on Rovers reaching the play-offs after their run of three defeats in January, so he decided to book a holiday to America instead.

"We started winning all these games and my friends kept telling me

I'd miss Wembley if we got there," he laughs. "I was contemplating coming back a few days early, but I knew if I did that and we got beat I'd be devastated. So I watched it whilst I was away in America, at 7am.

"I thoroughly enjoyed it and I was envious that I wasn't there, of course, but I know a lot of work had been put in by TROSC to get fans there. By all accounts, everyone had a great time. I was delighted to be going up!

"I actually told Mark Palios I wouldn't be there after the first leg of the semi-finals. He said 'I thought you were Tranmere through and through' and I said 'I am, I've got the club motto, 'Ubi fides ibi lux et robur', which means 'Where there is faith there is light and strength', tattooed on my arm.' And he said 'well you should fucking read it, shouldn't you!' It was an ill-timed holiday."

***

Newport were Tranmere's opponents, a side who had sneaked into the top seven late in the regular season, having to play catch up in terms of games for much of it due to a strong run to the fifth round of the FA Cup.

Their credentials were clear. They had beaten Premier League outfit Leicester and Championship side Middlesbrough en route to the last 16 before suffering a 4-1 defeat to eventual winners Manchester City.

That alone suggested Rovers were in for a tough afternoon. Michael Flynn had built a robust side, capable of playing attractive, slick football, although they were perhaps more used to scrapping and stifling their opponents.

Tranmere had already seen what Newport were capable of in the regular season, failing to score in either meeting. The game at Prenton Park ended in a 1-0 victory for the visitors, whilst a 0-0 stalemate at the back end of the campaign was played out at Rodney Parade.

The fixture on the Wirral had been a particular eye opener. The Exiles were pretty good for the opening half hour, taking the lead through a fifth minute strike from Fraser Franks.

Yet after the break, despite the standard they had set, the visitors merely decided to sit on their 18-yard line. It was as if a completely different team had come out for the second half. They were physical, they wasted time and they frustrated a home crowd who thought watching matches like this were a thing of the past after getting out of the National League.

The South Welsh side had booked their place at Wembley courtesy of a penalty shoot out victory over big spending Mansfield. The tie had ended 1-1 after 210 minutes of football, with the second leg at Field Mill finishing goalless.

Keeping an attack that included the likes of Tyler Walker, Christopher Hamilton and Danny Rose quiet was an impressive effort, especially away from home, but it came as no surprise, given they had conceded just three goals in the previous 11 matches.

Like Tranmere, Newport had recent experience of playing under the famous arch. A little over a year earlier, they faced Spurs, who were using Wembley as their home ground whilst White Hart Lane was rebuilt, in an FA Cup fourth round replay. They lost 2-0 to side that included Heung-Min Son, Moussa Sissoko and Toby Alderwiereld.

They were not, however, able to call upon the experience of such a do or die occasion. Yes, The Exiles had reached the 2013 National League play-off final where they beat bitter rivals Wrexham 2-0, but whilst manager Flynn was playing that day, only one of his starting teammates was part of the squad to face Tranmere, defender David Pipe.

Rovers, on the other hand, had been there and done it all before. "It was the calmest I've ever been going into a final," reveals Scott Davies. "I think it was my fourth or fifth one. The group were calm. It was business as usual.

"In the morning of the game, I was sat in the Costa opposite Wembley having a coffee and then I went for a wander around before a chill in the hotel. Nothing different really. It was the calmest I've ever been before a big game.

"Obviously you get your nerves, of course. I get them before every game. My tell tale sign, and everybody who's roomed with me before knows this, is I go to the toilet about five times on the day of a game! Jay Harris used to hate it! The room stinks! But they were good nerves that day. If I'm ever 'nervous' nervous, I'd be worried, but I wasn't."

Tranmere treated the game in a similar way to the play-off final against Boreham Wood 12 months earlier. They had learned from the experience of losing to Forest Green, where they over-egged things a touch, celebrating the achievement of getting back to Wembley after a 17 year absence. They could not afford to do that again. Therefore in 2018, Micky Mellon regularly reminded his side that the job was far from done.

Against Newport, it was exactly the same. There was a place in League One at stake, and that experience of having competed in two previous finals stood Rovers in a good position.

"I was so calm," says Mellon. "I just couldn't wait to see the team working at Wembley. They were purring like a big Lamborghini and they were comfortable. They were comfortable psychologically, because Wembley is a big thing. It's massive.

"The first time I went there, with Tranmere, the whole thing was massive. The second time it was less and the third time, honestly, I wasn't even bothered. That's not me trying to do it a disservice, because it is a fantastic place to go. But I was so calm.

"I was looking forward to the game and couldn't wait for it to start and was able to really take everything in. I slowed it right down and took every part of it in and really, really enjoyed it.

"That can't happen many times when you go to Wembley because it's such an emotional time, but even the national anthem, I loved it. I was really focused. We'd worked really hard.

"I knew how the team was going to perform. We knew Newport really well, so I knew where we'd have to be good and what we'd have to accept and not get my knickers in a twist about because it was two different shapes and all that kind of stuff. I really wanted the players to know that it was just about them going out and being them. They were very calm as well."

"I remember the gaffer's speech in the hotel after the team meeting," adds Davies. "I think his words were 'I can't fucking wait to watch my machine roll, because that's what you are. You're a well oiled, well drilled machine that's just going to go out there and do it'. And we did. We didn't bend. We stuck to our jobs. Every man had to stand up and be counted at some point and we did it."

Whilst Davies and Mellon have revealed they were totally relaxed any the occasion, the same cannot be said for all the squad. Liam Ridehalgh admits to feeling more than a few butterflies for what lay in wait.

He had been sent off in the play-off final against Boreham Wood 12 months earlier, receiving his marching orders after just 48 seconds for a foul on Ricky Shakes. In 2017, his error had allowed Forest Green to take a 3-1 lead just before half-time, as he had his pocket picked by Kaiyne Woolery after dwelling on the ball.

"I was very nervous because of what had happened the year before," he admits. "I was thinking 'blooming heck, I'm here again! What happens if something like that happens again? I'm finished.' I'm pretty proud of how I performed that day.

"But I don't think there was as much pressure on us for some reason. Obviously getting out of the National League was so important for the football club as a whole, but if we lost at Wembley against Newport, it wouldn't have been disastrous.

"So I think there was less pressure on us. And when you've got a goal scorer like James Norwood and you know how well the back four has been doing all season, we always knew that we could win."

Connor Jennings reiterates those thoughts, adding: "There wasn't as much pressure. It was a strange one. We had the big trophy there. You look around and you know it's a proper final, but it didn't really feel like it.

"We were all very calm. It helped that we'd had two good games against Forest Green where we had played well. We were all very confident. It was a bit of a weird feeling."

***

The game got underway and it was a cagey affair. The two sides knew each other pretty well and they were determined not to give in to the other's strengths.

James Norwood had the first chance, but it did not come until the 26th minute. Jake Caprice picked him out with a clever cut-back, and the striker powerfully struck a first time volley, only for goalkeeper Joe Day to save.

Norwood had another chance before the break, heading over the bar, whilst a third effort was deflected in the second half and fell to Jennings, but he could not quite get the ball out from under his feet.

Newport grew into the game. It was not until the second half that they started to test Tranmere, but when the chances came, they were good ones. Davies had to make one particularly sensational save, from Jamille Matt, somehow keeping out a header by pushing the ball on to the post.

Micky Mellon did not like what he was seeing. The Exiles were beginning to get the upper hand. He needed to shift things back in Rovers' favour, and to everybody's surprise, he turned to a man who had played just once since that 3-0 defeat to Mansfield back in January.

"I know Steve McNulty really well," says Mellon, "So I know when you come into that later part of the season, you need his kind of mentality. When it all becomes mental, people start to panic and they come off the plan. They start to revert into a safe place, instead of doing what we want them to do.

"McNulty was good at keeping people on track, because he could comfortably keep himself on track. He would never really get too flustered about what other people would say is a big game. It'd just be another game for him. He'd be quite calm, he would make sure he did his job and make sure the people around him did theirs.

"He was struggling with his knee and his Achilles in the second half of the season and Mark Ellis and Manny Monthe had built up a partnership. But even when he was injured, I kept him involved. I got him to help the back four and I had him sitting upstairs watching games, then he'd come down at half-time and tell me what he was seeing. I kept him in and among it and I kept him helping me around the place.

"There are a number of players who are good around the place in keeping the standards up. If anybody pisses around, and I don't see it, they wouldn't get away with it, because these guys know that if anything stops the boat moving forward and they want the boat to move forward and somebody's not pulling their weight, they know that they've got to stop that. They're very good at that. McNulty was great at that for us.

"Yes, he was a loss playing wise. But I tried to get everything out of him that I could in order to keep the thing moving forward. I also tried to keep him fit. If I needed him, I was going to use him. Thank God we did that, because on a sunny afternoon at Wembley, I looked at the game of football and I thought 'it's McNulty time'.

"I don't think anybody else in the stadium apart from myself looked at that and thought 'that's a fantastic decision, to play a guy who's not played since January'. But I just knew what he was like."

'McNulty Time', to be precise, was in the 82nd minute. Kieron Morris came off, allowing the manager to switch to a 3-5-2 formation, with Sid Nelson and Manny Monthe playing either side of McNulty.

"I could see the momentum swinging to them a touch until I switched McNulty on," Mellon continues. "That's why I did it. I thought we were just coming off our running a little bit and we weren't quite getting across the pitch to their wingbacks. There were a lot of crosses coming into the box and you don't like that because eventually one is going to land on somebody's head.

"I knew I needed to stop the wingbacks from getting the crosses into the box and when it does come into the box, I need us to be more commanding. I need to settle that down.

"So you think do I change the shape with who I've got on the pitch, or do I need to do a different thing? I'd always thought that with their three at the back, I had a three at the back in my locker with McNulty coming on.

"I knew I needed to do it now, or I'd regret it. There comes a time in a game where a manager either shits himself, and I've had many managers say to me before that they know when the end comes, because they can't make a decision - they shit it. So I'm at Wembley and it's decision time. Some managers make the decision to shit themselves. I thought McNulty.

"I turned around, I looked at him and beckoned him over. Honestly, I'll never forget this as long as I live, McNulty looked behind him! I went 'no, you! Come here'. He came down the stairs and I told him to go and play in the middle of the back three for me. The game was becoming stretched.

"I said 'are all you alright with that? Can you handle that?' He said 'aye gaffer', so I told him to go and put his shinguards on.

"I then turned to Mike Jackson and Steve Banks and said 'get big Macca on'. They'll tell you this themselves, honestly, they said 'Big Macca?' I said 'Yes'. 'Steve McNulty gaffer?' 'Yes!'

"Every time I meet Banksy now, he says 'I don't know anybody else who'd have made that decision at that time. It was unbelievable. I still can't believe what you were doing, because he hadn't played.' But I was sure.

"He goes right in the middle of the back three and makes sure he squeezes up. I said to him 'don't go too deep and on the overloads get out to the centre-backs'.

"Adam Buxton came on and he is a talented lad too. He can play. If you free him up with the ball he's got a great range of passing. That's what we did. It just started to click in.

"Macca was winning the headers. Players like him being in and about them. They, Newport, didn't like that he started to win all the headers and dominate them, and you could just see the thing starting to rise again.

"Honestly, from that moment on, I thought we would win it in normal time. When it went to extra time, I thought we'd do it in extra time. I never thought we'd leave it until the last second! But I just thought we'd do it.

"Sometimes as a manager you can see it happening. I could see Adam Buxton getting more and more of the ball and Ben Pringle coming into pockets and turning, whilst Jennings and Norwood were starting to get free."

Even McNulty's teammates were surprised when they saw him getting ready to come on. The defender had played in Tranmere's final game of the season, a 3-1 defeat to Crawley, but that was a match in which Mellon rotated his squad in order to keep his first choice players fit and firing for the play-offs.

"It was a weird one," says Jennings, "But when you watch it back, it wasn't a weird one at all. Obviously the gaffer trusts him massively. Even if you just take the last three or four minutes, you can see why he came on. Every ball hit his head. It was like a magnet.

"When somebody like him comes on, it can be a massive boost for you. He'll help you out defensively and he'll get you through it.

"It's another sign of just how good the manager is tactically. He trusts everybody who is in the squad and knows what they're capable of. We had a great squad with a lot of character. Ben Pringle comes on as well and he does really well, because it's not an easy game to come into."

Scott Davies had been captaining Tranmere with McNulty out of the side. The moment he saw the club skipper waiting to come on, he sprinted over to hand him the armband.

"That was a nice moment for me," smiles the 'keeper, who has known the defender longer than most. "Away from everything, that was a thank you. He's led me through my whole career. I love him to pieces. He's been an unbelievable captain for me.

"He deserved that moment. He came on and cometh the hour, cometh the man. It was the kind of game where we needed him, and he was there for us."

***

As the game wore on, the weather started to have an effect on the game as well. It was a roasting hot day. The Tranmere fans were bathed in sunshine, and that perhaps took its toll on them as the weather sapped their energy and quietened their chanting a little.

The players were feeling the heat too, especially as the match wore on and then got taken into an extra 30 minutes.

"You don't really train for extra time," says Liam Ridehalgh. "How can you? It's just something you've got to get on with. It's hard physically, obviously, but mentally it's really tough. It's the last stages of the game, you don't want to make a mistake and you want to win.

"Because of the heat, I had to cut my socks. I had cramp in my calves in the second half of extra time. I literally could not run. I always laugh when I see it back on the video, because there's a ball that comes into the box, I've headed it and landed and I've just collapsed."

Connor Jennings felt the temperature too, adding: "I hit rock bottom in about the 75th minute. I played about 50 games last season, the clock hits 75 minutes and I was gone. I was so tired.

"It wasn't until extra time that I got my second wind. I felt fine after that! But it was a tough game mentally and physically, and the longer it went on, it was just about trying to stay in it. We had Norwood there, we were confident with our defenders, we knew we were going to get one chance."

***

Neither team was able to break the deadlock before the 90 minutes was up, but Tranmere fans were left with hearts in mouths when Matt took a tumble in the box. The striker poked the ball away from Monthe, who subsequently brought him down. Appeals for a penalty were waved away, and half the ground breathed a huge sigh of relief, including Scott Davies.

"I know Jamille well and played with him at Fleetwood," he says. "I think if he doesn't throw his arms in the air, he gets a penalty. For me it's a penalty. I've watched it back. It's a stonewall penalty. I think that moment changed the game to be honest. After that I knew we'd win."

Minutes later, Newport were reduced to ten men, losing captain Mark O'Brien who was shown a second yellow card for hauling down Norwood.

Remarkably, it was the fifth consecutive play-off match in which Rovers had been involved that had seen a sending off; four in favour of the opposition, alongside Ridehalgh's dismissal twelve months earlier.

Connor Jennings insists it did not have too much of an impact, though. "When they had the man sent off, you're kind of happy," he says. "But then you think that a lot of the time a team is harder to beat with ten men. That was definitely the case. We just had to keep going and keep going and try and unlock the defence."

With the game heading towards extra time, Tranmere would have one more chance, and it fell to the man who had scored 32 times for them in the season already. Unfortunately, Norwood could not add to his tally, dinking a volley over Day but just wide of goal.

Therefore, another 30 minutes was required to decide who would go up. But if anything, extra time was more cagey than the initial two halves of football. Neither team wanted to give an inch, especially with so much at stake.

Matt Dolan had one chance for Newport, a cheeky attempt from near the half way line that Davies easily saved, whilst the 'keeper also got down well to keep out Padraig Amond's header.

It was still 0-0 at half-time in extra-time. It looked like penalties were looming, especially when Norwood saw another shot deflected for a corner and Day saved from Ollie Banks.

Tranmere even brought on their spot-kick specialist, Adam Buxton, who replaced Sid Nelson on the right side of that back three.

"I wasn't fearing penalties," laughs Davies. "I was buzzing about it! We'd planned it, me and Steve Banks. We always go through them the day before. He actually said he was writing down on a water-bottle what we thought they'd do, just so it was refreshed in my mind, and then Connor headed it in.

"Do you know what was weird, though? Even though it was the 119th minute, I don't know if it's because I was so in the zone, I didn't realise the time. I never felt like we were going to penalties.

"I never even thought about it, even when Adam Buxton comes on. Genuinely. I never considered it getting to that stage, because I thought there was a goal in the game. I think they felt like that too."

Jennings is of the same mindset. He just felt like something was going to happen, regardless of how little time was left in the game.

"I didn't think of penalties at all," he adds, "Because I knew that we were going to score. I had a feeling, a bit weirdly, that I was going to get a chance, and what was really strange is that Liam Ridehalgh had said to me 'you're going to score a header' a few days before hand.

"I was waiting for that moment! But when I saw Buxton come on, I thought maybe we were settling for penalties. In the end, the ball went down his side and that moment comes."

Every supporter believed Buxton had been brought on with penalties in mind. But who else would have taken one? "I'd have put myself forward," says Ridehalgh, "But I don't know if I'd have been on the list.

"Norwood would have obviously taken one, then you had Banks and Buxton, who's a great striker of the ball. It would have been interesting to see what happened."

Thankfully, it never came to that. With the game petering out towards a draw, the chance that everybody had waited for finally came.

Jake Caprice picked up the ball on the right and Buxton went on the overlap. As he can so cleverly do, the defender freed up some space with a drop of the shoulder and cut inside before laying off to Ben Pringle, who passed back out to Caprice, who had continued his run.

"I've seen him hit those first time crosses so many times," says Micky Mellon. "He does it every day in training. I remember thinking to myself 'just connect with it right' because sometimes he balloons it, but he is good at it when he does that side footed bender.

"He connected with it right and then immediately you look into the box and I'm thinking 'go and put your head on that'. I'd seen Jennings storming in. 'Go and put your big loaf on that'. It came in and he just went bang. And it went in."

It was not the most powerful of connections from the forward. He headed the ball down into the ground, but the direction was perfect, back across goal and past an already committed Day, who could do nothing to stop the ball bouncing into the back of the net.

1-0. Jubilation. Sheer joy. Incredible scenes. Limbs flying everywhere. A collective roar from one end of the stadium, jumping up in unison to hug and kiss strangers. A moment encapsulated in time that will never be forgotten by Tranmere supporters.

"The thing with Adam Buxton is that you know he's going to chop inside," explains the goal hero. "Nors and I are coming back out when he chops. The ball goes out to Pringle and then to Caprice. He takes a touch, and we make our run again, that's when the cross comes in.

"To be fair, I didn't really see it until late because the guy in front jumped and it's just missed him. I've tried to head it down, back to where it's just come from. There was so much relief when it hit the net.

"I've scored at Wembley before, but this felt miles better. At the time, it was relief that it was over, although there was still four or five minutes to go when we were under plenty of pressure.

"But after what had happened with my family over the past three weeks, this was special. It put a smile on their faces, along with all the other fans. Lots of my family came!

"I actually got cramp in the celebrations. They all jumped on me and we were on the advertising board. There's this poor man on the other side of it and I don't think you can see him on the TV footage, but he's basically holding the board up! I'm facing him, face to face, and he's like 'get them off you', I couldn't!"

"The goal is crazy," adds Ridehalgh. "I somehow found myself on the penalty spot, which is bizarre. The cross from Caprice is incredible. Connor's header is great. When I saw the ball hit the back of the net I just sprinted after him. When it went in, I just knew we'd done it.

"I felt full of belief and every emotion you can think of. I was so happy for Connor, with what had happened to him the week before with his family.

"That pile on after the goal, I was trying to get to him and I just couldn't get near him! I think it was Jay Harris who was next to me and I just cuddled him instead! I wanted to get to Connor and I did in the end and I just said 'unbelievable'."

The devastated Newport fans had suddenly been silenced. Their hope had evaporated. With only ten men on the field, they knew their race was run. But Micky Mellon had to make sure his team stayed focused.

"I could see people running all over the place but I was calm, because it wasn't done," he says. "The place went mental. I was calm and I told Manny and Macca to keep them calm and see it out.

"I knew it was going to become launch time, and who else do you want in your 18-yard box at launch time than Steve McNulty? He's going to win everything. So I just thought 'see it through'."

Jennings' strike came in the 119th minute. Two minutes of added time were signalled, although it felt like a lifetime to everyone associated with Tranmere.

Mellon was right; Newport did throw the kitchen sink at Rovers, getting the ball into the box as quickly as possible. And he was right about McNulty too, who gobbled up everything and eased the pressure on his thankful teammates. And so the Exiles ran out of time. At 5.35pm, the final whistle blew. Game over. 1-0. Two in a row.

A few minutes later, Davies and McNulty climbed the 107 Wembley steps side by side to lift the League Two play-off final trophy, which is significantly more impressive than its National League counterpart.

"That was an unbelievable moment," reflects Davies, "The best moment of my career. I'll never forget it. In fact I can't forget it, it's on the walls all over the training ground!

"But to be fair to Macca, if he'd have said 'I'm doing it on my own', I'd have let him, but he came to me at the final whistle and said 'you've been captain for half of the season, let's do it together,' which I thought was nice.

"He's one of my best friends in football and you don't get many. So to be able to do it, one, for the fans and two, with somebody I've had a good relationship with for my whole career, was even better. It was a great moment and one I'll never forget and one, seriously, I'm truly thankful for."

The celebrations were very different to 12 months earlier. Whereas in 2018, players streamed across the pitch in relief, this time they hugged and kissed in exuberance and pride.

"We're good at celebrating now," jokes Mellon. "Trust me! It was mayhem the first time, but everybody this time was really determined to take everything in. They wanted to make sure they enjoyed the bus, which was mental and hilarious, but they didn't want it to pass them by.

"We got back to Prenton Park and even the fans were ready! We enjoyed that and then went down into town. I couldn't stay out because it was just madness. You couldn't move. So I went home early and I woke up in the morning with that feeling in your stomach.

"We had the town hall, the beer tent at the club, the pubs in Birkenhead. I slowed right down and really made sure I took everything in and I'm glad I did that."

Chapter Thirty Four
Individual Emotions

Winning that second Wembley play-off final meant different things to different people. To some, it was the finest moment of their career. Others, who had been driven by the desperation to prove people wrong, were simply over the moon to get back to a level at which they believed they belonged. Here is a collection of thoughts from some of those involved.

Micky Mellon

"I'm struggling to see what it means to me, because I don't really think that way. I think about the club and I think about the people; the chairman and my players, and I think about my family. And I think about how important it is to all of them, a lot.

"So really, that's the way that I am. All the time when Tranmere are playing, I'm thinking about the fans, the club, the chairman and my family and making sure that I'm getting everything out of the players and doing the best that I can.

"I'm having to be really patient at the minute. At the start of the 2019/20 season, I knew that I was going to have a lot of players with whom I didn't know how they were going to do in League One.

"So I wrote behind my eyelids 'patience'. Be patient, work hard, get the principles, allow them to try and hit the tempo as quickly as they can and sustain the tempo of League One football. It's massively different.

"The intensity is the difference. Make sure that you give them the opportunity to hit the tempo as quickly as possible and then make them sustain it. Train every day to sustain it. That's exactly where I am in the minute.

"In terms of League One, I get a lot of enjoyment when I see Tranmere at Ipswich, or Rotherham, or Portsmouth, or when we're at home and the ground's full.

"I take satisfaction out of that, knowing that the fans can go out on a Friday night and say they're going to watch Tranmere tomorrow and they're playing Ipswich or Sunderland, instead of what they've had to say, with all due respect, in the past.

"I think that we've brought pride back. But I have to try and make us competitive all the time in order to keep moving it forward. Keep improving everything and try and get the best out of what we've got.

"So what does it mean to me? All of that. I don't really sit here and say 'I'm so proud of me'. No. I still have work to do. I'm engrossed in the work at the minute and I'm enjoying seeing the improvement.

"I'm working hard at being patient and rolling with the punches, because I don't like getting beat and I don't like Tranmere getting beat, but I understand that it's a development job.

"I'm grateful that the fans have been understanding of that, and the guys in the press, because I needed people to understand that that's what it was: a development job. I wasn't trying to buy time or worry about me. No, it's a development job.

"As long as you can see development and the team growing and getting better, I'm alright with that, but obviously I'm greedy for that. I want more and more and more. That's all I'm trying to do; keep it moving ahead.

"I enjoy taking the fans to bigger stadiums and more high profile clubs. Long may that continue because that's where we deserve to be. But I won't really ever sit down and give myself a big pat on the back. I'm absolutely not like that."

Connor Jennings

"I've watched the game back quite a few times, mainly for the celebrations! When the goal goes in, it's such an amazing feeling, knowing that you can give 14,000 fans emotions like that, all off their seats and happy. That's what football is all about.

"It was my second favourite moment on a football field. Nothing will get better than the first promotion, when we beat Boreham Wood. That was the first promotion of my career, not just at Tranmere. It makes you a lot more hungry for success. And as they say … you always remember your first! They're both special moments.

"But it's odd to say how the two promotions compare. There was a lot more pressure on us in 2018, but looking back, and I mean this with no offence to Newport, there should have been more pressure and I should have felt a lot more pressure in 2019. We should have been expected to win it easily.

"But the year before, the club needed it. In that 2017/18 season, there were some real tough times. We were 18th in the National League at one point. That was low, very low, especially around the training ground. It wasn't a good place to be. But we went on and finished second in the table, which is incredible considering the start we had with those first ten games.

"As for the Newport game - it was exactly the same as the league match we played against them a couple of months earlier, which ended 0-0.

"Compared to the season before, it felt like a bigger game. They brought a lot more fans than the Boreham Wood and Forest Green in the previous two years. It was a great atmosphere, despite the heat! It was a tough game to play in.

"We knew what they were good at and it was just trying to stop that, as well as trying to do what you're good at. I can't really remember much about my performance though. There was some good stuff and some bad stuff.

"If I look back to when I signed, I honestly believed that I could get back to League One, having played in the division with Scunthorpe. Maybe I didn't expect it as quickly as back to back promotions though!

"Once I knew Tranmere were interested in signing me, I wanted to come here. I knew that the club were going to take a turn and only go upwards. Since I arrived in 2016, things have changed massively around the place.

"I actually played against Tranmere the season before joining them with Wrexham, and we had two matches at Prenton Park, one in the League and one in the FA Trophy. It wasn't the nicest of places to come, but more for the home team than the away team. It was very eerie.

"I wasn't apprehensive about joining though. The first thing I wanted was a promotion. I knew I was going to get it at Tranmere. I thought I would get it in the first year, but that wasn't meant to be. I knew I'd go up though, and I turned out right!

"I've seen the club transform massively since then. It's been brilliant ever since. It's been a special few years. The sky is the limit."

Liam Ridehalgh

"It's unbelievable really, what we have achieved as a group. It doesn't happen often in football. We've been to Wembley three times. We've won twice. I'm very proud of that.

"It's the best feeling I've ever had in football, 100%, certainly on the pitch. But off the pitch, it was when James Norwood scored against Boreham Wood. That's probably one of the best feelings I've ever felt.

"But I felt a lot more a part of this win. Obviously I was in a tracksuit and off the pitch for the majority of the win against Boreham Wood. I was buzzing that we'd got promoted, of course, but personally I didn't feel a part of it as much as I did the League Two promotion.

"It was more about having a little moment to myself as well. I remember being in the changing room and there's champagne everywhere and everybody is jumping around, but I remember taking myself out of there and just having a little moment to myself which I appreciated.

"It really does mean everything to me, to be the only one who has been on the whole journey, from League One, to the National League and back again.

"Say I did decide to leave for whatever reason, or I sulked about what happened or had my bottom lip out, I wouldn't have experienced what I have experienced. I'm really glad that I stuck with it.

"So the second promotion means more to me, because it means getting back to where I started. I'm a loyal person. Loyalty is so important to me because of how I've been brought up, I think. I'm from quite a tight knit family. I believe there isn't enough of it in football. Staying was all about me showing I am loyal and I'm thankful for it.

"It was important for me to stay at Tranmere after what I'd been through. I'd signed for the club when they were in League One. Two years later, I found myself in the National League. I said in one of my interviews that if the contracts kept coming, I'd stay until we were back in League One. I always believed we would get back.

"This place feels like home. It always has. It's quite rare now, but I've only signed permanently for two football clubs throughout my career. I want to keep it that way really.

"Nowadays, you see players signing one year contracts here, there and everywhere. You can't get any structure or have a place that feels like home.

"I feel like Tranmere are my second Huddersfield Town. I was in the development centre there when I was eight and signed full academy terms at the age of 12. I still take an interest in their results now.

"It was very hard for me to leave. But what do you do when you're not getting selected? I had a similar situation there as what happened with Iain Hume at Tranmere - I was training with the youth team. I was at an age where I felt I should be playing first team football, so I guess it was a choice that was made for me.

"So here I am. And this club means a lot to me. I've spent a quarter of my life here. Whatever happens in the future, I'll always look at it like I do with Huddersfield Town.

"I've actually started quite a few seasons out of the team here, but often end up back in it come the end. I think that's because I never get too disappointed. I always believe that things happen so quickly in football, so a day can change things.

"Somebody might be ill or pick up an injury. You've just got to keep yourself right and ready for when the chance comes, because if you're not, you might not get that chance again for a while.

"It's paid off with two medals which are lying around in the spare bedroom and when you walk in there for whatever reason, you see them and you don't really think about it, but subconsciously it makes you feel brilliant."

Scott Davies

"Last season was 100% the greatest moment of my career. I've had some good ones, I've had some special ones, but getting promoted up to League One felt like the full circle of a journey that at one point I'd given up.

"I fell back in love with the ambition of that journey and I made it. To share it with the people I shared it with and the pride and emotion I had within that will live with me for a life time.

"2018 was all about relief. I was in tears after this one though. It was more of a reality check of 'fucking hell, you're back where you said you'd be'.

"When the whistle went, I dropped to my knees and I'm in tears straight away. The year before, because we knew we should go up, it was a cry of relief. For this one, though, nobody believed we were that good. Nobody believed we were League One players.

"Everybody wrote us off four years ago. Now where are you? Where are the people from January who said what they said? That was my overriding emotion. Where's everyone now?

"I'm a big believer that you find your level. We were at the level we were at for whatever reason, but as men, not just footballers. To be able to come back from that and get to where I've come from gives me so much pride.

"I'm proud of myself. When I left Fleetwood, I said I'd get back to where I was. When I decided to come to Tranmere, I said I'd get back to League One. It made me emotional.

"Me and Connor had a running joke when we were celebrating in Magaluf. I'd point at him and say 'you deserve it Connor' and he'd point back and say 'no you deserve it'. He really did though.

"Nobody has done more for the cause than Connor Jennings.

Nobody works harder than him or is a better person. He deserves everything he gets. He was probably written off as a National League player, but we all knew how good he was.

"I'm proud of Liam Ridehalgh for the way he's come back from what he's been through. It's unbelievable. If anybody deserves it, Rides does. Emotionally, he dealt with it unbelievably.

"I'm proud of Nors. I'm proud of McNulty because people told him he was retired in January. He came back and got us over the line. Jay Harris was probably written off at one point. I'm proud of him.

"I was lucky enough to captain these lads. I'm proud of every single one, as men, not just footballers. Questions were asked of every single one of us at one point and we all answered them.

"If I look at this club now, compared to when I arrived, it's unrecognisable, and I don't think it's just the football side of things. I think when you rock up to this football club now, you think of the Championship. When I rocked up previously, you'd think they were a run down Football League club who are stuck in Non League.

"I think it's everything that surrounds it that has changed. If you go out in the surrounding areas, it's Tranmere. I'd go as far as saying the ground was dark and dreary. It's not now. The people are positive. The training ground is positive.

"You've got to credit the chairman, but I also think a huge amount of credit needs to go to the manager. When he came in, he recognised the disconnect between the club, the players and staff and the fans. I think if you asked him, he'd probably say that's his biggest achievement. Yes we've won promotions, but he's connected everyone back together. I personally think that's the biggest difference. Everyone is as one."

Shaun Garnett

"I could feel that the club was starting to go downhill, but I didn't think it would go to the depths that it did. That was a bit of a shock to me.

"I left the club in 1996 and they were still on that upward curve. The success we had under John King brought an atmosphere and belief to the club and there was financial stability under Peter Johnson.

"When I came back in the mid-2000s, we were forever plugging holes. There was always the financial side of things to anything; the budget had been cut, we'd dropped out of the Championship and had a different owner. I think if I'm being brutally honest, there was definitely a different smell to the club.

"I had a lot more belief once we dropped into the National League. Yes, it was the making of the club, in a sense, but I think we could also have done the same if we'd stayed in League Two.

"I don't think we had to drop into the National League to get that injection of hope again. We could have got that in League Two. But things happen for a reason. What the relegation did was allow us to become a big club in a small league again. People embraced that. The name of the club improved again all of a sudden.

"I say this from a fan point of view - I always believed we'd win the Boreham Wood game, even when Liam Ridehalgh got sent off. I always thought we had too much for them, having experienced the game the previous season when we just weren't focused enough for it. I knew we'd learnt from that. We showed some resilience and desire and got the win with a manager who made tactical decisions in the first half which set up the victory. It was great.

"Newport on the other hand was always going to be tough. They were a good cup team and had potential on the day to play above their ability. I knew it was going to be tough, but I also knew if we kept a clean sheet, we had enough in our locker to score goals. From a supporter's point of view, there was hope going into both games.

"I was on the bench for the Newport game and when Connor scored, I was just jumping up and down and hugging the nearest person. I knew we'd done it. There was so little time left. There was this belief of going up again. We were back in League One. It was a bit surreal.

"I've been lucky enough to be involved in seven of Tranmere's eight Wembley trips, as a player, coach or supporter. It's surreal really. To win again there was just fantastic.

"Tranmere Rovers in 2019 is a different club compared to Tranmere Rovers in 2015, both on and off the park. From a business point of view, it's different. Footballing wise, you've got an up and coming manager, still, although he's got loads of experience and five promotions.

"He's got ambition and he's also very much Tranmere through and through. You've also got a chairman who owns the club and wants the best for them long term, not just short term. In football, just when you think things are working out, it's got a habit of slapping you in the face. At the moment, we're in a good place.

"If you can realise what your club is, what makes it tick and know that, yes, there are dark days in football, but if you have belief that you're doing things right, the outcome will be right. If you don't change what you're doing, the outcome will never change.

"That's what Tranmere have done in the last few years. We've done things differently, and therefore the outcome has been different. In the dark days, the outcome was always going to be the same because we didn't change. We just went with the flow, patched things up a little bit and hoped it would work. It won't. It never does. We did change, we're in a better place. In football, you have to move on.

"For Micky Mellon to get the back to back promotions, similar to what Johnny King did but in different circumstances, it's given the club the life that it badly needed. Would I recommend the play-offs to anybody? No! It's a nerve-racking procedure! You've got to win the semi-finals and then win the one off game at Wembley. But what it does do is get the buzz around the place.

"I'm very proud to be involved in the club. It's a bit corny, but it's back where it belongs. We know where we're at as a club. We've been a Championship club and we've got the potential to go there again.

"Where we are at the moment gives us that platform to push on, which is what we did in the 1990s. It's going to take a massive effort again, both on and off the pitch, to do so, but our ultimate goal has got to be the Championship."

Steve Jennings

"My time with Tranmere has been an absolute roller coaster. I had some great, fantastic years early on. I then went away and people say you should never go back to a club you've been at, but I couldn't see past coming back to Prenton Park and working under Ronnie Moore and John McMahon at the time.

"In hindsight, yes, I probably shouldn't have returned. I wouldn't have those two relegations on my CV if that was the case. But I wanted to. I wanted to do well and never give up. I thoroughly enjoyed the early parts and saw the other sides of football in the second part.

The first year under Ronnie was okay, we had enough to get out of it, but the second time, we didn't have anywhere near enough. We only had three or four players pulling their weight. It was quite embarrassing to be honest.

"I remember towards the end of the season, we had some games at home and the fans were waiting outside. There were a few of us who literally couldn't show our faces outside, whereas half the team were twenty minutes on the motorway going home.

"Now the club are back in the Football League, I can bring my head above water, having gone through the embarrassment of what happened. League One is the minimum level they should be at and with the way the club is moving forward, you literally do not know what is around the corner.

"I am back here doing some coaching now and the difference compared to 2015 is night and day. You're training at a different place, the new owners have had an impact. This club is going from strength to strength. It's a club massively on the up and it's not far away from knocking on the door for the Championship."

Mark Palios

"When Connor scored, I was thinking 'we've still got a couple of minutes to go'. People say I looked pretty miserable, but I don't tend to celebrate goals that much.

"Now and again I will. They'll get me out of my seat, but I don't tend to celebrate that much because you're in the box with directors of the other club and especially at Wembley it's a massive disappointment. You shouldn't rub it in their faces at all.

"The other things is that we've been great recently with late goals. It's not over until it's finished and that was my thought at the time.

"But it was slightly surreal. It's almost like you read it in books. You scored with a minute to go in the 119th minute and it's Connor again. It was great to watch. Well, it wasn't a very good game, but it was great to watch the fans celebrate.

"When I do presentations, sport has always been very rich in terms of the content you can put on. When we did the AGM, I didn't talk about what had gone on on the pitch in the last five years. I did a video instead which is four minutes and just covered the last five years.

"It takes you through the nadir of going out of the league, Bury celebrating on our pitch, where are they now? And then it's about us getting back into the league and League One. Three Wembley appearances. Two promotions, back-to-back.

"I think getting back to League One was obviously very satisfying. When I came in, we were a League Two side with a negative momentum. Now we're a League One side with a positive momentum. From a turnaround perspective, you would say that gives you a great deal of satisfaction.

"As a fan, and recognising the pain of being in the non-league for this club, obviously getting back into the Football League was massively important for the fans and added to the pride that people had.

"I think what made that Boreham Wood win extra special was the way it happened. It was against total adversity. We came through it. I think it was the drama of the event, as well as the significance of it, in terms of the reputation and status and how the fans would feel about their club being a League club again.

"It's hard to say the Newport game was equally as dramatic or heartwarming, because it wasn't. That's not being unemotional about the club. You just believe that if you keep doing the right thing, then you will progress.

"That's what we've done. We need to finish off doing the right things. We went up about a year ahead of plan. Now I'm focusing on what are the right things to do to make us a Championship club? It may not be for me to do it but it's to put the club in a place whereby it's capable of doing that.

"After I'd been here for a few years, one of the employees gave me a picture of James Bond and said 'it's you'. The Three Ps. Be polite and professional and have a plan to kill everybody you meet. To be quite honest, that's what Tranmere Rovers should be. We should be polite and professional and have a plan to beat everybody that we play.

"You're looking at this and thinking 'as long as we do it the right way, I'll feel it's been worth it'. Well it's been worth coming back anyway, at this stage certainly, but you just want to make sure that you can hand it on. That's the next stage that I've got to be cognisant of. In a way I'll be sad to hand it on, but we can't hang around forever.

"I knew it could be done, getting us back to League One. I think it's doing it in adversity that makes it so special. Getting relegated was massive in terms of increasing the difficulty.

"Turnarounds don't take that long, maybe two or three years, but if you extend it out, things start to depreciate and deteriorate. You need more cash. I just think it is a turnaround in extremist with lots of difficulties, so it is quite satisfying and it's not without rewards.

"I've got a wall of redemption that I'm going to put up in my office. That's to go from the Plymouth game, from which I've kept the programme, right the way through to the promotion back.

"People come up to you in the street and say 'thank you for saving my club, I'm proud of my club again'. You can't buy that. It's an absolute privilege to have the opportunity to do it with your own club. Not in terms of owning it. I hate being called the owner of Tranmere Rovers, because I'm not. The fans own the club.

"You'll see this with Bury. They'll come back at some stage in the future and it will be the fans. The corporate entity is only the physical manifestation, because you've got to have one. It's the club. The essence and the spirit of the club is in the fans. If we've created new fans, that's fantastic. It's takes the club on.

"If we've made old fans happy, that's great. I would have preferred to have got us back into the league before a couple of them died. I said to Norman Wilson 'we'll get back' and he said 'do it quickly, mate' and we didn't unfortunately. I took a second to think of them at the end of every Wembley appearance."

2018/19 Statistics

Date	Opponent	Result	Line-Up
04/08/2018	Stevenage	D 2-2 (Norwood x2)	Davies, Caprice, McNulty, Sutton, Bakayogo, Smith (Tollitt), Banks, Harris, Jennings, Norwood, Stockton
11/08/2018	Cheltenham	W 1-0 (Norwood)	Davies, Caprice, McNulty, Sutton (Monthe), Bakayogo, Smith, Banks, Harris, Jennings, Norwood, Stockton
18/08/2018	Swindon	L 3-2 (Smith, Norwood)	Davies, Caprice (Mullin), Ellis, McNulty, Monthe, Smith (Mottley-Henry), Banks, Harris, Jennings, Norwood, Stockton (Gilmour)
21/08/2018	Mansfield	D 0-0	Davies, Ellis, McNulty, Monthe, Caprice, McCullough, Banks, Jennings, Smith (Mottley-Henry), Jennings, Stockton
25/08/2018	Port Vale	W 1-0 (Norwood)	Davies, Ellis, McNulty, Monthe, Smith (Mottley-Henry), McCullough, Banks, Jennings, Caprice, Norwood, Stockton (Mullin)
01/09/2018	Northampton	D 1-1 (Norwood)	Davies, Ellis, McNulty, Monthe, Caprice, McCullough, Banks, Jennings, Smith (Mottley-Henry), Norwood, Stockton (Bakayogo)
08/09/2018	Colchester	D 1-1 (Norwood)	Davies, Caprice, McNulty, Monthe, Bakayogo, Smith (Mottley-Henry), McCullough, Banks, Jennings, Norwood, Stockton (Mullin)
15/09/2018	Carlisle	W 0-2 (Parkes og, Mullin)	Davies, Caprice, McNulty, Monthe, Bakayogo, Mottley-Henry (Smith), McCullough, Banks, Jennings, Norwood, Stockton (Mullin)
22/09/2018	Newport	L 0-1	Davies, Buxton, McNulty, Monthe, Bakayogo, Mottley-Henry (Smith), McCullough, Banks, Jennings (Cole), Norwood, Mullin (Stockton)
29/09/2018	MK Dons	D 1-1 (Smith)	Davies, Buxton, McNulty, Monthe, Bakayogo, Smith (Mottley-Henry), McCullough, Banks, Jennings, Norwood, Stockton (Gilmour)
02/10/2018	Lincoln	W 1-0 (Norwood)	Davies, Buxton, McNulty, Monthe, Bakayogo, Smith (Mottley-Henry), McCullough, Banks, Jennings, Norwood, Stockton (Gilmour)
06/10/2018	Morecambe	W 3-4 (Banks, Gilmour x2, Smith)	Davies, Buxton, McNulty, Monthe, Bakayogo, Smith (Mottley-Henry), McCullough, Banks, Gilmour, Jennings (Ellis), Mullin (Akammadu)
12/10/2018	Macclesfield	W 1-0 (Gilmour)	Davies, Caprice, McNulty, Monthe, Buxton, Smith (Cole), McCullough, Banks, Gilmour, Jennings, Norwood
20/10/2018	Yeovil	D 0-0	Davies, Sutton, McNulty, Monthe, Caprice, McCullough (Harris), Banks, Gilmour (Mullin), Smith (Cole), Jennings, Norwood
23/10/2018	Forest Green	L 3-1 (Mullin)	Davies, Sutton, McNulty, Monthe, Caprice, McCullough, Harris, Gilmour (Tollitt), Smith (Cole), Jennings, Norwood

Date	Opponent	Result	Team
27/10/2018	Crawley	W 5-1 (Jennings, Norwood x2, Buxton, Mullin)	Davies, Caprice, McNulty, Monthe, Buxton, Cole (Smith), McCullough, Banks, Jennings, Mullin (Gilmour), Norwood
03/11/2018	Exeter	W 2-0 (Norwood x2)	Davies, Caprice, McNulty, Monthe, Buxton, Cole (Gilmour), McCullough, Banks (Harris), Jennings, Mullin (Smith), Norwood
17/11/2018	Crewe	L 3-2 (Norwood, Mullin)	Davies; Caprice, McNulty, Monthe, Bakayogo, Smith (Mullin), McCullough, Banks, Gilmour (Cole), Jennings, Norwood
24/11/2018	Oldham	D 1-1 (Jennings)	Davies, Caprice, McNulty, Monthe, Bakayogo, Mottley-Henry, McCullough, Banks, Jennings, Mullin (Stockton), Norwood
27/11/2018	Grimsby	L 5-2 (Norwood, Mullin)	Davies, Caprice, McNulty (Sutton), Monthe, Bakayogo (Ridehalgh), Mottley-Henry (Cole), McCullough, Gilmour, Jennings, Mullin, Norwood
08/12/2018	Cambridge	W 1-0 (Norwood)	Davies, Buxton, McNulty, Monthe, Ridehalgh, Smith (Caprice), McCullough, Harris, Jennings, Norwood, Stockton (Mullin)
15/12/2018	Notts County	L 3-2 (Smith, Jennings)	Davies, Caprice, Ellis, Sutton, Bakayogo, Smith, McCullough, Harris (Gilmour), Jennings, Cole (Mullin), Norwood
22/12/2018	Bury	L 2-1 (Sutton)	Davies, Ellis, McNulty (Sutton), Monthe, Caprice (Smith), Harris, McCullough, Jennings, Ridehalgh, Mullin (Stockton), Norwood
26/12/2018	Morecambe	W 3-1 (Stockton, Norwood, Harris)	Davies, Ellis, Sutton (Gilmour), Monthe, Caprice, Harris, McCullough, Jennings, Ridehalgh, Norwood, Stockton (Mullin)
29/12/2018	Yeovil	D 0-0	Davies, Ellis, McNulty, Sutton (Mullin), Caprice, Harris, McCullough, Jennings, Ridehalgh, Norwood, Stockton (Smith)
01/01/2019	Macclesfield	D 1-1 (Jennings)	Davies, Buxton, Ellis, Monthe, Ridehalgh, Caprice, Harris, McCullough, Smith (Cole), Jennings, Norwood
12/01/2019	Cheltenham	W 1-3 (Norwood, Miller, Banks)	Davies, Ellis, McNulty, Monthe, Caprice, McCullough, Perkins, Banks (Harris), Ridehalgh, Norwood, Miller (Mullin)
19/01/2019	Swindon	L 1-2 (Norwood)	Davies, Ellis (Buxton), McNulty, Monthe, Caprice, McCullough (Smith), Perkins, Banks, Ridehalgh, Norwood, Miller (Jennings)
26/01/2019	Mansfield	L 3-0	Davies, Buxton, McNulty (Pringle), Monthe, Ridehalgh, Jennings, McCullough, Perkins, Banks, Caprice, Jennings
05/02/2019	Northampton	L 1-2 (Norwood)	Davies, Caprice, Nelson, Monthe, Ridehalgh, Morris (Smith), McCullough (Gilmour), Perkins, Pringle (Dagnall), Jennings, Norwood
09/02/2019	Stevenage	W 2-0 (Morris, Norwood)	Davies, Caprice, Nelson (Ellis), Monthe, Ridehalgh, Morris (Smith), McCullough, Perkins, Pringle, Jennings (Dagnall), Norwood
16/02/2019	Cambridge	D 0-0	Davies, Caprice (Buxton), Ellis, Monthe, Bakayogo, Morris, McCullough, Perkins, Pringle (Smith), Jennings, Norwood

Date	Opponent	Result	Team
19/02/2019	Port Vale	W 1-2 (Norwood x2)	Davies, Caprice, Ellis, Monthe, Bakayogo, Morris (Smith), McCullough, Perkins, Pringle (Gilmour), Jennings, Norwood
23/02/2019	Notts County	W 1-0 (Jennings)	Davies, Caprice, Ellis (Nelson), Monthe, Bakayogo, Morris, McCullough (Banks), Perkins, Pringle (Smith), Jennings, Norwood
02/03/2019	Exeter	W 0-1 (Norwood)	Davies, Caprice, Ellis, Monthe, Bakayogo, Smith (Gilmour), McCullough, Perkins, Pringle (Nelson), Jennings, Norwood
08/03/2019	Crewe	W 1-0 (Norwood)	Davies, Caprice, Ellis, Monthe, Bakayogo (Buxton), Smith (Banks), McCullough, Perkins, Pringle (Gilmour), Jennings, Norwood
12/03/2019	Grimsby	W 4-1 (Jennings, Monthe, Norwood)	Davies, Caprice, Ellis, Monthe, Ridehalgh, McCullough, Perkins, Jennings, Banks (Harris), Pringle (Gilmour), Norwood
23/03/2019	Colchester	W 0-2 (Norwood, Perkins)	Davies, Caprice, Ellis, Monthe, Ridehalgh, McCullough, Perkins, Jennings, Banks (Harris), Pringle (Morris), Norwood
30/03/2019	Carlisle	W 3-0 (Banks, Norwood, Monthe)	Davies, Caprice, Ellis, Monthe, Ridehalgh, McCullough (Harris), Perkins, Morris (Gilmour), Banks (Smith), Jennings, Norwood
02/04/2019	Oldham	L 2-0	Davies, Caprice, Ellis, Monthe, Ridehalgh, Harris (Smith), Perkins, Morris, Banks, Jennings, Norwood
06/04/2019	Newport	D 0-0	Davies, Caprice, Ellis, Monthe, Ridehalgh, Morris, Perkins, Banks, Smith (Dagnall), Jennings, Norwood
13/04/2019	MK Dons	W 2-1 (Perkins, Jennings)	Davies, Caprice, Ellis, Monthe, Ridehalgh, Morris, Perkins (Harris), Banks, Pringle, Jennings, Norwood
19/04/2019	Forest Green	L 0-1	Davies, Caprice, Ellis (Nelson), Monthe, Bakayogo, Morris, Harris (Dagnall), Banks, Pringle (Mullin), Jennings, Norwood
22/04/2019	Lincoln	D 0-0	Davies, Caprice, Nelson (Gumbs (Buxton)), Monthe, Bakayogo, Morris, Harris, Banks, Jennings, Mullin (Gilmour), Norwood
30/04/2019	Bury	D 1-1 (Norwood)	Davies, Caprice (Buxton), Nelson, Monthe, Ridehalgh, Morris, Harris, Banks, Pringle (Mullin), Jennings, Norwood
04/05/2019	Crawley	L 3-1 (Norwood)	Davies, Buxton, McNulty, Monthe, Bakayogo, Tollitt (Banks), Perkins (Morris), Gilmour, Smith (Jennings), Dagnall, Norwood
10/05/2019	Forest Green	W 1-0 (Banks)	Davies, Caprice, Nelson, Monthe, Ridehalgh, Perkins, Harris, Morris (Smith), Banks (Gilmour), Jennings, Norwood
13/05/2019	Forest Green	D 1-1 (Norwood)	Davies, Caprice, Nelson, Monthe, Ridehalgh, Perkins, Harris, Morris (Gilmour), Banks, Jennings, Norwood
25/05/2019	Newport	W 1-0 AET (Jennings)	Davies, Caprice, Nelson (Buxton), Monthe, Ridehalgh, Perkins, Harris (Pringle), Morris (McNulty), Banks, Jennings, Norwood

Statistics (League and play-offs)

Games Played: 49 (W22, D14, L13)

Goals Scored: 66

Goals Conceded: 51

Biggest Win: 5-1 (v Crawley)

Biggest Defeat: 5-2 (v Grimsby)

Most Appearances: Scott Davies (49, including 21 clean sheets, the most in League Two)

Top Scorer: James Norwood (30, Golden Boot winner for the Football League)

Players Who Made A First Team Appearance: 29